IMAGES
of America

MOUNT HOPE AND OTISVILLE

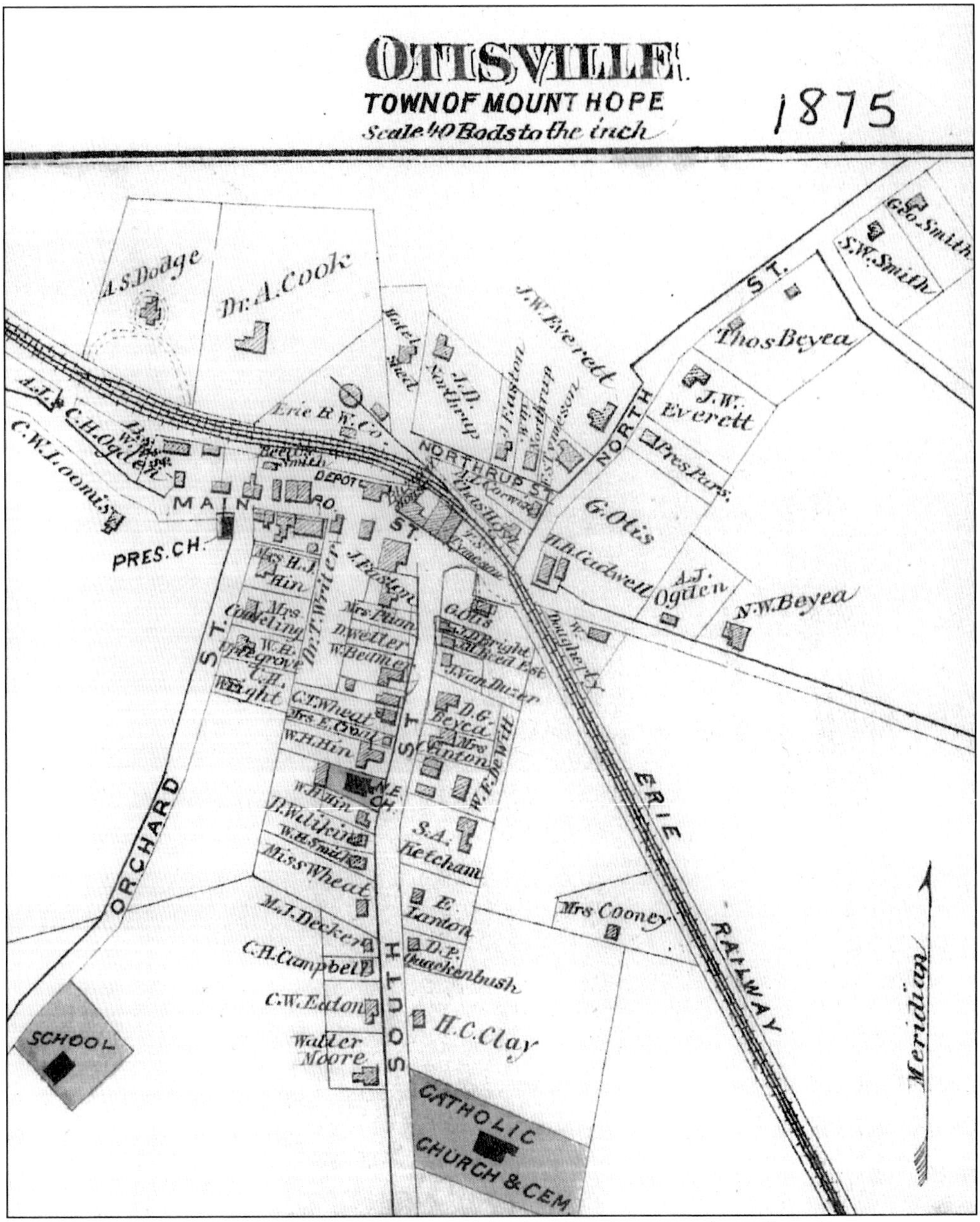

This 1875 map of Otisville gives the names of the families living in the village. It is interesting to note that Highland Avenue is identified as South Street, and on the other side of the railway, the road is identified as North Street. The only route to the school was by way of Orchard Street as School Street had not yet been constructed.

On the cover: Taken in 1906, this photograph of the Greenleaf Hotel shows proprietor Oscar S. Greenleaf in a white hat. During the construction of the Erie tunnel, the hotel provided room and board to various tunnel engineers, including Frank J. Cavanaugh, who was the masonry contractor for the tunnel project. (Courtesy of Nancie Craig.)

IMAGES
of America

MOUNT HOPE AND OTISVILLE

Nancie Craig and Anita Goldsmith

ARCADIA PUBLISHING

ISBN 978-0-7385-5702-1

Published by Arcadia Publishing
Charleston SC, Chicago IL, Portsmouth NH, San Francisco CA

Printed in the United States of America

Library of Congress Catalog Card Number: 2007939166

For all general information contact Arcadia Publishing at:
Telephone 843-853-2070
Fax 843-853-0044
E-mail sales@arcadiapublishing.com
For customer service and orders:
Toll-Free 1-888-313-2665

Visit us on the Internet at www.arcadiapublishing.com

This book is dedicated to the pioneer families who came to the area now known as Otisville and the town of Mount Hope before and shortly after the American Revolution. These include the Finch, Gumaer, Seybolt, Loomis, Ketcham, Corwin, Pierson, Harding, Woodward, Dodge, Mapes, Hawkins, Greenleaf, Beyea, and Otis families. They endured many hardships, and we are indebted to them for their struggle to tame a wilderness and make it their home.

Contents

ACKNOWLEDGMENTS

There are many people to acknowledge for their monumental contributions to this book. Without their unparalleled assistance, this book would not have been possible. The Mount Hope Historical Society is a relatively new organization, having been founded in 1988 by Mount Hope historian Dolores Hawkins. Therefore, the historical society has a limited collection of vintage photographs. We depended on many individuals in our area and elsewhere to loan us their family photographs for the completion of this project. We are grateful to everyone who contributed information and treasured family photographs for this book. It was truly a community effort that extended to descendants of our early settlers who now live throughout the United States.

Our gratitude is given to Ray Decker, who was tireless in his pursuit of the perfect picture. He spent many hours scouring the countryside for vintage photographs for this book. He then graciously volunteered endless hours to review and scan the images.

John Holley, an Otisville native, deserves special recognition for the extensive amount of historical information that he has provided to the Mount Hope Historical Society since its formation. If we have a question about a historical event, a person, or a house in the town of Mount Hope or village of Otisville, he is the one we turn to for the answer.

Countless hours were contributed by Larri Vreeland Jarosz, who contacted many of her relatives and convinced them to loan us their family photographs. Her Ketcham ancestors came from Long Island and settled in Mount Hope in 1774. In 1872, her great-great-grandfather Andrew Mitchell discovered a mastodon on Shoddy Hollow Road. The mastodon is now on display at the Peabody Museum of Natural History at Yale University.

Many individuals contributed valuable information and photographs for our project. They are as follows: John Gray, Larri Vreeland Jarosz, Denege Patterson, Patty Butzgy Pierce, Sylvia Corwin Butzgy, Dolores Hawkins, James "Kayo" Stanfield, Shirley Grebeldinger, Bob Beebe, Mike Hornbuckle, Lamira Ketcham Bowles, John Holley, Orrin Pierson, Jackie Pierson, Al Wessels, Evelyn Pierce, Millie Crawford, Joan M. Lexau, Don Yonskie, Doris Yonskie, Mary Ann McDonough, Anita Goldsmith, Lloyd Goldsmith, Lois Gambino Adamson, Harvey Collins, Gladys Craig Loeven, Ann Hayes-Rader, Lee Runnalls, Charles Wilbur, Nancie Craig, Blanche Michelitch, Dick Vreeland, Dot Bedford Culver, Joanne Vreeland Hosking, Hale Hawkins, James Mapes, Glenda Teabo-Sandoe, Lori Soller, Rudy Van Dunk, Sid Green, Bonnie Gray Green, Frank Graziano, Jens Artus, Eldred Carhart, and Ed Sisson.

INTRODUCTION

Otisville and Mount Hope are located in a lovely area of western Orange County bordered by the Shawangunk Mountains. Early settlers came from Connecticut, Massachusetts, Long Island, and other areas looking for fertile land to farm and raise a family. They were often the younger sons of a family who had to look elsewhere for a plot of land to call their own.

The John Ketcham family arrived in what is now Mount Hope in 1774. They built a log cabin and soon erected a gristmill on the Shawangunk Kill, which crossed their land. Ketcham's grandson later built a sawmill and had a patent in 1821 for a dog-powered butter churn, which was used by many households in Orange, Sullivan, and Sussex Counties.

Josiah Pierson settled near Otisville shortly after the close of the Revolutionary War. The Pierson family has remained on the family farm since the late 1700s. The family burial ground sits on a knoll overlooking the vast pastures of the farm. It is an amazing accomplishment to have passed down this land from generation to generation and to continue operating it as a working farm.

When Isaac Otis arrived in Deerpark Four Corners in 1817, he built the first major mercantile establishment. He also constructed a distillery nearby. Money was scarce, and Isaac bartered with the settlers. There were no banks, and this was the accepted manner of conducting business. In 1825, Otis became the first postmaster, and Deerpark Four Corners was renamed Otisville in his honor. Many members of the Otis family came and settled in Otisville. Otis's half bother William owned and operated a woolen mill on Shoddy Hollow Road.

The New York City Department of Health selected Otisville for the site of a tuberculosis sanitorium, and in 1906, the first patients were admitted. It was built on the side of the Shawangunk Mountains by Dr. Thomas Darlington and Dr. Herman Biggs. Biggs believed in giving the patients nutritious food, and clean, cool mountain air. Biggs did not believe in coddling the patients, and everyone had a work assignment according to his capabilities and talents. Gus Sefranka, a patient at the sanitorium, was a gifted architect and designed many of the buildings there. Officials from the French government came to the Otisville sanitorium to study the sanitary techniques developed by Biggs.

Although many lovely historic homes remain in Otisville and Mount Hope, many others no longer exist. Photographs of homes and businesses that were built in Otisville and Mount Hope but have never been seen by local residents appear in this book. Over the years, many houses and businesses were destroyed by fire. In the early years of the village, fires were prevalent and hard to control. In 1875, when the Loomis barn caught fire and burned to the ground, the Presbyterian church nearly became a casualty. It was the quick thinking and fast action of the bucket brigade that saved the historic church from destruction.

This is a glimpse into the history of Otisville and Mount Hope. It is hoped that the pictures of historic homes and townspeople will encourage readers to learn more about the village and town. The Mount Hope Historical Society continues to collect and preserve artifacts and photographs of the area's early beginnings and welcomes new members.

All of the authors' proceeds from this book will go the Mount Hope Historical Society for restoration of the carriage barn that will house a library and research room on the grounds of the Harding farm in Otisville.

One

Main Street and Businesses

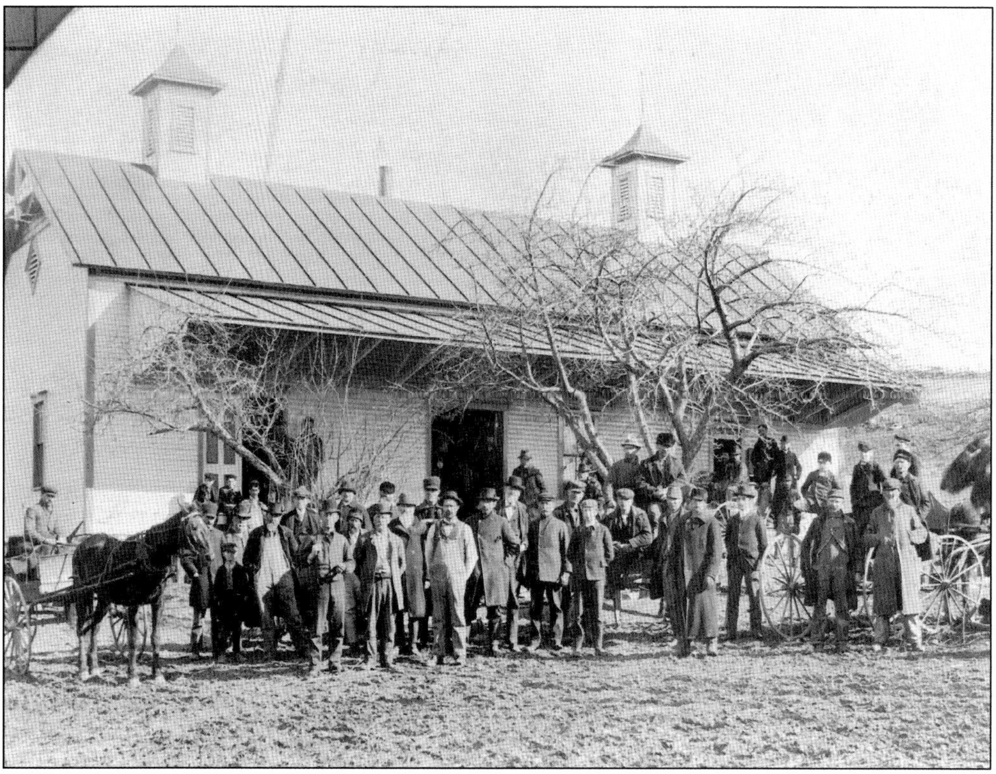

In the early 1900s, a butter factory was built by the Greenleaf family on the state road. It became a major supplier of butter for the New York City market. When the Borden Company opened a condensary in Otisville, the butter factory went out of business. They could not compete with the price that the Borden Company was paying the farmers for their milk.

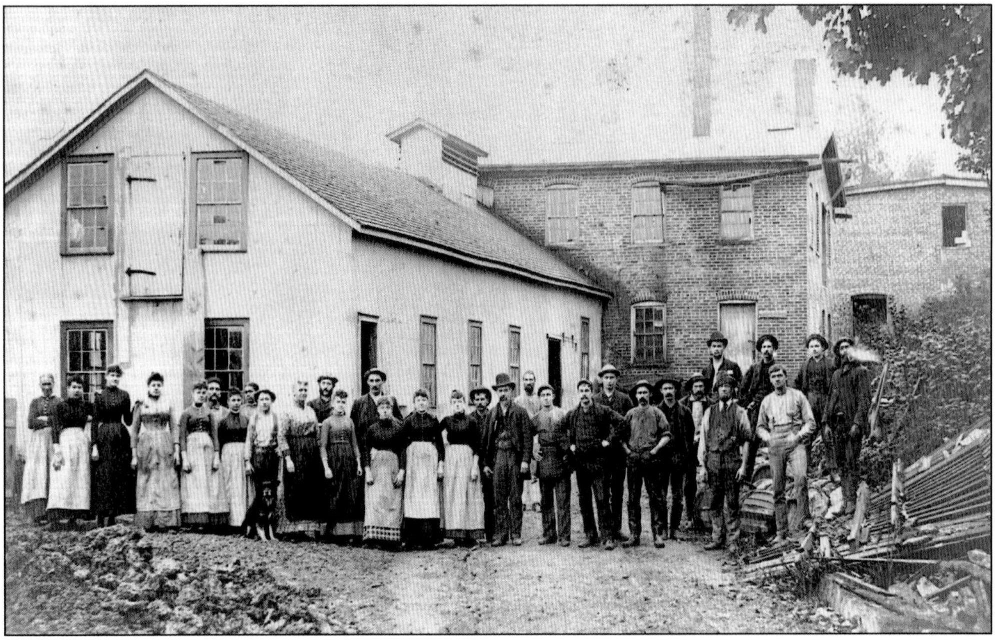

Joshua Oldroyd manufactured felt boots in his factory near Shoddy Hollow Road in the 1880s. Barrels of water were kept by the shredding machine to douse the small fires that were as frequent as five times daily. Sparks from the shredding machine ignited the material, which would result in a fire. The building was made of brick with a stone floor because of the danger. The site was once operated as a woolen mill by William Otis.

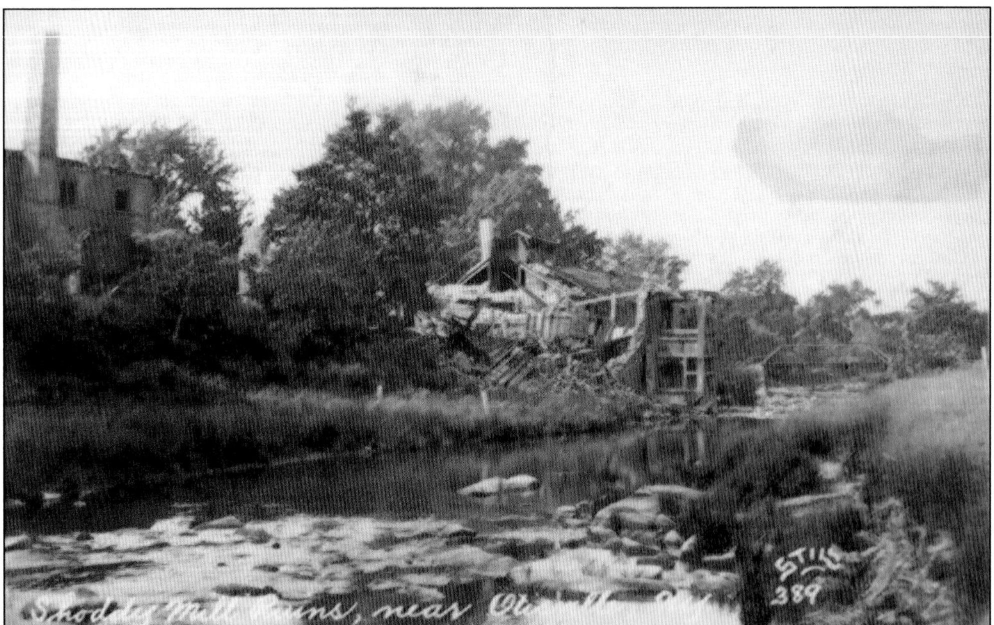

The ruins of the Otis factory and Oldroyd's mill are found on the kill near Shoddy Hollow Road. A fire destroyed a major portion of the factory and mill, and years later, a flood on the Shawangunk Kill destroyed the remainder of the buildings. William Otis was operating this site as a woolen mill as early as 1818, making woolen cloth and wool stocking material.

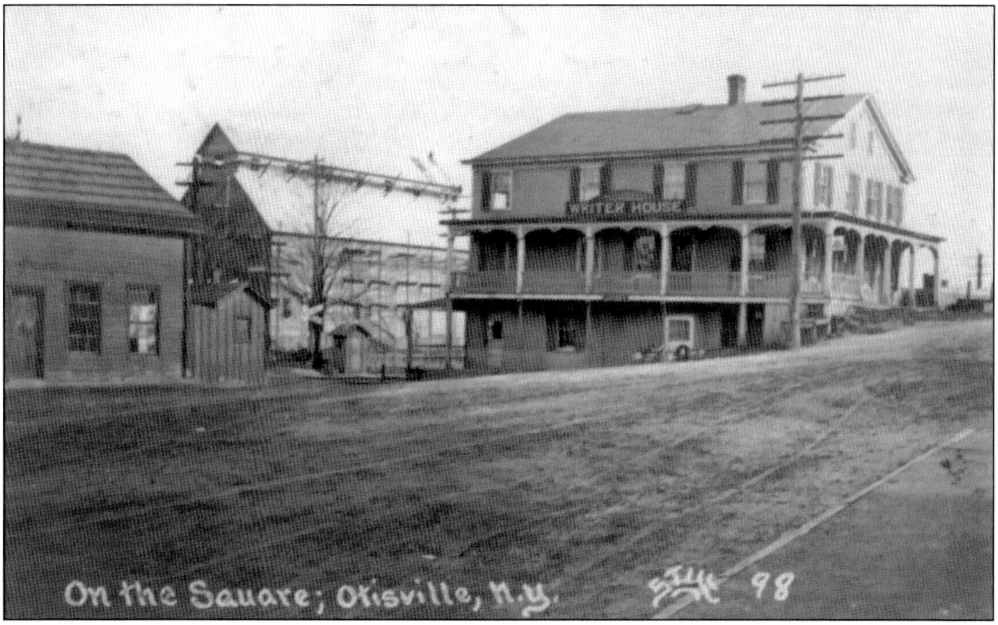

Shortly after the completion of the Erie line in 1846, Ambrose Green and his brother John built this hotel in Otisville. The hotel was once owned by George S. Writer, the son of Jasper A. and Arminda Ketcham Writer, and was known as the Writer House. Over the years, several derailments caused trains to crash into the side of the hotel due to its close proximity to the tracks.

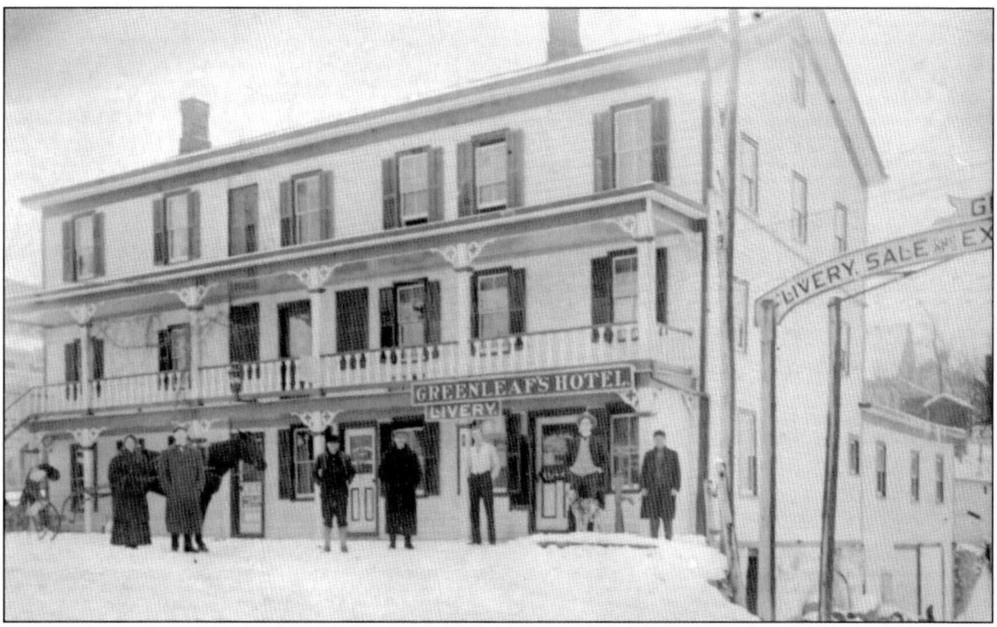

Ambrose and John Green built this stately hotel around 1835 in Otisville. When the Erie Railroad arrived in town, they sold this hotel and built another hotel across the street. In the early 1900s, the hotel was owned and operated by Oscar S. Greenleaf and his wife, Mary Craig Greenleaf. During the construction of the Erie tunnel, they served many hot meals to Col. James Bennett and Robert Talbot, who were the engineers that designed the tunnel.

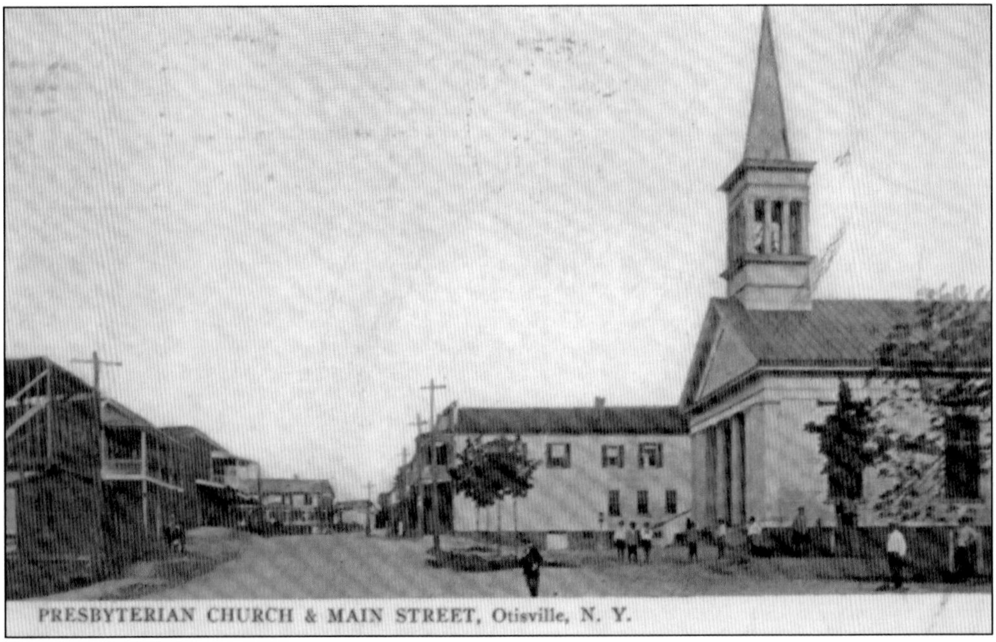

When Isaac Otis settled in Otisville in 1817, only a few houses had been built. Early settlers included the Loomis and Seybolt families. Ephraim Loomis donated land for the erection of a Presbyterian church. The church was completed in 1856 and has been in continual operation since that time.

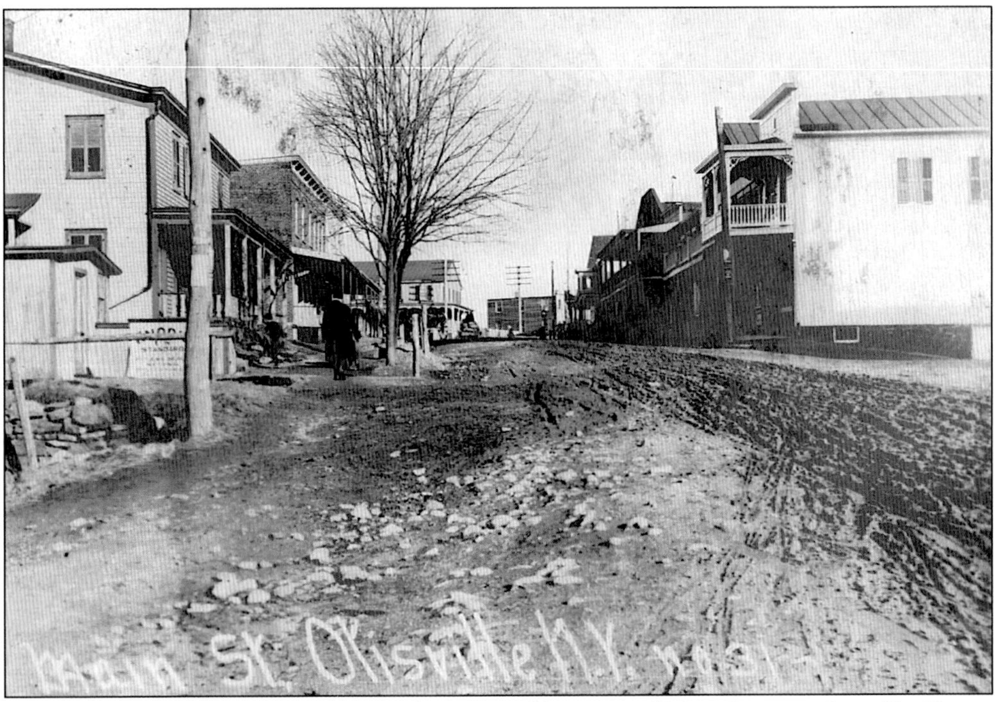

This early photograph from about 1900 shows a muddy, unpaved Main Street in Otisville. Horses and buggies were used to traverse the streets of Otisville and Mount Hope. During the snowy winter months, sleighs were used to get from one point to another.

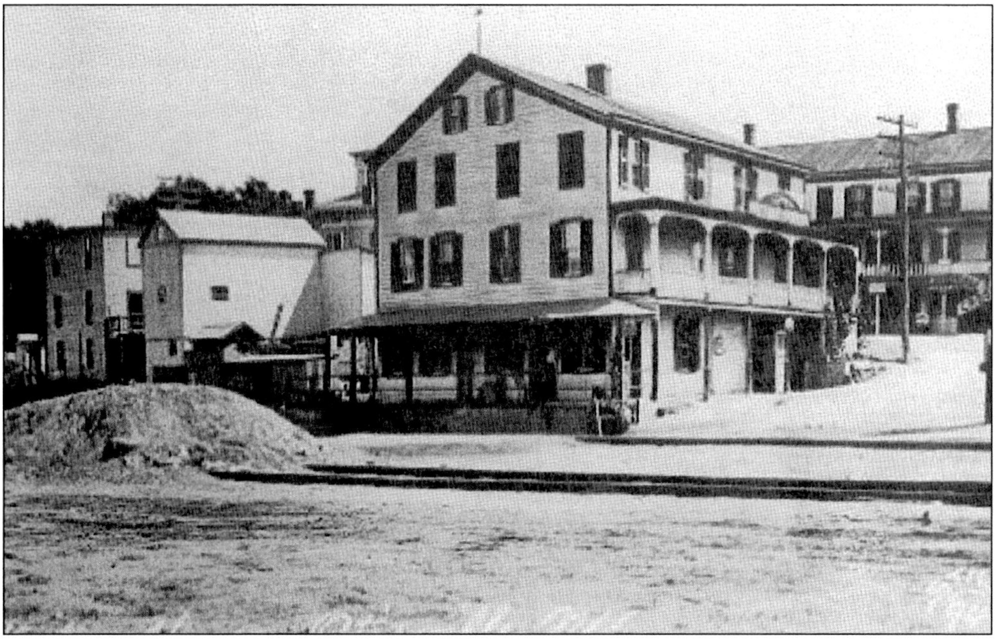

The Writer House hotel provided accommodations and meals to businessmen and tourists who were staying overnight in Otisville during the early 1900s. In 1906, William Loeven, who was originally from Honesdale, Pennsylvania, purchased the hotel. It remained a popular spot for travelers on the Erie Railroad to stop and have refreshments before continuing on their journey.

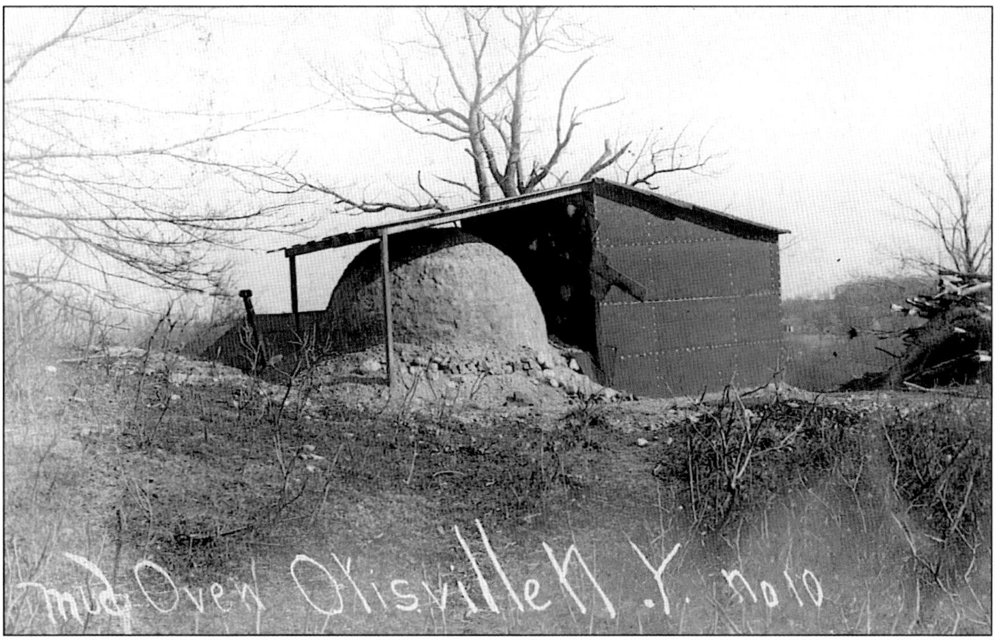

This mud oven was used by a local baker in Otisville to bake bread. Perhaps this was built in response to a fire in November 1907 that was caused by a lit oven in a bakery in the basement of the Bailey building. The baker was accustomed to leaving his wood oven stoked with hot coals throughout the night in order to have a hot oven in the morning when he was ready to bake bread. The fire in 1907 destroyed the building the bakery was in as well as the house next door.

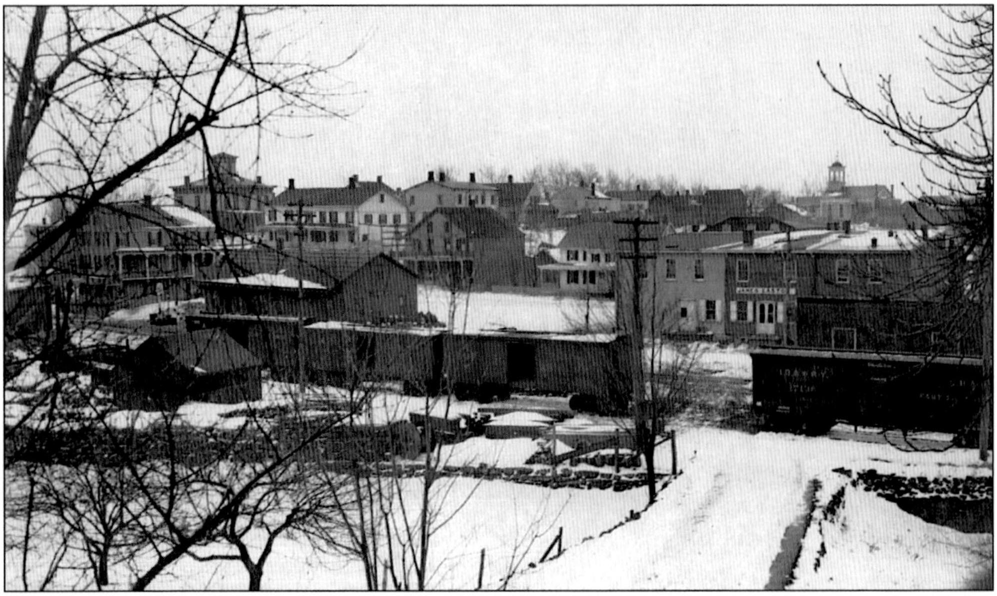

This photograph was taken from present-day Route 211 looking down onto Main Street in the village of Otisville. The depot is to the left, and the back of James Easton's store can be seen on the right. In the early 1900s when this picture was taken, a road connected the state road to Main Street.

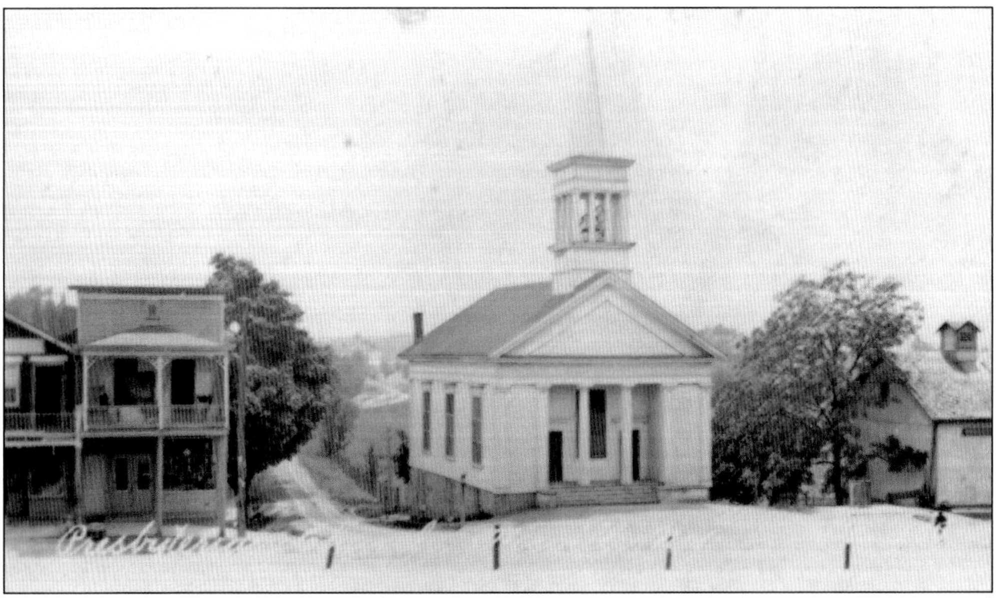

During the late 1930s, a very small grocery store was located on the corner of Main Street and Orchard Street. John Holley, an industrious local boy, delivered groceries with his wagon to customers in the village. In the mid-1900s, Joseph Cinotti operated the adjoining store. A fire in 1984 destroyed the buildings on this side of the street.

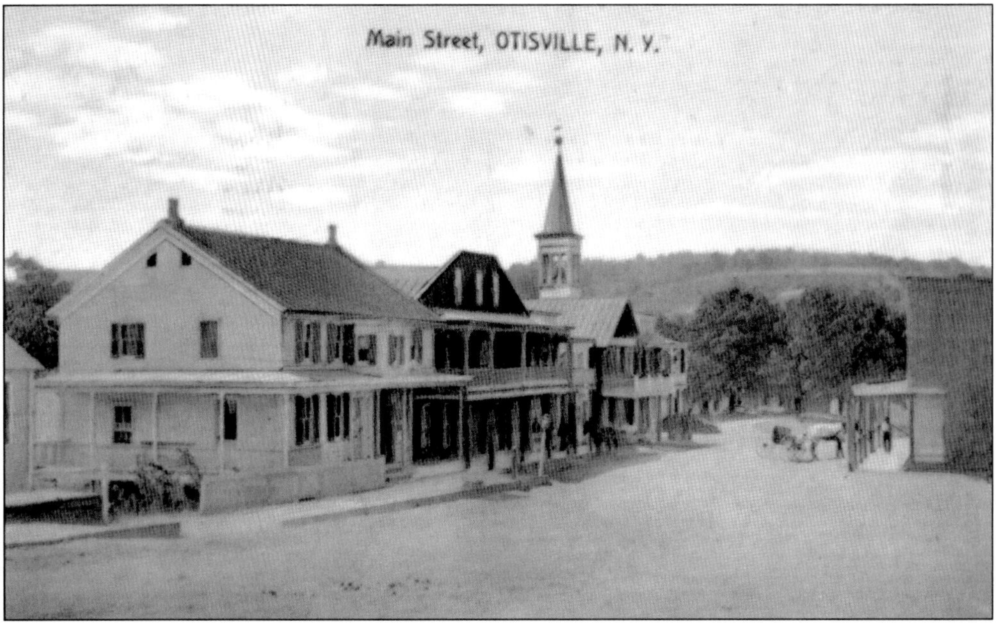

The white building on the left side of the photograph has been a fixture on Main Street since its early days. It was once a drugstore owned by Dr. Avery Cook, a longtime Otisville physician. The building presently houses a liquor store and gift shop. In the middle of the photograph, the steeple of the Presbyterian church can be seen.

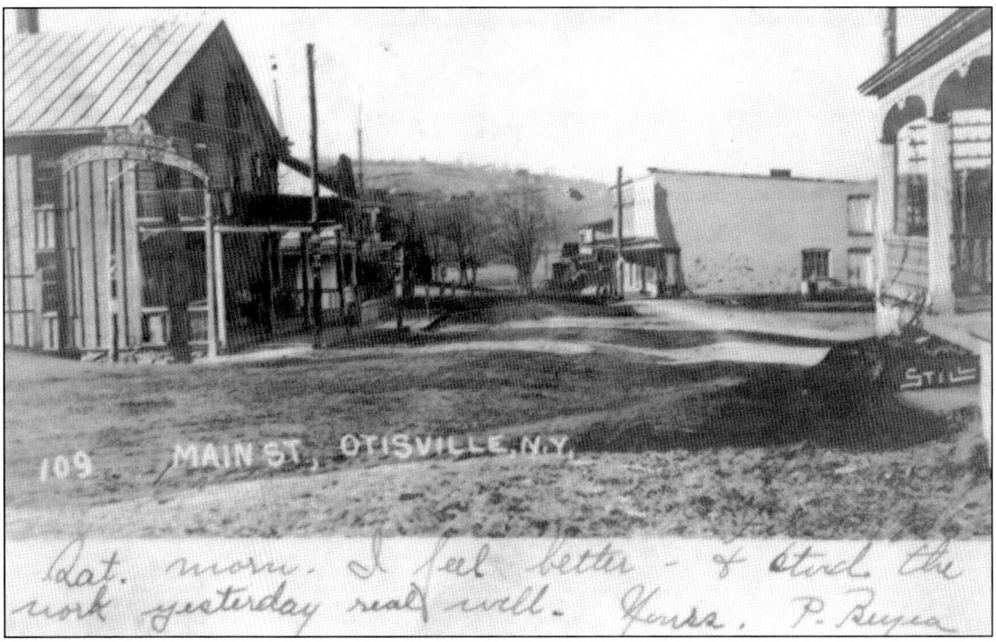

Main Street in Otisville is photographed from the top of the street looking down onto the village center. Beyea's store was located in the large frame building on the left side of the photograph. It was destroyed by fire, and a one-story building was erected at the same location. The building later contained a barbershop operated by Mr. Carpentier, who was known as "Carpy" to all his loyal customers.

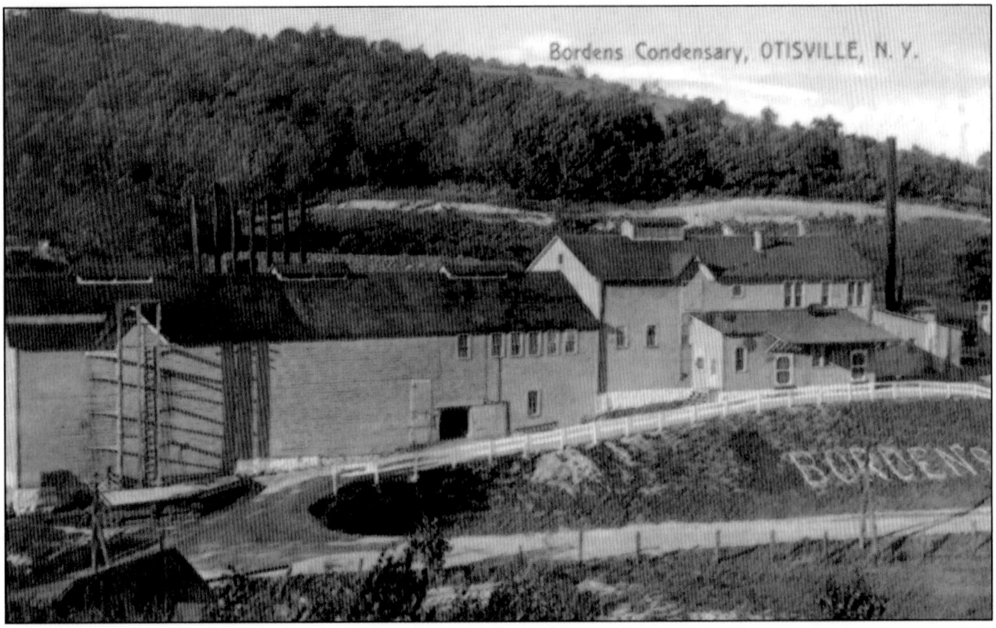

The Borden Company built a condensary in Otisville at the end of Main Street across from present-day Veterans Park. The Borden plant was located directly in front of the Erie Railroad track. This enabled the company to easily ship their milk products to New York City and other markets.

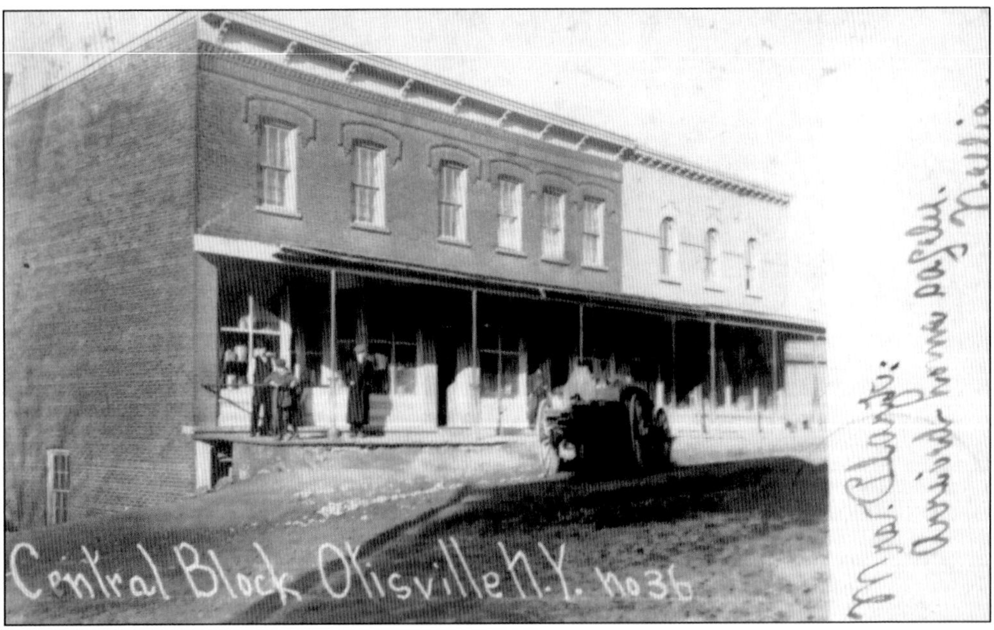

In 1884, a massive fire destroyed a large section of the business district in Otisville. Later that year, the buildings were rebuilt. Harry Reed and George Smith had a general mercantile business where Mick's store is now located. The central portion of the building was occupied by Kuykendal's ale saloon and Judson VanDuzer's tinsmith shop. VanDuzer made various articles out of tin and also constructed tin roofs on houses.

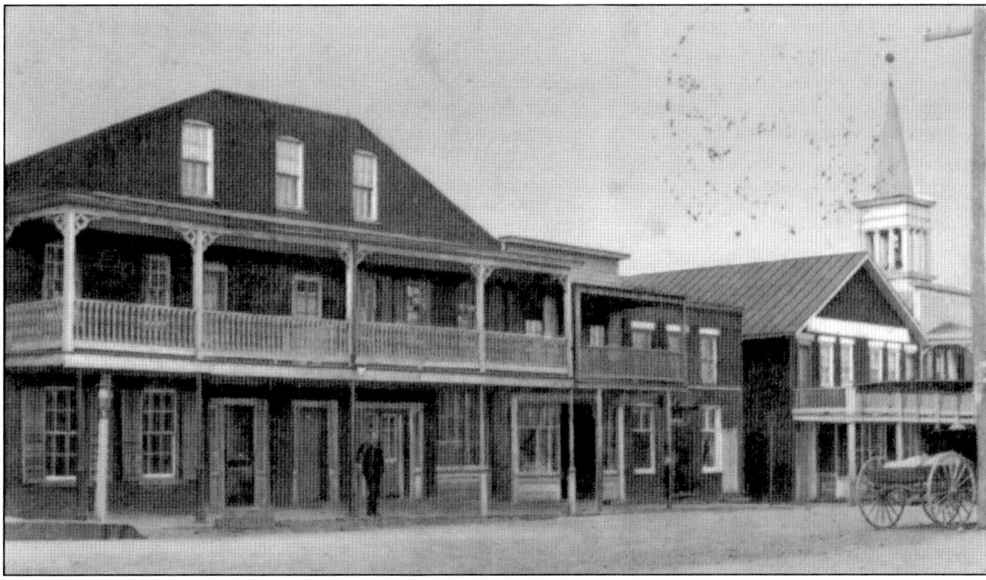

At the time that this photograph was taken around 1906, the Otisville Post Office was operated out of this building. During the mid-1900s, Mary McCollough had a confectionery and general mercantile business at this location. Next door, Harry Cherney had a hardware store, where he sold a little bit of everything. If someone needed an item in a hurry, he could find it on one of his shelves.

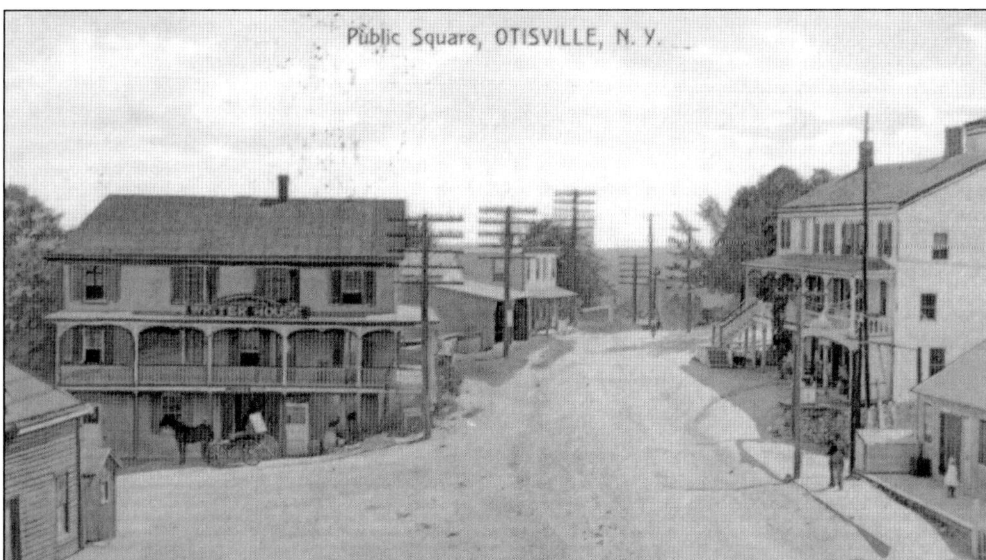

Ambrose and John Green erected the two hotels shown in this vintage photograph. Ambrose came to Otisville about 1835 and was one of the proprietors of the old stage line between Ellenville and Forestburg. Ambrose was also one of the first operators of the mines in the Shawangunk Mountains near Otisville.

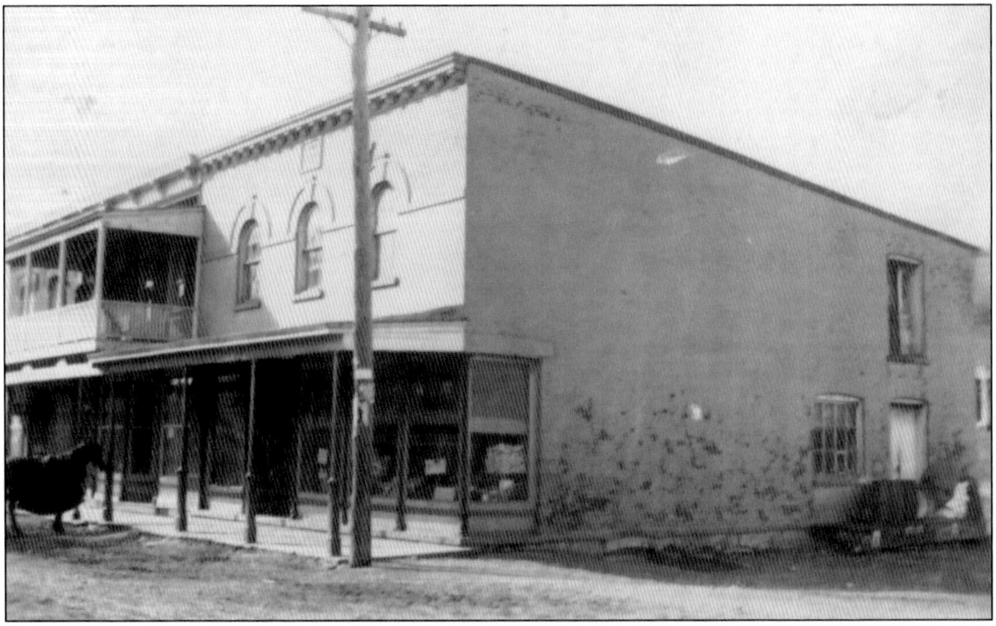

George Smith and Harry Reed conducted a general mercantile business at this store on Main Street. Smith was a merchant in Otisville for more than 40 years. The store was built in 1884 after their previous store was destroyed by fire. The store sold everything from vegetables and eggs to pots, pans, and summer hats.

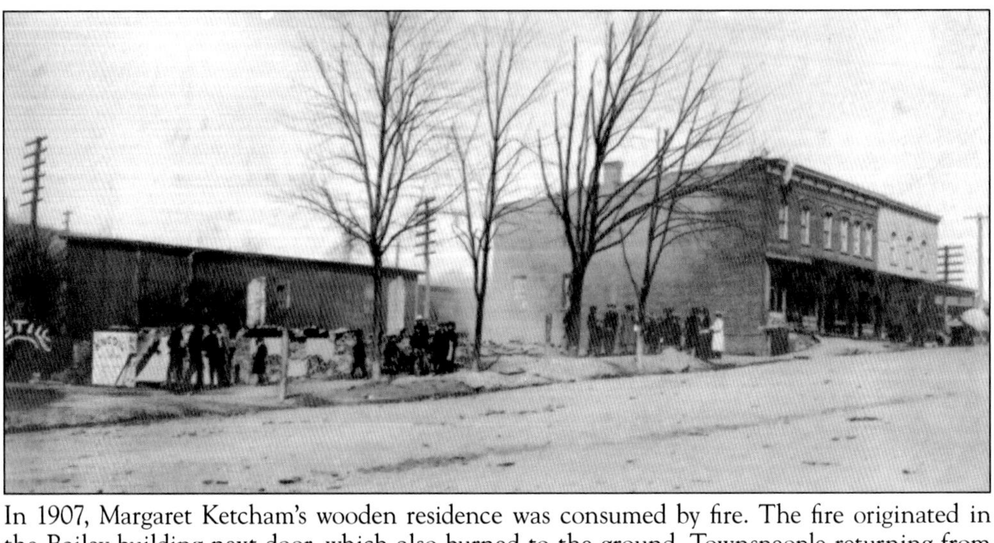

In 1907, Margaret Ketcham's wooden residence was consumed by fire. The fire originated in the Bailey building next door, which also burned to the ground. Townspeople returning from a function at the sanitorium saw the flames and issued the alarm. Despite valiant efforts by the citizens of Otisville, the fire was beyond their control and both buildings were leveled.

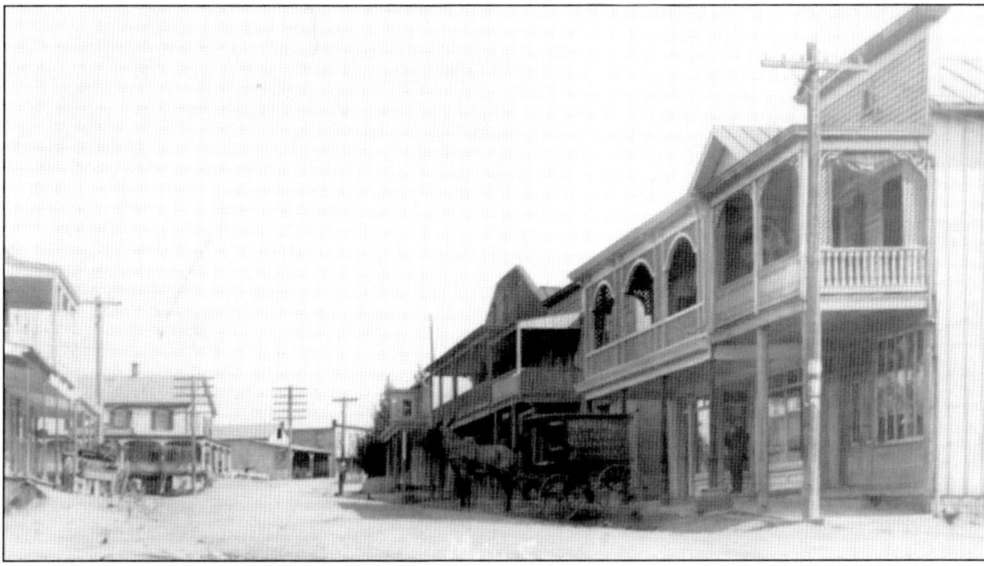

When the buildings on Main Street were built in the mid-to-late 1800s, many featured balconies that overlooked the street. During parades, it was the perfect vantage point to observe the processions. Many of these balconies were removed in the 1940s in an attempt to give the buildings more modern facades. Mr. Rockwell had a general store in the building on the right side of the street in the early 1900s. In this photograph, Rockwell's horse and delivery wagon are waiting outside the store. The writing on the side of the wagon reads, "L. N. S. Rockwell, General Merchandise Otisville."

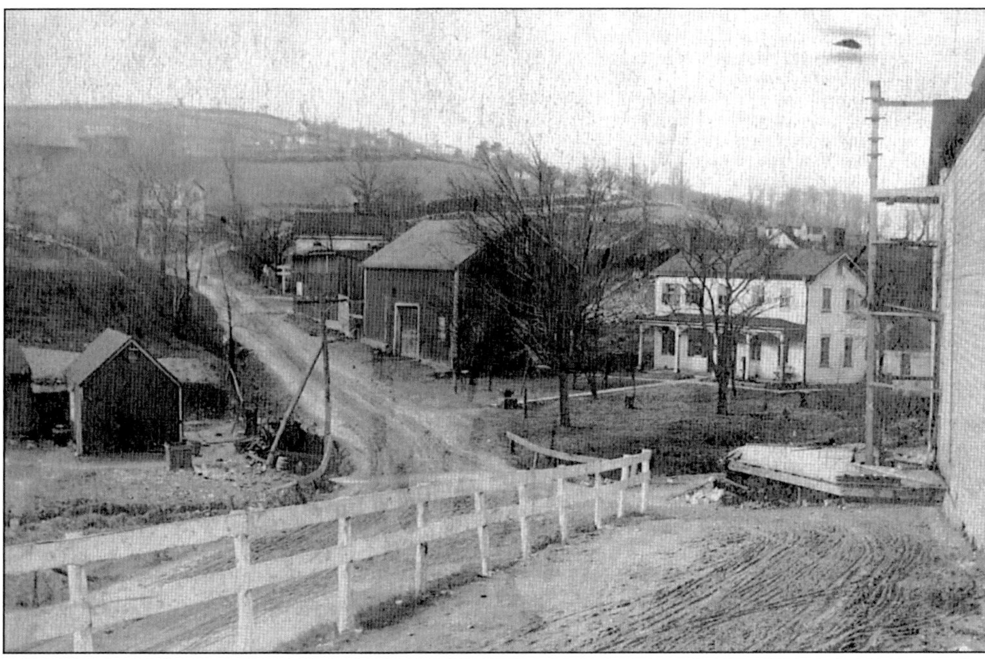

This photograph is a view taken from the Borden condensary on Main Street, looking toward Field Road on the left and Walker Street on the right. The house in the picture is still located at the terminus of Main Street. Stone foundations from the Borden plant can be found in the woods beside the street.

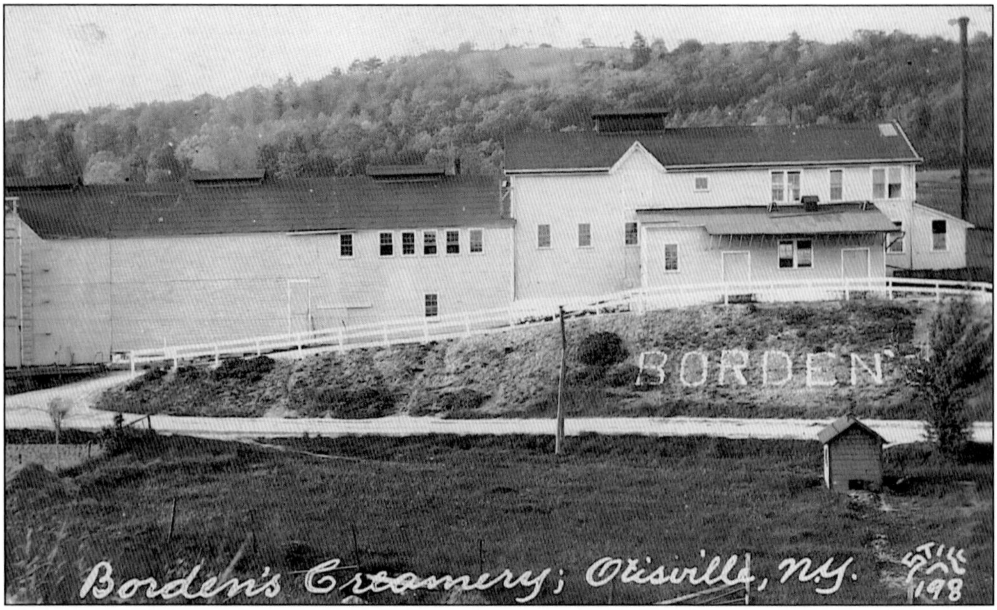

This photograph shows an impressive view of the front of the Borden condensary in Otisville. The plant was eventually closed for fear of possible lead contamination from the mines on the hill above the town. The Borden Company then built a creamery in another location in Otisville.

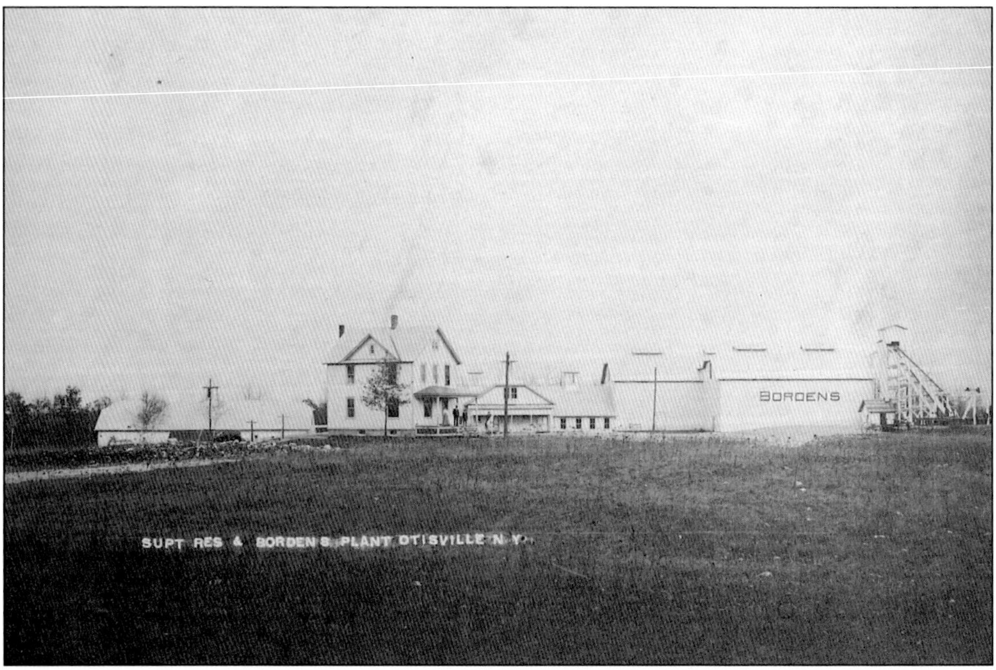

In the early 1900s, a large Borden creamery was built in Otisville on a street named for the company. The plant on Borden Street employed many men in the area, including a few local farmers who appreciated earning some extra money during their shifts at the Borden creamery. The Ketcham Fencing Company currently has their offices in part of the original Borden building.

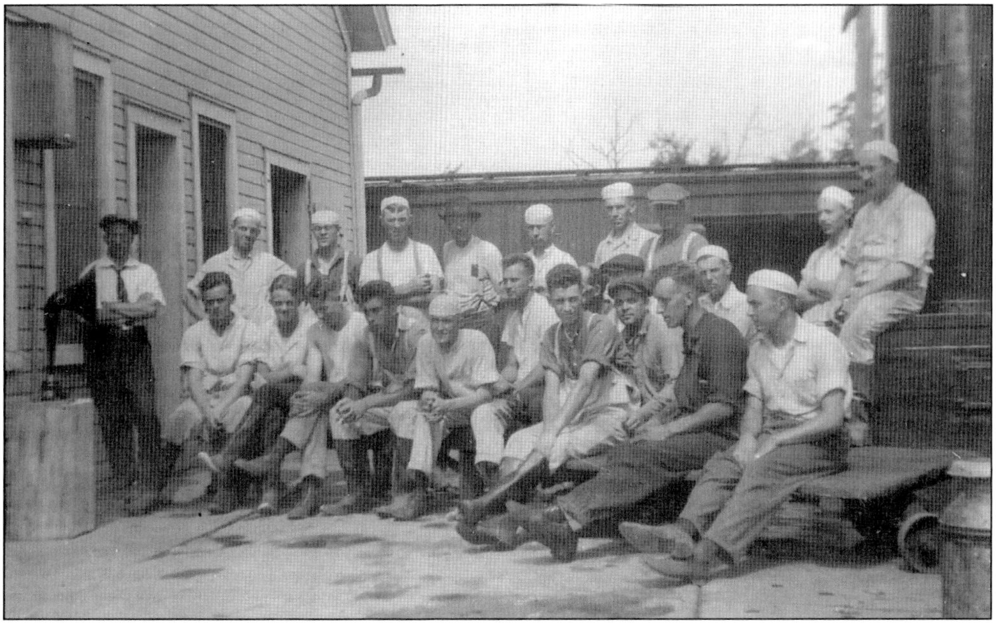

Employees of the Borden creamery pose for a photograph. The men in the photograph from left to right are (first row) unidentified, William Donahue, Abijah Ketcham, Walter Miller, Harry Collins, Curtis Carter, unidentified, Ronald Walker, Harold Nourse, unidentified, and Archie House; (second row) E. L. Walker, Fred M. Penney, K. R. Walker, William J. Smith, Alfred Smith, H. Kirkander, unidentified, unidentified, C. Drews, and William House.

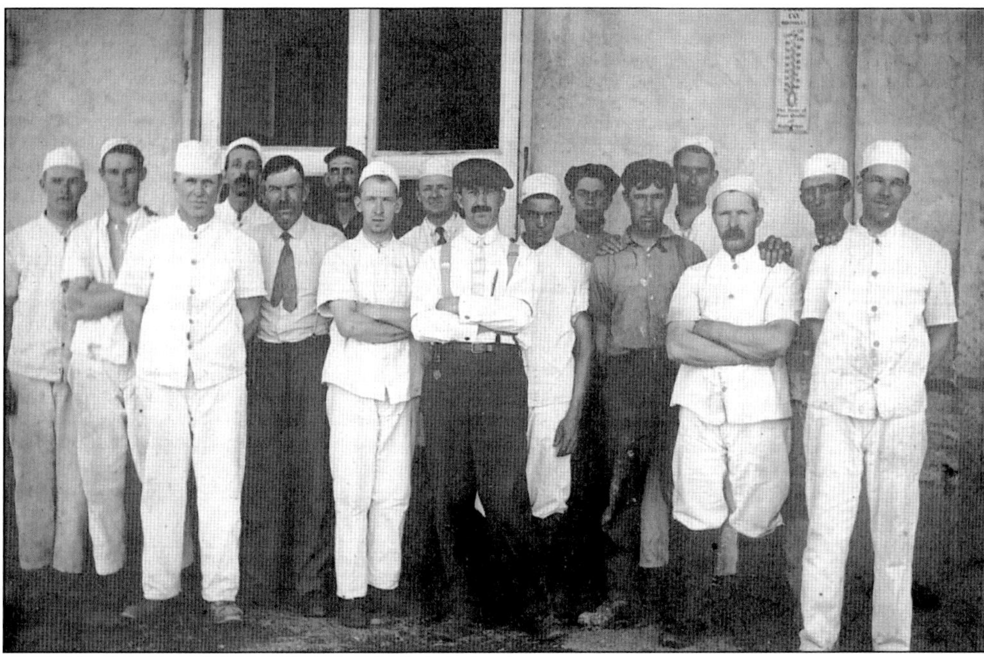

Posing for the camera is another group of employees at the Borden creamery. Pictured are Willard Moore, Albert Collins, Lewis Writer, Mat Writer, Alfred Ketcham, Clarence Glass, William Green, Loton Horton, superintendent E. L. Walker, Ronald Walker, William Smith, ? Collins, and Frank Hull.

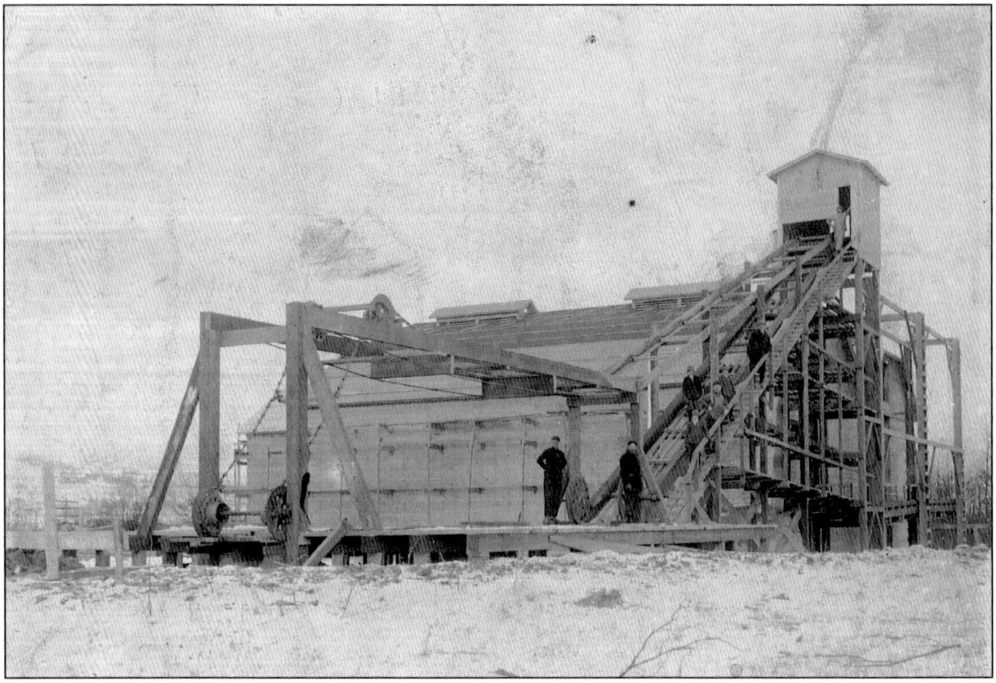

The ice flume at the Borden plant in Otisville is shown in this vintage photograph. Ice was harvested from Borden's pond, which was located on Mount Hope Road. Then the ice was taken by horse-drawn cart back to the plant to be used in producing various milk products. In the early 1900s, there were many dairy farms in the town of Mount Hope that produced milk that was purchased by the Borden Company.

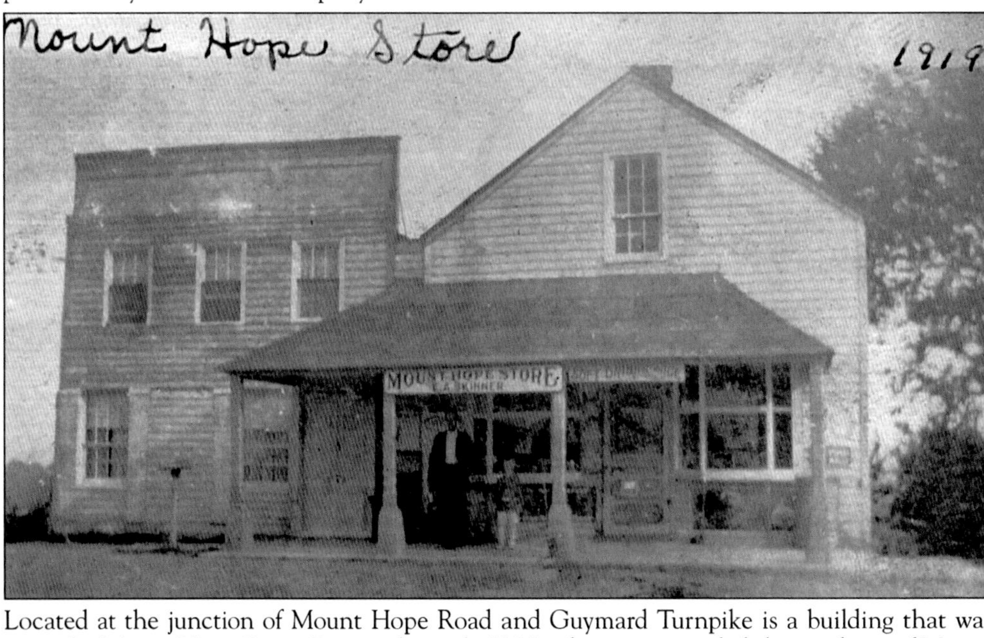

Located at the junction of Mount Hope Road and Guymard Turnpike is a building that was once the Mount Hope Store. During the early 1900s, the store provided the residents of Mount Hope with all types of general merchandise from eggs to nails. In the mid-1900s, the store was operated by the Dodd family.

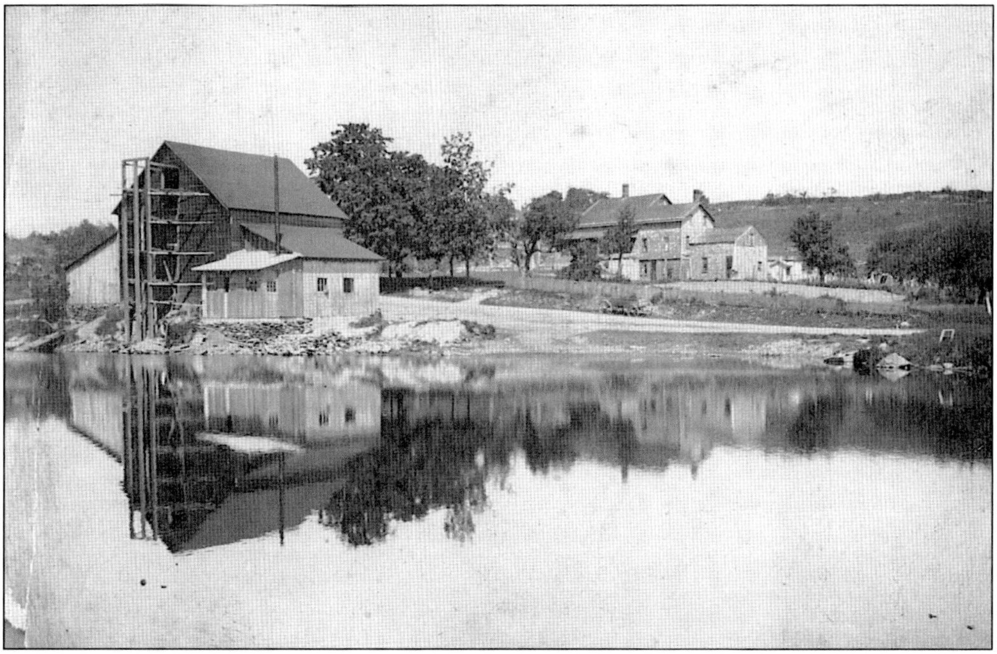

In 1774, the Ketcham family settled in Mount Hope on land adjacent to the Shawangunk Kill. John Ketcham and his three sons operated a gristmill and plaster mill on their property. Ketcham's grandson Joseph built a sawmill on the kill in the early 1800s, and in 1821, he invented a dog-powered butter churn that was used in households throughout the area. Many Ketcham descendants still live in Otisville and Mount Hope.

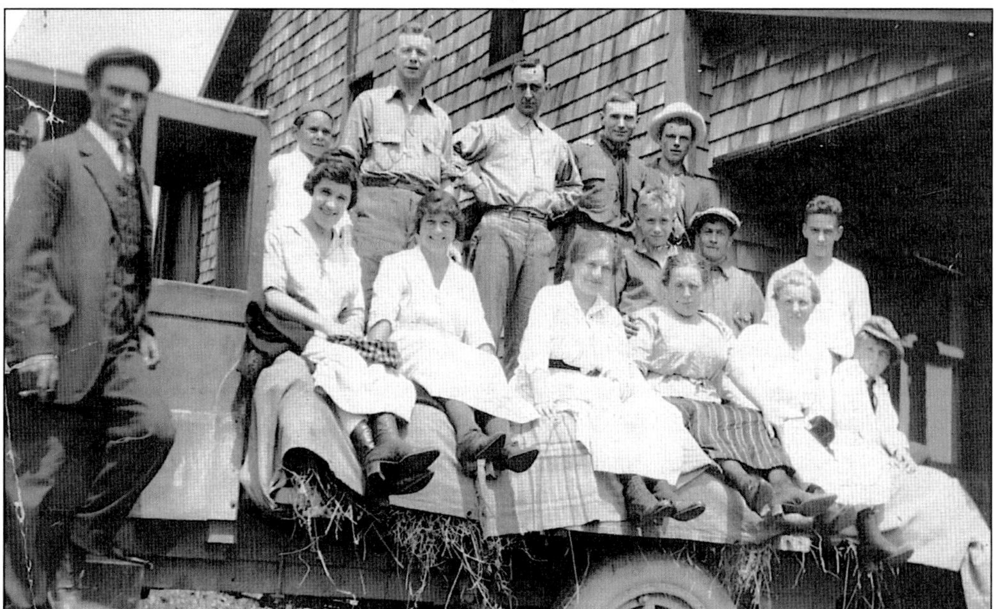

The Ketcham family once operated a summer boardinghouse on Guymard Turnpike across from the millpond. Tourists came to enjoy a few days in the country. In this photograph, they are getting ready to take a ride on one of the country lanes nearby. The old millpond later became the popular summer locale known as Old Mill Beach.

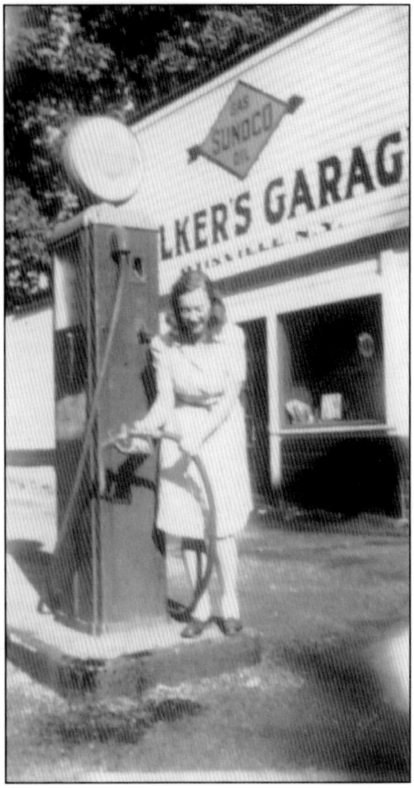

Walker's garage was located on the corner of the state road and Walker Street in Otisville. At Walker's garage one could fill a tank with gas or have a flat tire fixed. In this picture, Dolores Meisener is getting ready to pump some gas at Walker's garage.

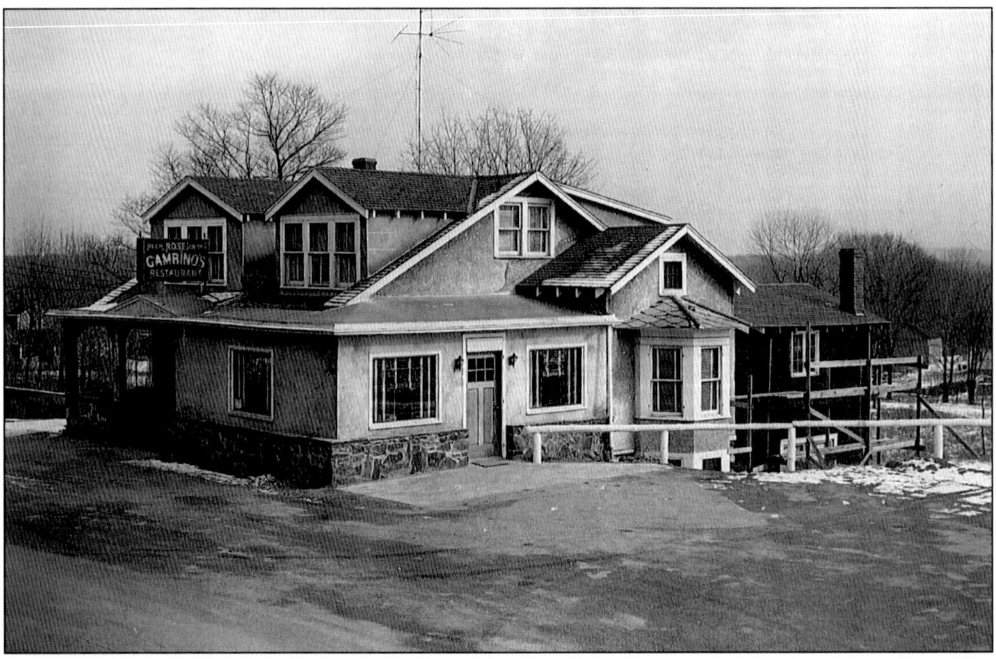

Rose Gambino's bar and grill was a popular gathering place on Sanitorium Avenue in Otisville. Rose's authentic Italian cuisine was unsurpassed. She was also a prominent democratic supporter, who was photographed with John F. Kennedy during his presidential campaign in 1960.

Two

RESIDENCES AND STREET SCENES

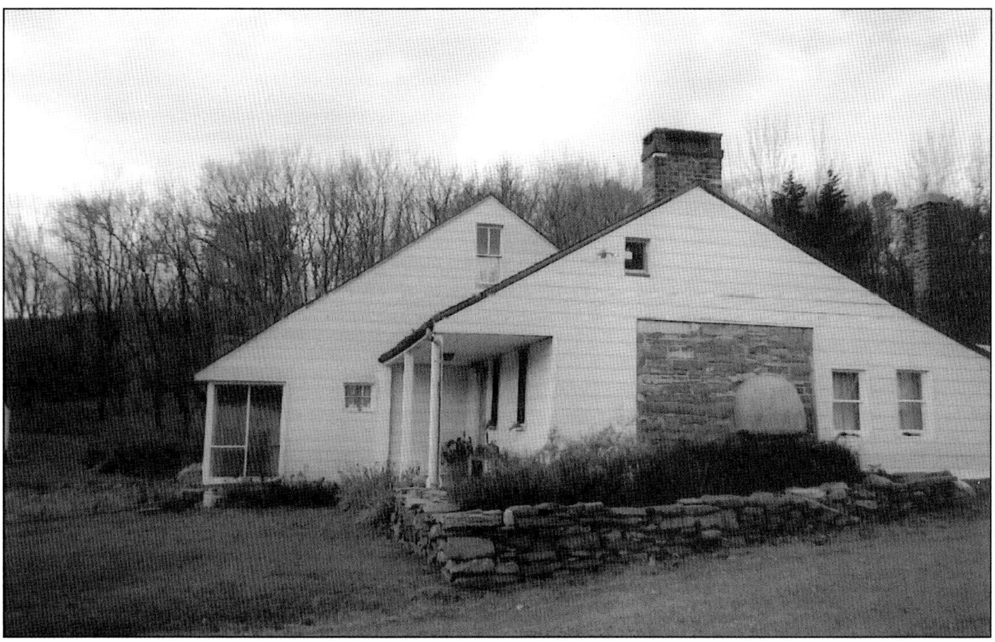

The Harding house was built around 1790 and was inhabited by many generations of the Harding family. A large beehive oven and open-hearth fireplace are original to the house. In the early 1800s, an addition to the house was built that included a dining room, sitting room, and bedrooms. Prior to this addition, everyone slept and ate in one room. The Mount Hope Historical Society maintains this home, and it is open to the public once a month.

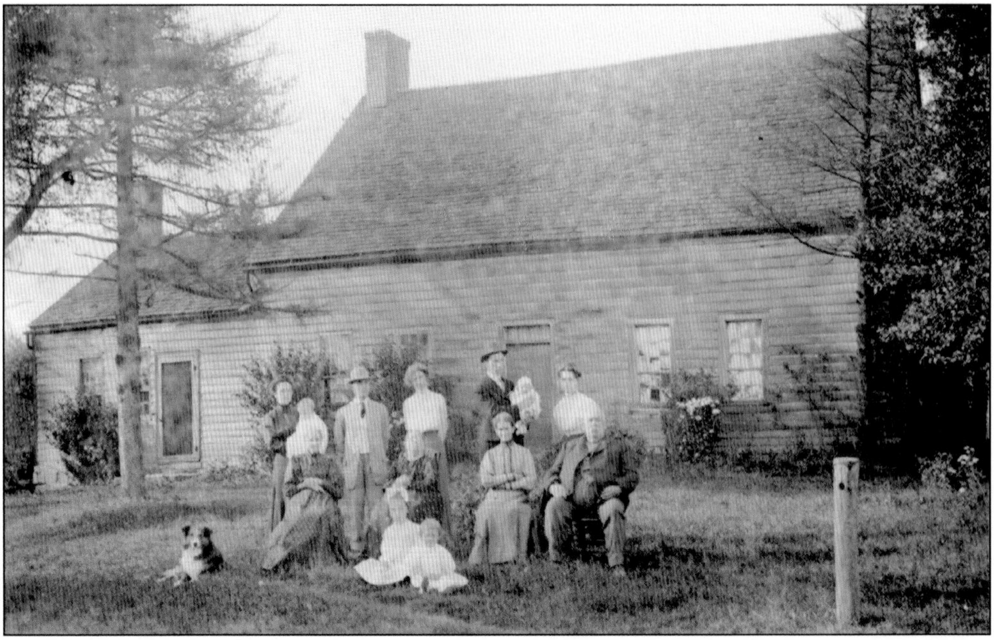

Johannes Seybolt and his son built this house in 1789 in Otisville. Both Seybolts served in the 2nd Regiment of the Ulster County Militia during the American Revolution. During the ownership of Lewis A. Seybolt, it was the center for village justice. There was a courtroom on the second floor and a whipping post stood in the yard. Gideon C. and Lamira Seybolt Harding are pictured with their family outside their home.

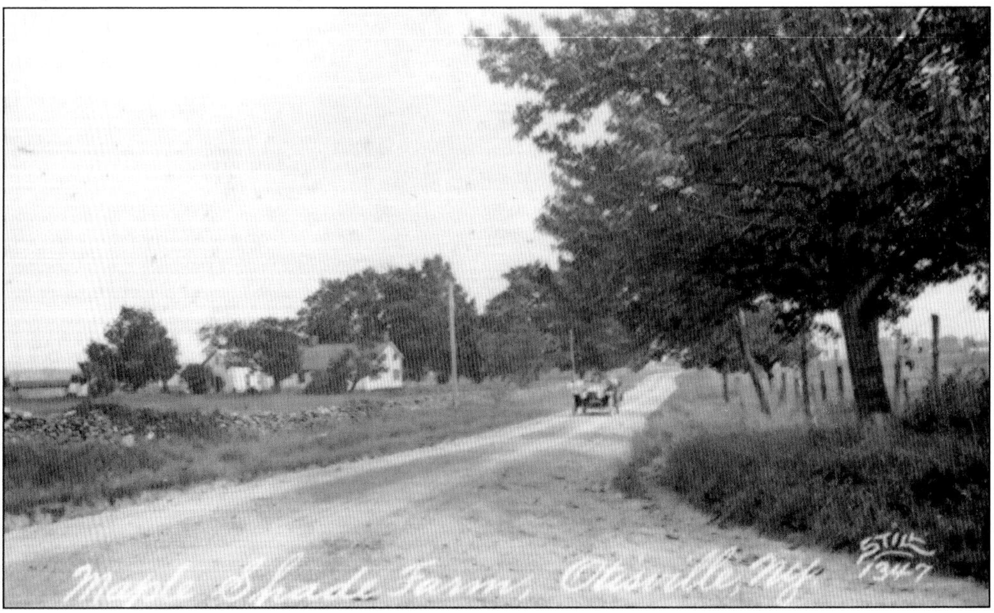

An early horseless carriage chugs down Mount Hope Road during the early 1900s. This was a time when villagers counted how many cars traveled through town on a Sunday afternoon. Alfred H. Still is credited with taking this photograph as well as many others that appear in this book. Still was related to the Easton-Holley family, and when visiting Otisville, he captured these wonderful images.

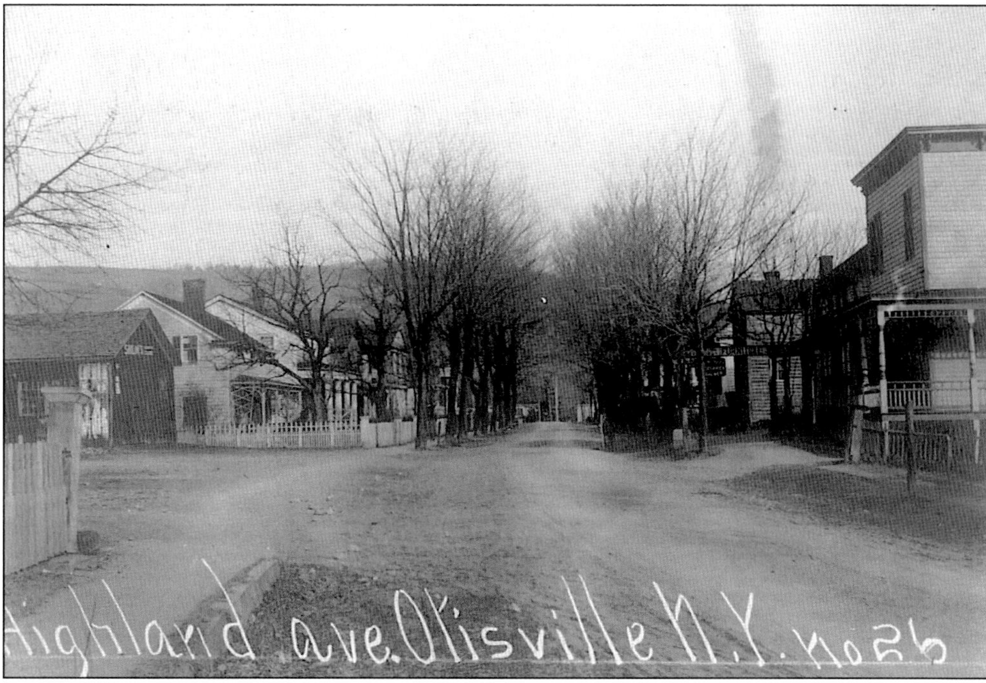

During the early 1900s, Highland Avenue was unpaved and horses and buggies were used to travel from one point to another. Until long after the automobile arrived, the road remained this way. In the winter, people used sleighs to traverse the snow-covered streets. This view of Highland Avenue was taken in front of the Methodist church looking toward the former home of Dr. Kaback.

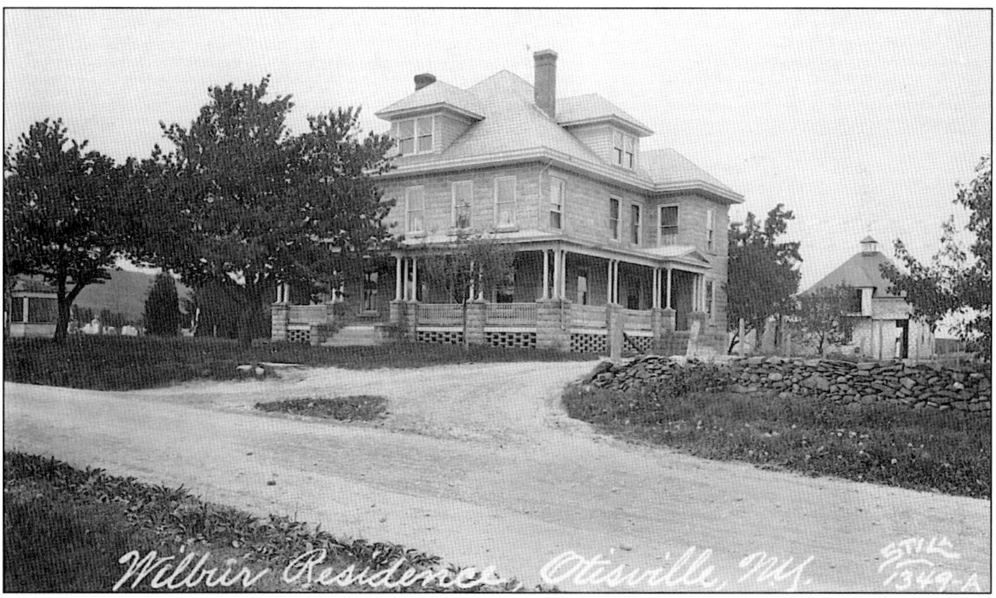

The expansive Wilbur home located next to the Mount Hope Plains Cemetery was constructed from formed concrete blocks in the early 1900s. The Wilbur family owned a sand and gravel business in Otisville. This means of construction was used to build several other homes on Highland Avenue in the village of Otisville.

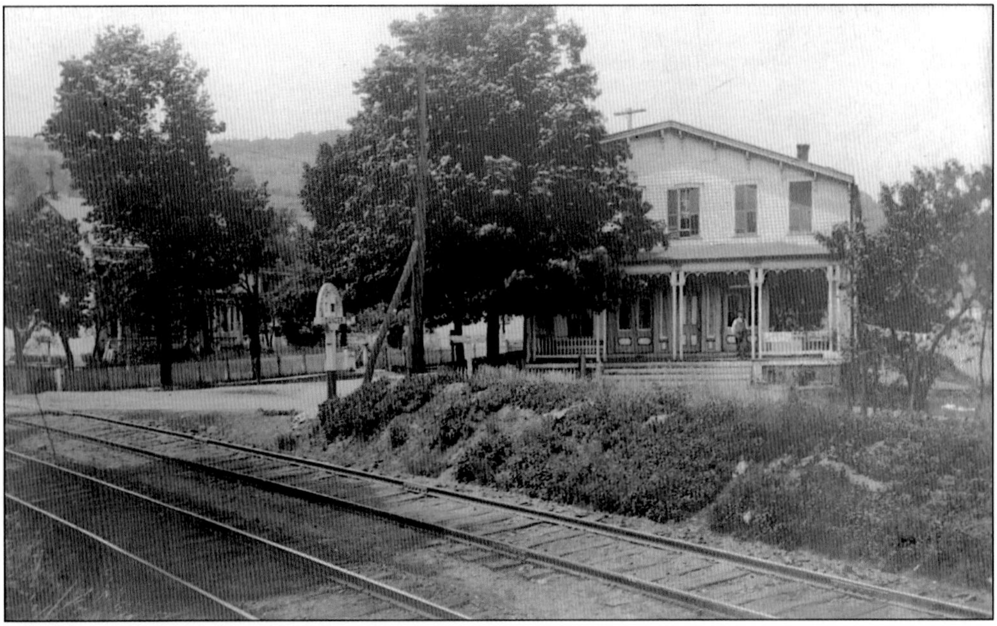

Located at the top of Kelly Hill is the Beyea house. This multiple-family dwelling was built on a portion of the former Cadwell farm. It is known by many people as the "beehive" because of its unusual shape. Cadwell's crossing for the Erie Railroad was situated in front of the Beyea dwelling.

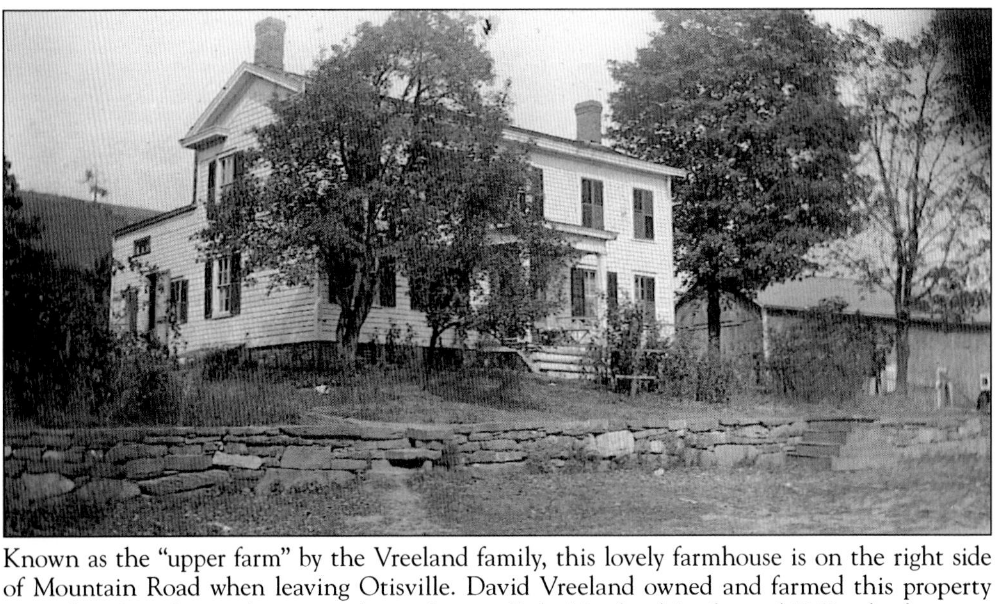

Known as the "upper farm" by the Vreeland family, this lovely farmhouse is on the right side of Mountain Road when leaving Otisville. David Vreeland owned and farmed this property around 1913, and it was later passed on to his son Rube Vreeland. In the mid-1950s, the farm was sold to the Easkold family.

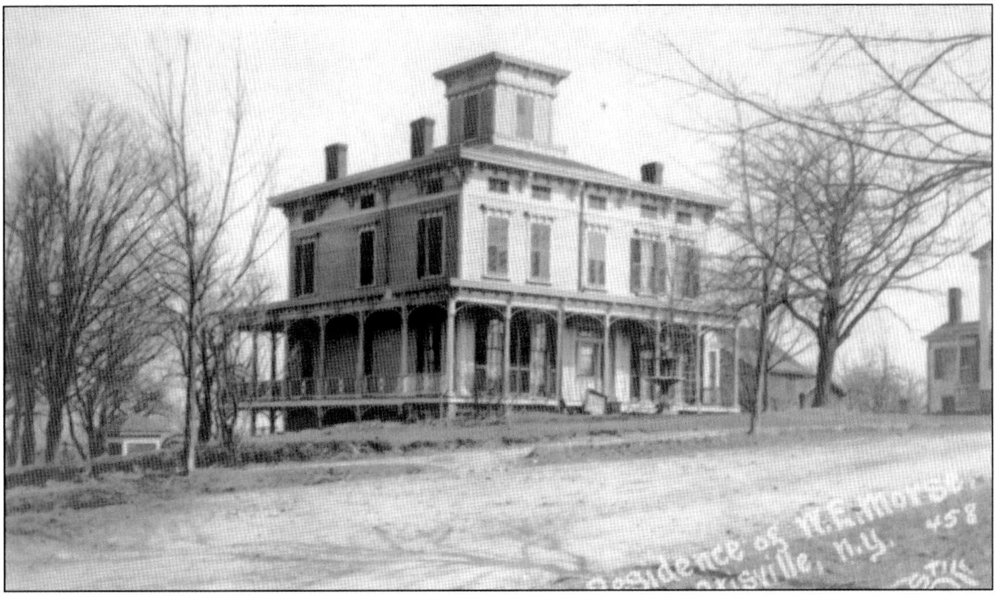

Galen Otis came to Deerpark Four Corners in 1817 with his brother Isaac. The two brothers opened a general mercantile business and operated a distillery. Galen built this large Victorian with a cupola next to the bridge on Highland Avenue and lived there for many years with his wife, Fanny King Otis, and their seven children. In 1929, the house was destroyed by fire during the ownership of Dr. Cahill.

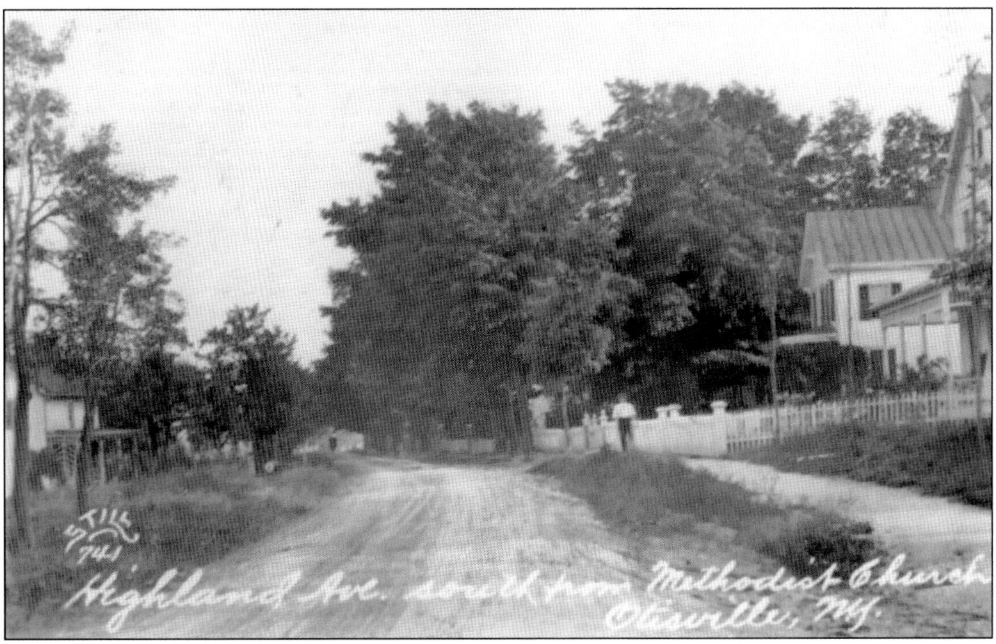

This photograph is an early view of Highland Avenue looking toward the south from in front of the Methodist church. Note the white picket fence that was commonly found in front of homes during the early 1900s. In early newspapers, Highland Avenue is often referred to as the "upper road" and Orchard Street is called the "lower road."

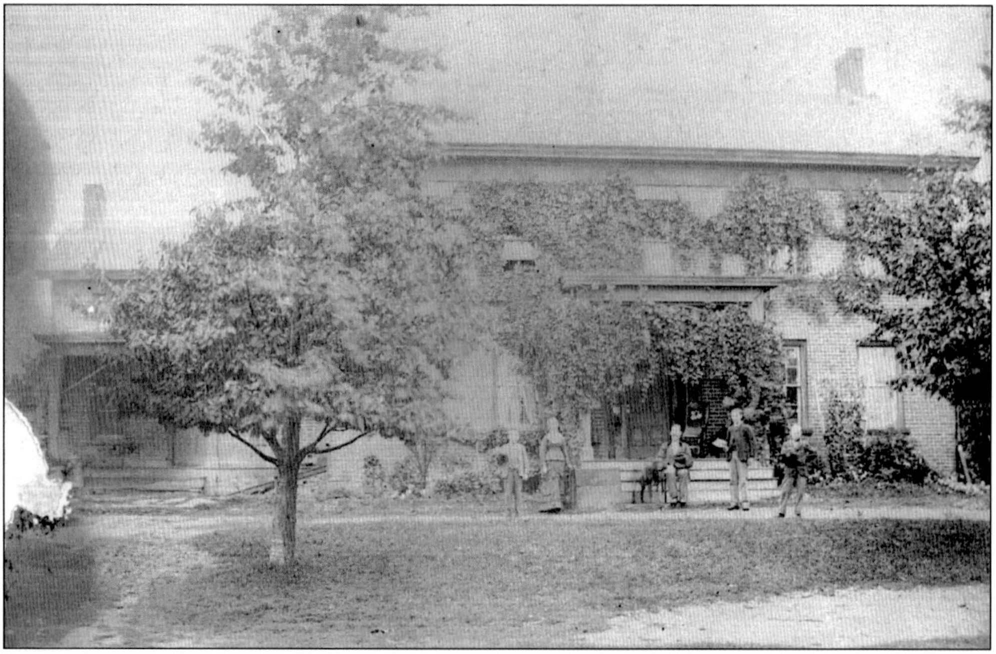

The Joshua Corwin family came from Southold on Long Island and settled on a large tract of land in Mount Hope during the late 1700s. In the early 1800s, an impressive brick residence was erected on the property. According to family members, the bricks for the construction of this house were brought by cart from Goshen. Many Corwin descendants remain in the area today.

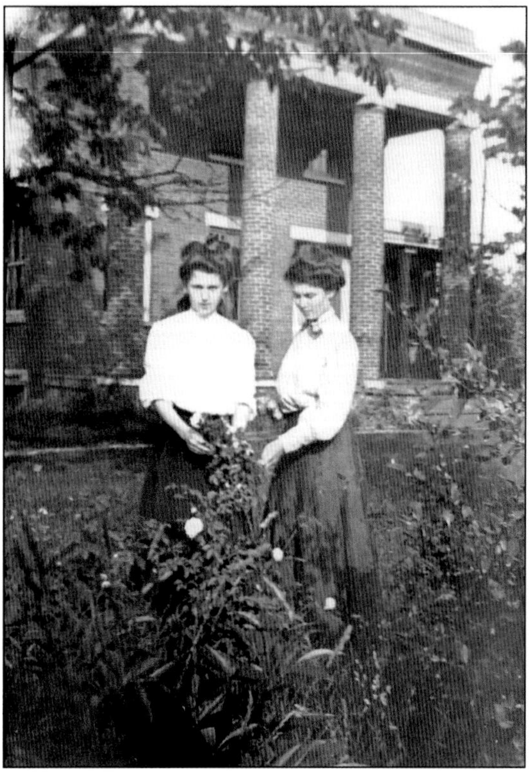

Ida Craig and her friend Elsie admire the roses in front of the Craig house on Sanitorium Avenue. The house was purchased in 1877 by Ida's grandfather James Craig. Ida and her sisters, Mary, Grace, Bertha, and Edna, and one brother, James, were all born in this house. When the house was built, a large, brick barn was also constructed on the property.

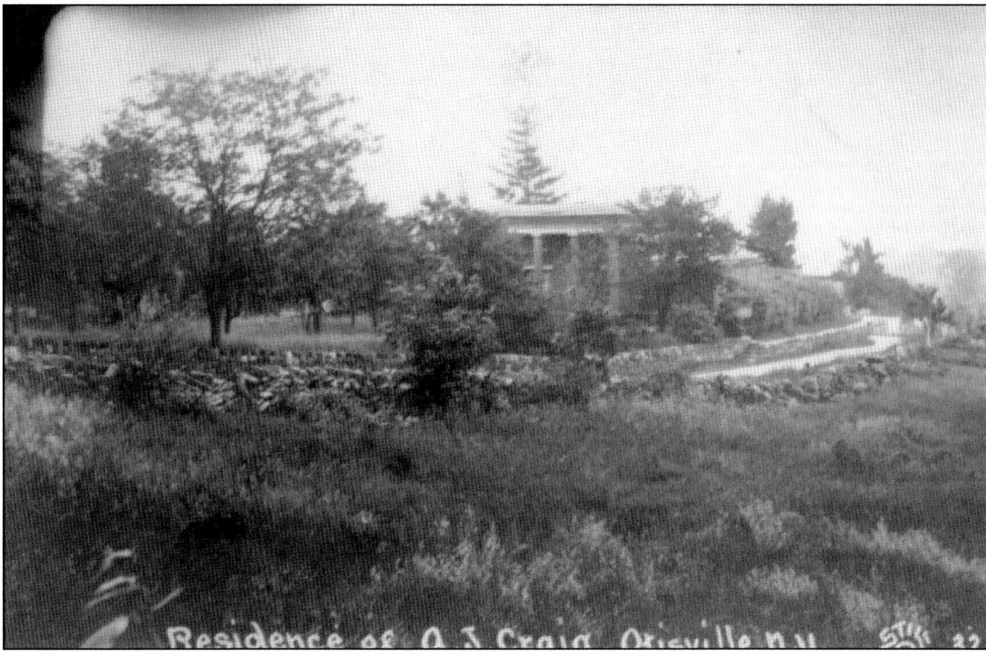

The brick house purchased by Ida's grandfather James Craig in 1877 was built for William Brown and his wife, Laney, in 1853. Brown was born in a log cabin on the property in 1819, and between 1851 and 1853, the home was built from bricks made in a kiln on the property. After James died, the house was held in trust for his grandson James Bailey Craig.

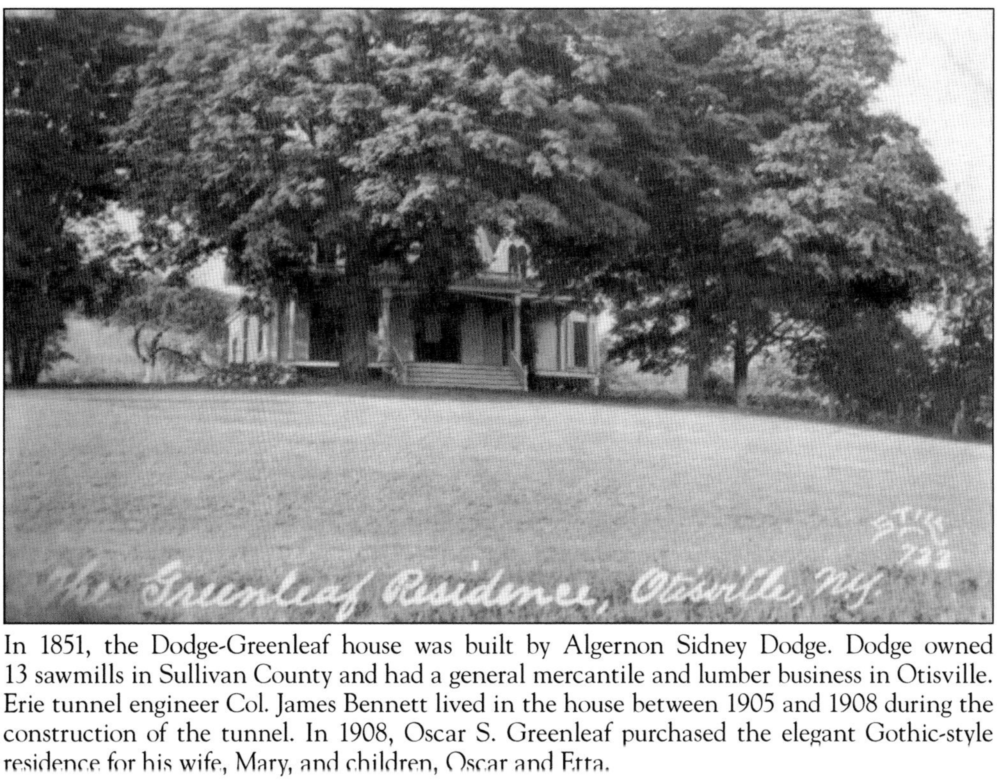

In 1851, the Dodge-Greenleaf house was built by Algernon Sidney Dodge. Dodge owned 13 sawmills in Sullivan County and had a general mercantile and lumber business in Otisville. Erie tunnel engineer Col. James Bennett lived in the house between 1905 and 1908 during the construction of the tunnel. In 1908, Oscar S. Greenleaf purchased the elegant Gothic-style residence for his wife, Mary, and children, Oscar and Etta.

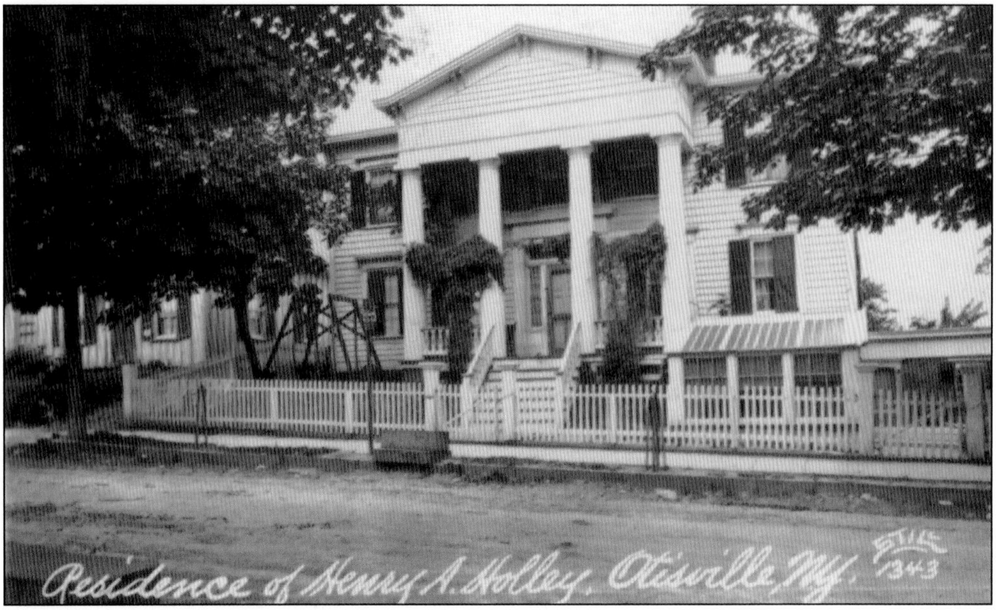

James Easton and his wife, Hannah Corwin, lived in this stately Greek Revival residence on Highland Avenue for many years after moving to Otisville in 1869. The house was erected around 1840. Easton was a leading merchant in Otisville and had a general mercantile business on Main Street. After Harriet Easton married Henry A. Holley, the house became known as the Holley house.

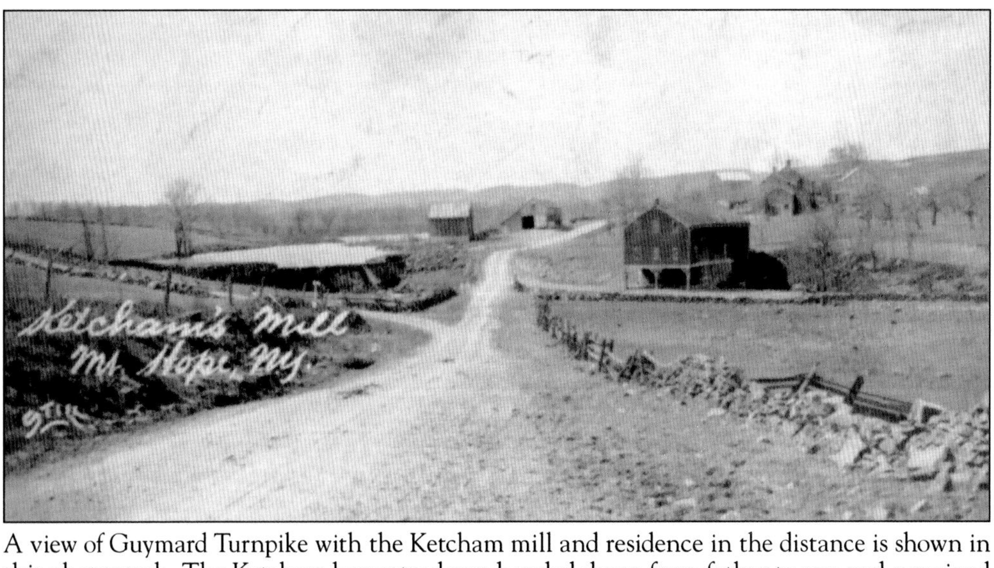

A view of Guymard Turnpike with the Ketcham mill and residence in the distance is shown in this photograph. The Ketcham homestead was handed down from father to son and remained in the family for many generations. In the late 1800s, the mill was operated by Isaac E. Ketcham and his brother Charles Clifford Vail Ketcham. The mill closed in the early 1900s.

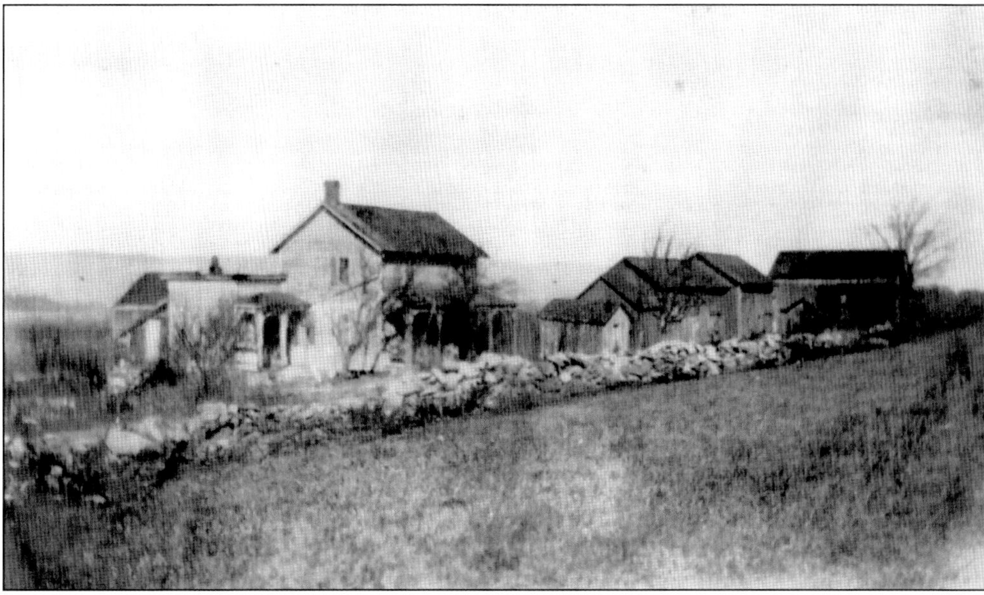

The early farmstead in this photograph was once owned by the Wilson family and is located on White Bridge Road in Mount Hope. Many dairy farms once dotted the landscape of Mount Hope. The farmers produced milk that was sold to the butter factory or the Borden plant. Only a few farms in Mount Hope still operate as working farms.

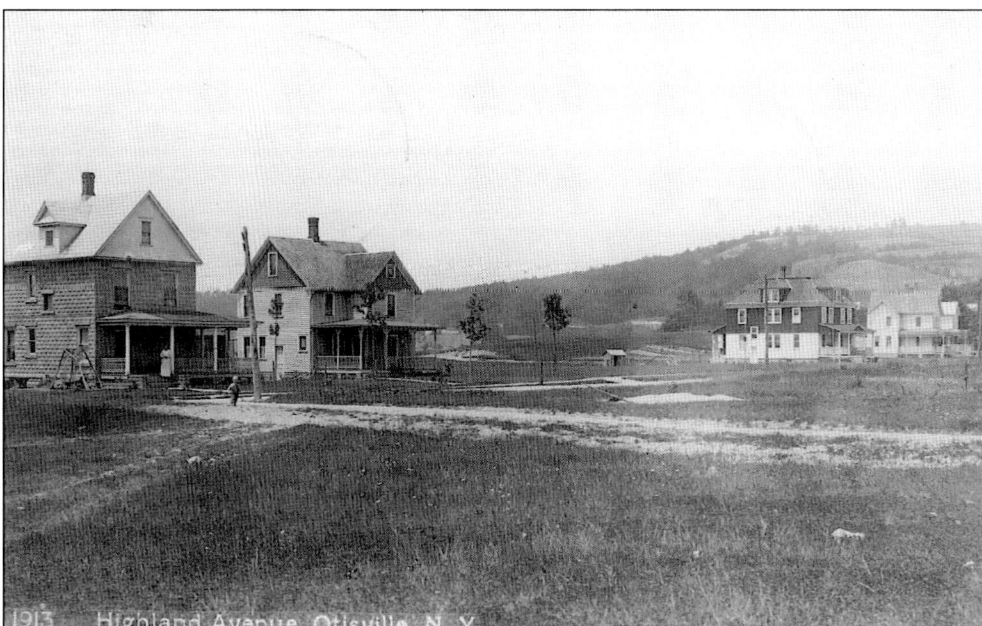

In 1913, this photograph was taken on Highland Avenue in Otisville near the intersection of School Street. The first house on the left was constructed from formed concrete blocks as was the Wilbur residence. The house to the far right was once occupied by Dr. Yetta Schevell, who was a physician in Otisville for many years.

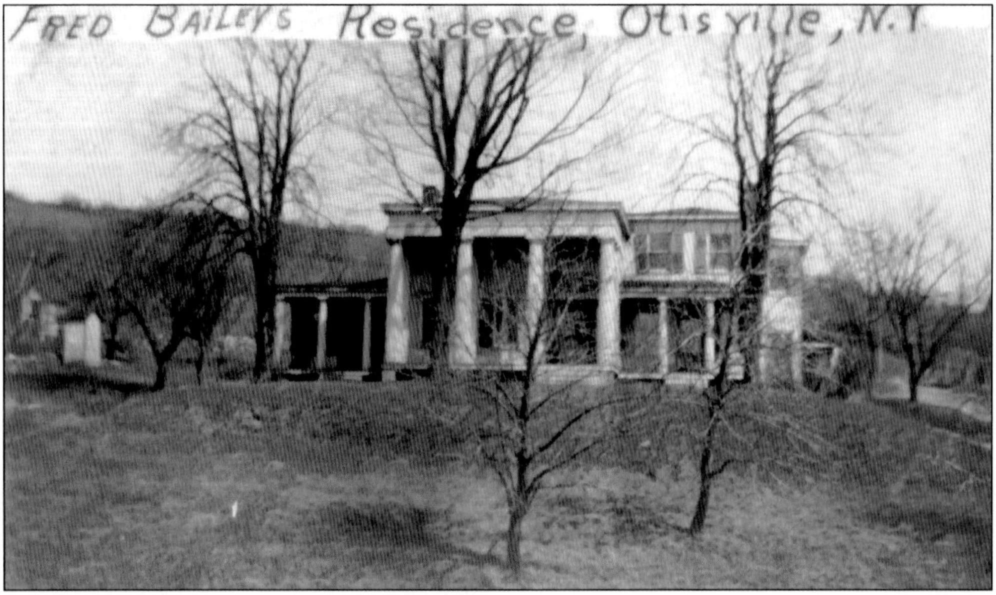

Dr. Avery Cook first came to Otisville in 1835 and practiced medicine with Dr. Silas Loomis. He fell in love with Loomis's daughter Pamela. Cook remained in Otisville and practiced medicine for almost 50 years. The Cooks built their impressive residence around 1840 on a knoll overlooking the village. Cook trained Dr. John Logue, who was a surgeon on the Civil War vessel, the *Monitor.*

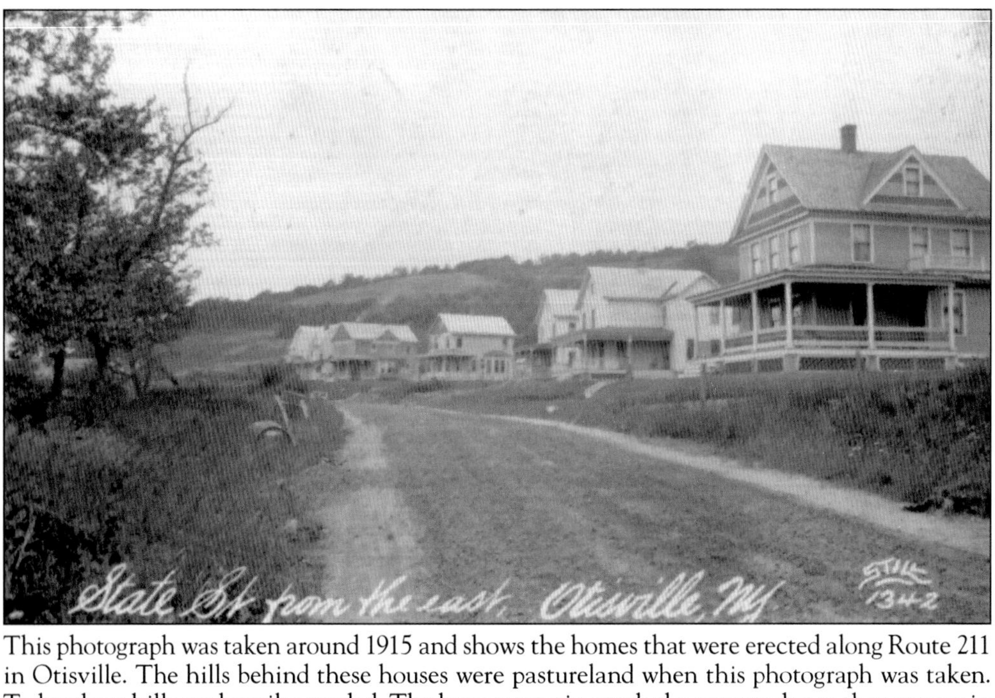

This photograph was taken around 1915 and shows the homes that were erected along Route 211 in Otisville. The hills behind these houses were pastureland when this photograph was taken. Today these hills are heavily wooded. The homes remain much the same today as they appear in this picture. The U.S. Army once had a hospital that was located behind these homes.

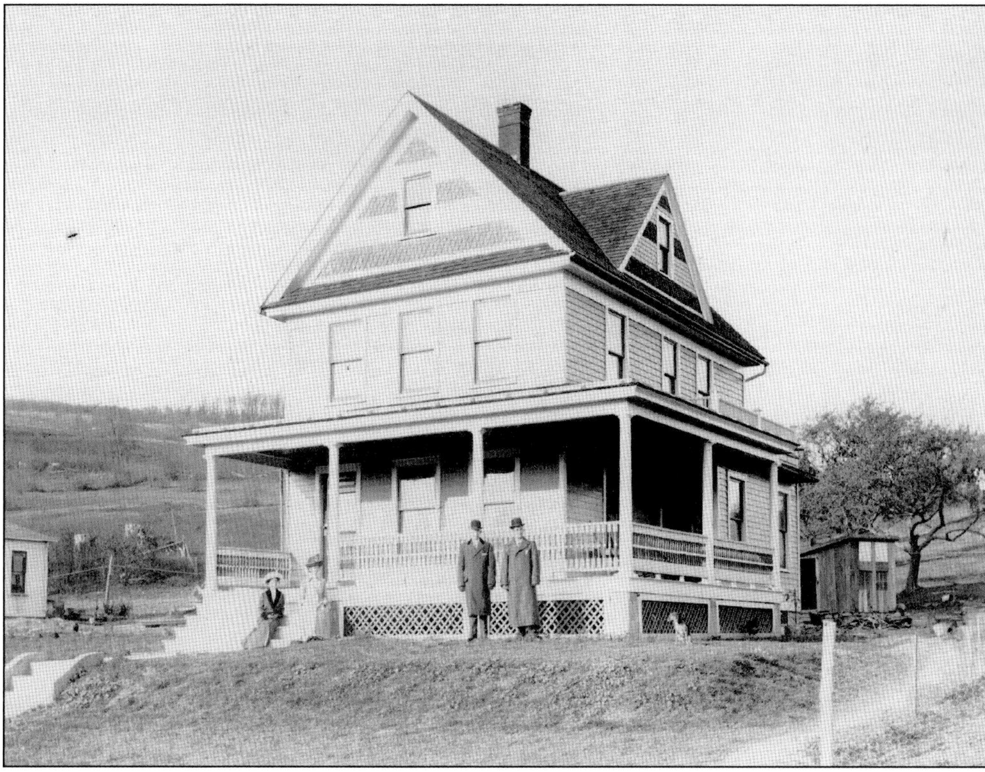

Florrie and Oliver Ketcham built this home on Route 211 in Otisville in 1914 for $3,000. It is the first house on the right after turning left from the bridge to head toward Port Jervis. The house features a large, wraparound porch. Pictured in front of the house from left to right are Florrie, Dora Green, Bill Green, and Oliver.

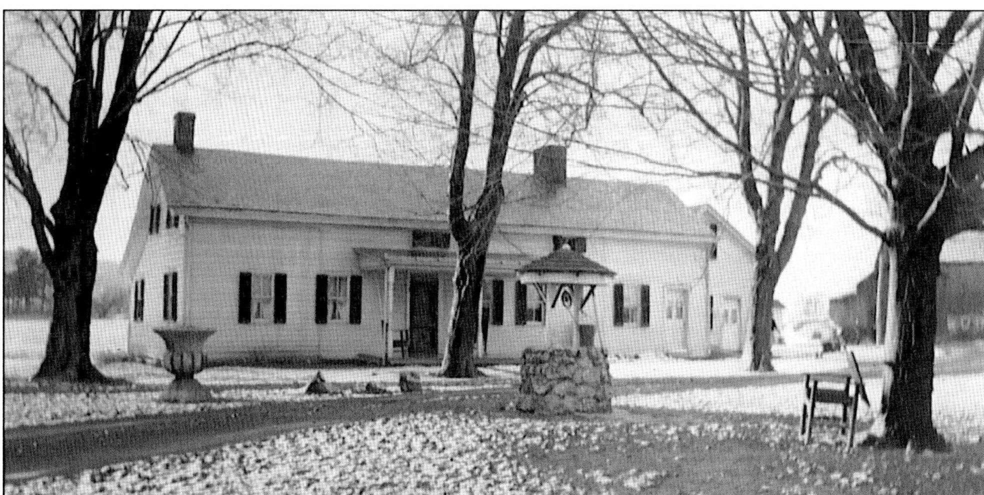

Daniel Osborne built this Colonial farmhouse around 1793 on the Mount Hope Road. It was one of the oldest houses in the village. Andrew Mitchell and his wife Molly once owned the Osborne farm. The farm was later in possession of Rube Vreeland and his wife, Anna Mae Mitchell. Vreeland held his very popular yearly auctions at this historic farm in Otisville.

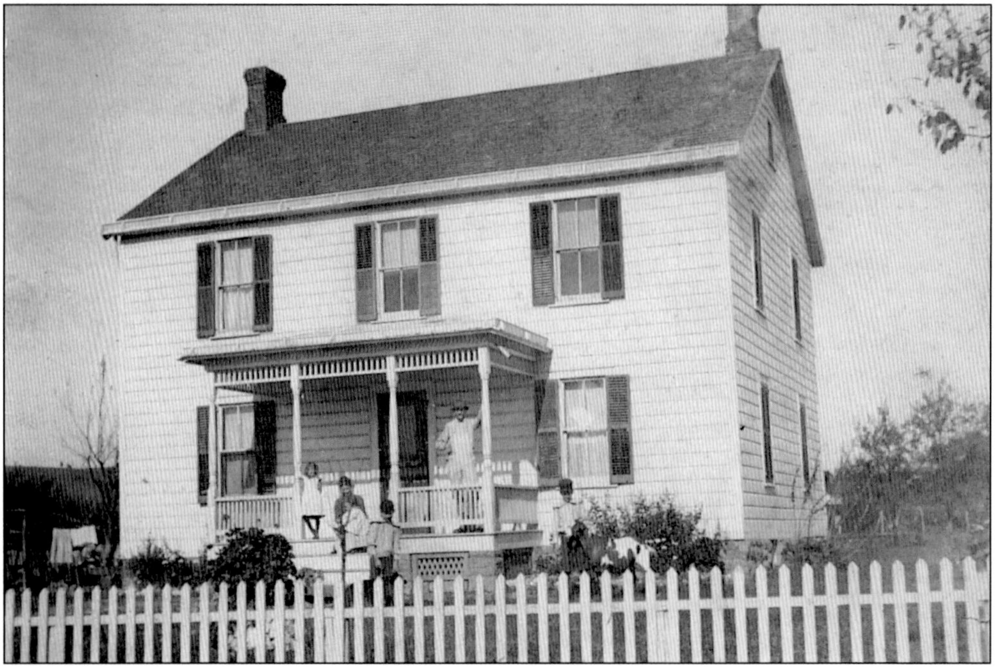

In 1902, this photograph was taken of the Andrew Mitchell family in front of their house on the corner of Mount Hope Road and Finchville Turnpike. Mitchell is standing, and his wife Molly is sitting and holding their daughter Anna Mae. Daughter Florence and sons Joseph and Andrew are also pictured. The Mitchells later moved a short distance down the road to the Osborne farm.

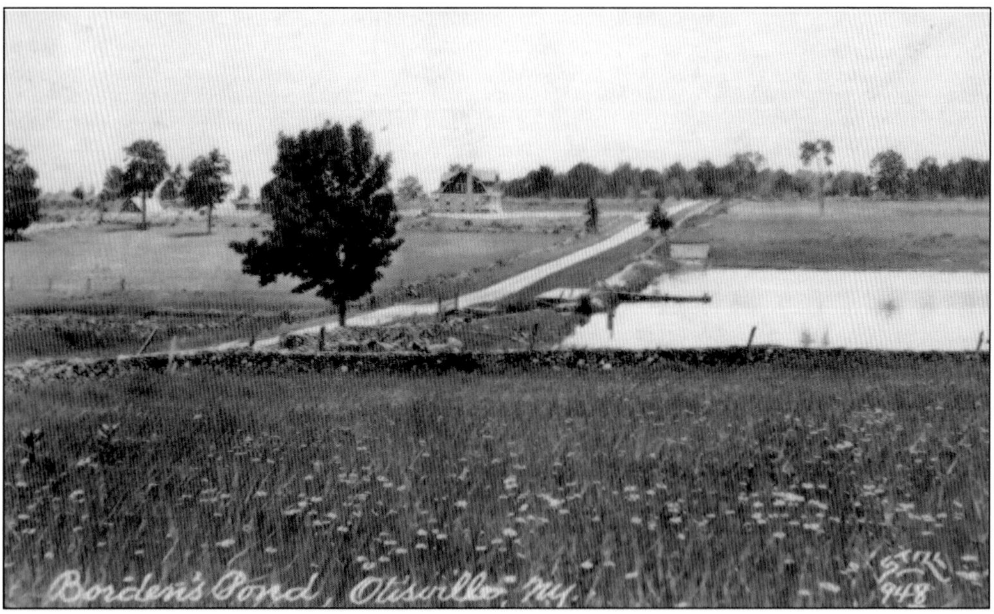

Borden's pond on Mount Hope Road was used by the Borden Company for ice harvesting. In the winter when the ice became thick enough, it was cut and taken by cart to the company's plant on Borden Street. In the early 1960s, the Otisville Lions Club sponsored an ice-skating program at the pond and many children in Otisville and Mount Hope enjoyed skating there.

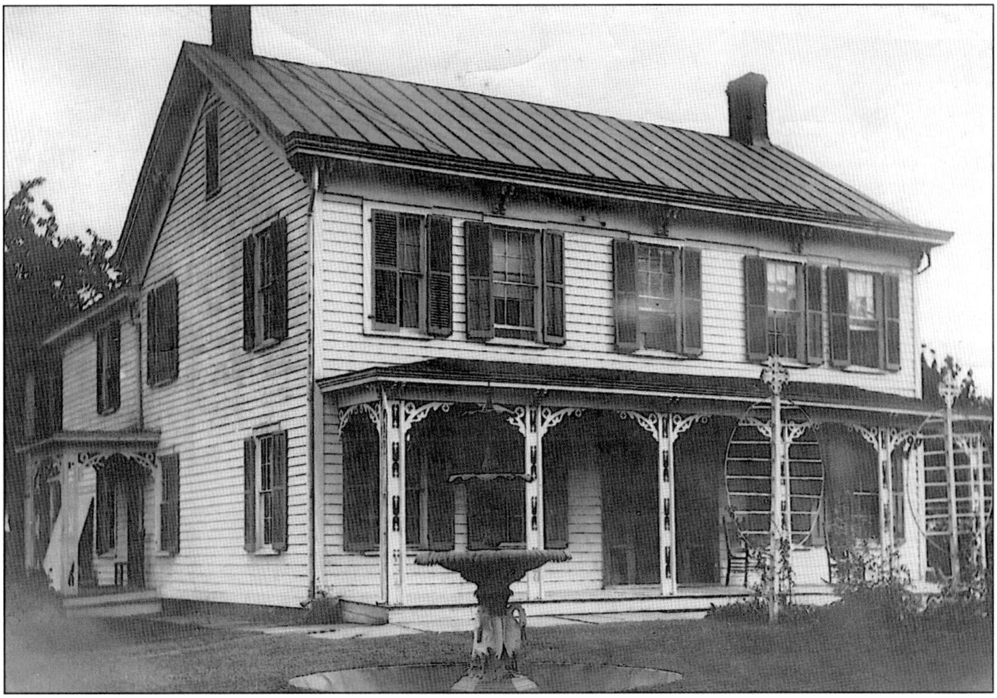

George Smith and his wife, Cynthia Green, lived in this spacious home on Sanitorium Avenue. Cynthia was the daughter of hotel builder Ambrose Green. She was also a lineal descendant of the fire-and-brimstone minister Rev. Cotton Mather. Smith was a supervisor of the Town of Mount Hope and owned a general store in Otisville. The house was later owned by the Cannon family.

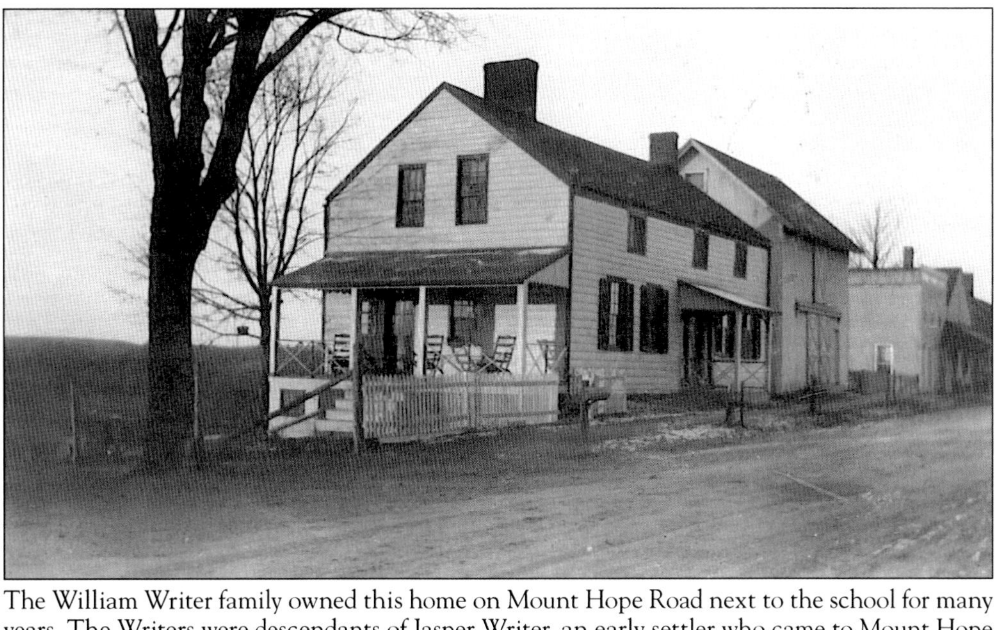

The William Writer family owned this home on Mount Hope Road next to the school for many years. The Writers were descendants of Jasper Writer, an early settler who came to Mount Hope in the late 1700s.

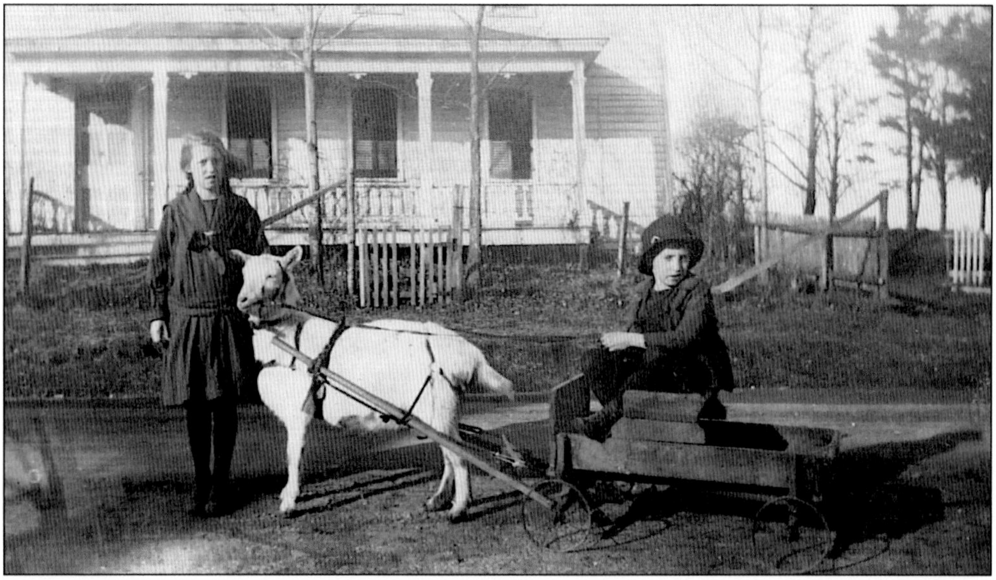

In this charming photograph taken in 1921, the Writer children are traveling the roads in Mount Hope with their goat cart. William Writer is sitting in the cart and Marion Writer is standing by the goat to keep it under control while the photograph is taken. Their parents were William and Nettie Writer of Mount Hope.

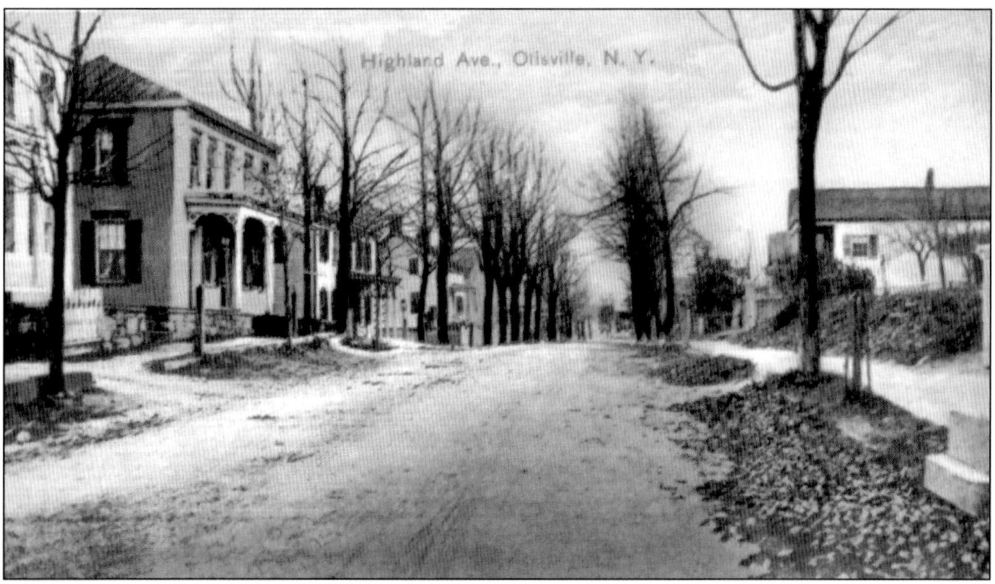

This photograph is an early view of Highland Avenue looking south from the Easton-Holley house. On the left is a home constructed from bricks made in a kiln on the William Brown farm. The third house on the left was owned by Judson VanDuzer. VanDuzer was the local tinsmith and had a shop on Main Street in Otisville.

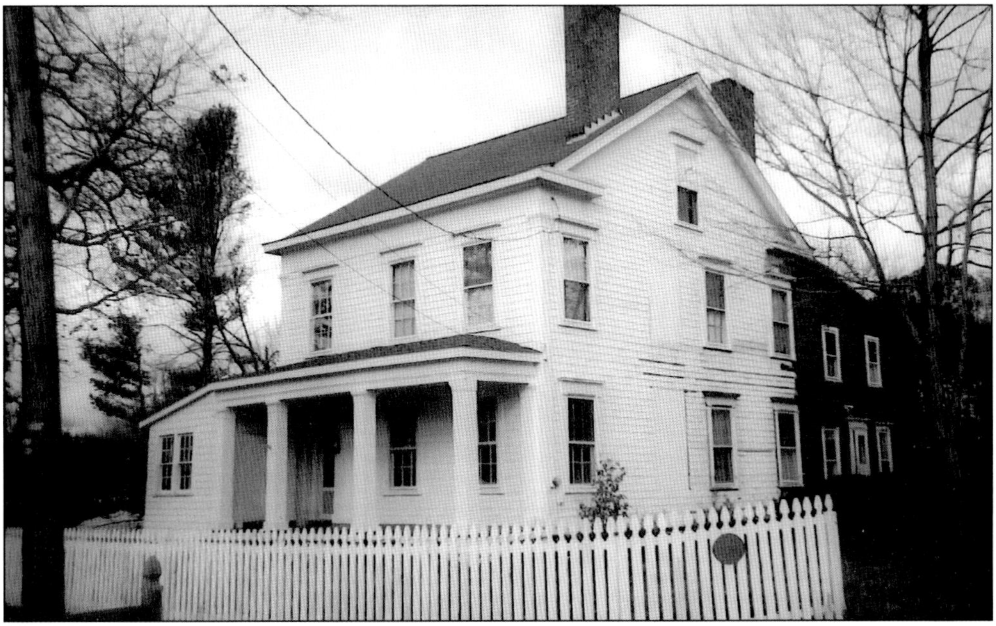

The Charles S. Woodward home is located on Mount Hope Road. In 1807, Woodward was born in Mount Hope, the son of Benjamin Woodward, who later became a New York State senator. Charles's grandfather Hezekiah Woodward was in the advance guard at the Battle of Minisink. This bloody battle with Joseph Brant, an English general and Mohawk warrior, took place north of Port Jervis in 1779.

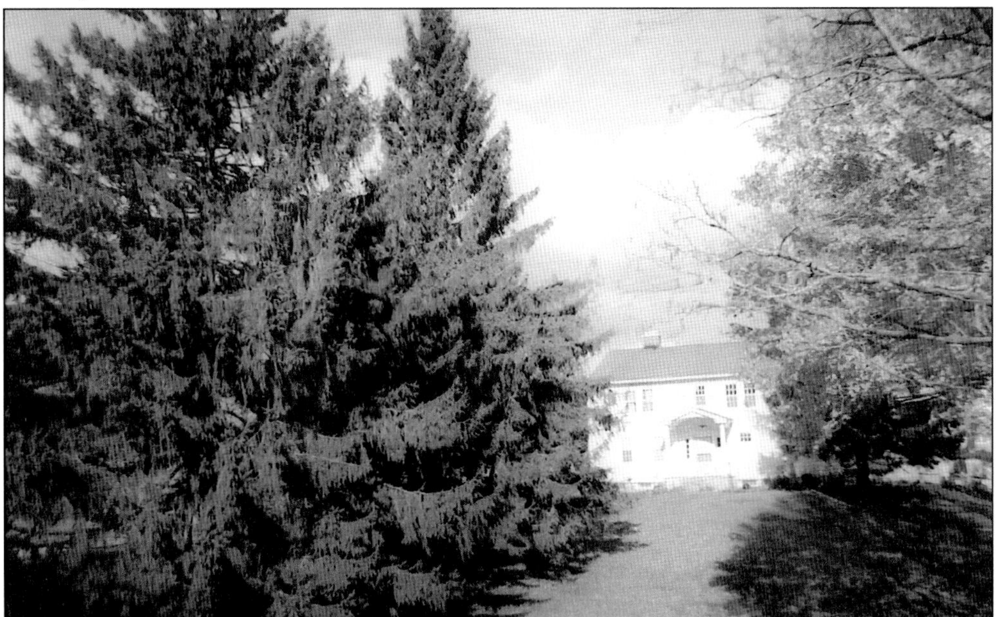

In 1785, when Josiah Pierson settled on 640 acres near present-day Otisville, the area was almost a wilderness. The Pierson house in this photograph was built by Silas Gilbert Pierson in 1834. One of the earlier Pierson homes is located a short distance past this house. The Pierson family burial ground is located on a hill overlooking the vast pastureland of the farm.

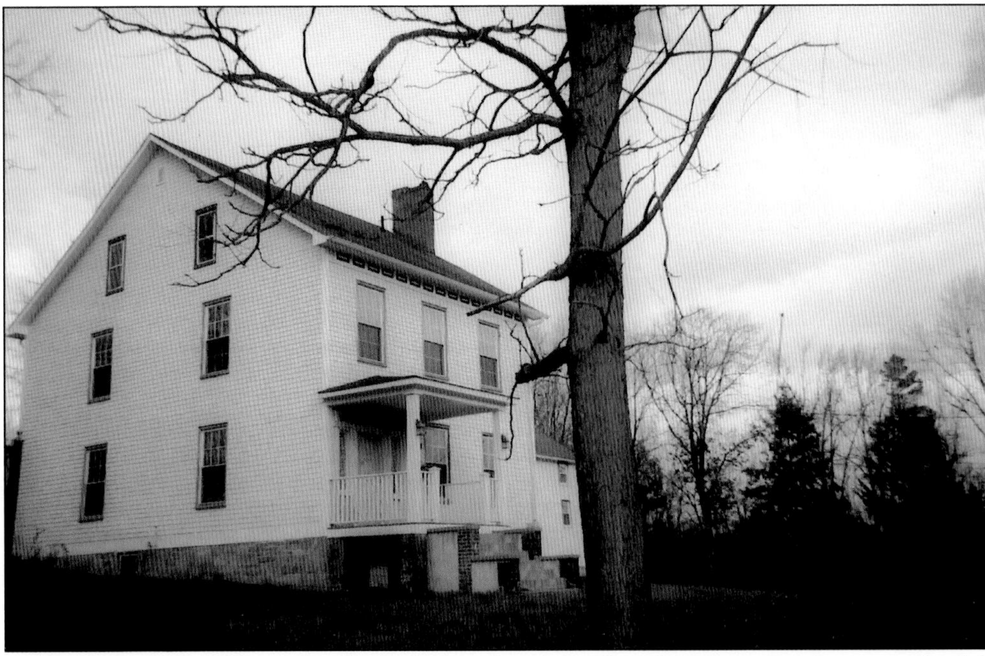

Benjamin Dodge and his wife, Elizabeth Woodward, lived in this impressive house on the hill in Mount Hope. Dodge was a well-to-do lumber dealer and had a general mercantile business in Mount Hope. The stately residence retains original woodwork, with acorn embellishments over the doorways. Original wall sconces are present in the spacious entryway. The Dodge house served as the Presbyterian manse from 1869 to 1922.

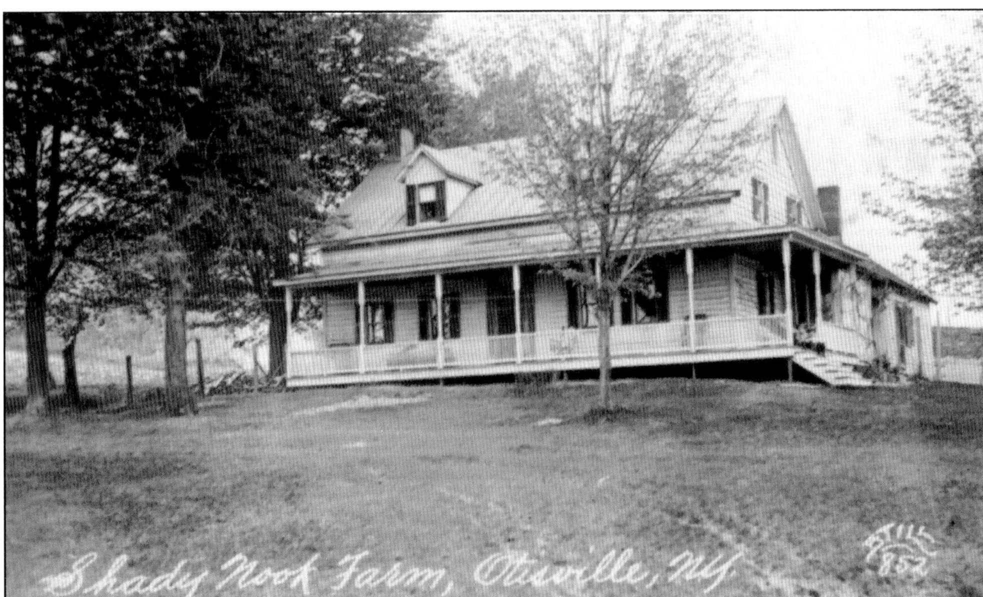

Shady Nook farm was located on Grange Road a short distance from Otisville. This photograph was taken by Alfred H. Still. The farm belonged to the T. Horton Easton family. Easton was the son of local merchant James Easton and his wife, Hannah Corwin. The farmhouse can still be found at this location.

Three

Citizens of Mount Hope and Otisville

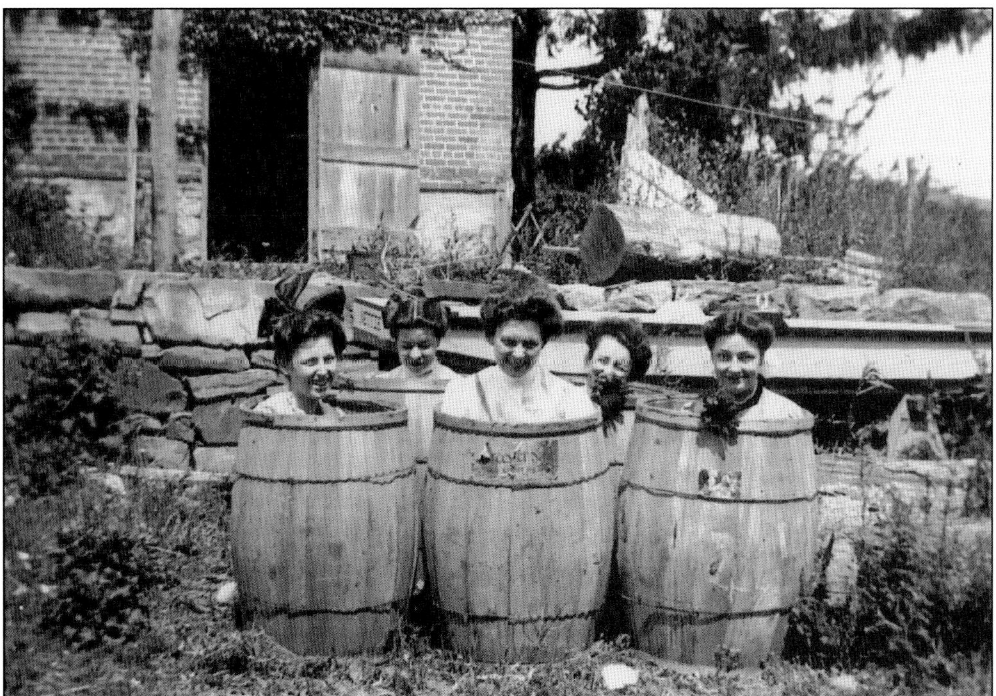

This early-1900s photograph was taken on the Craig farm in back of the woodshed. This image was used on a postcard that was sent to their friends. Pictured from left to right are Bertha Craig, unidentified, Ida Craig, Grace Craig, and unidentified. Bertha, Ida, and Grace were the daughters of Andrew J. Craig and Etta Bailey Craig of Otisville.

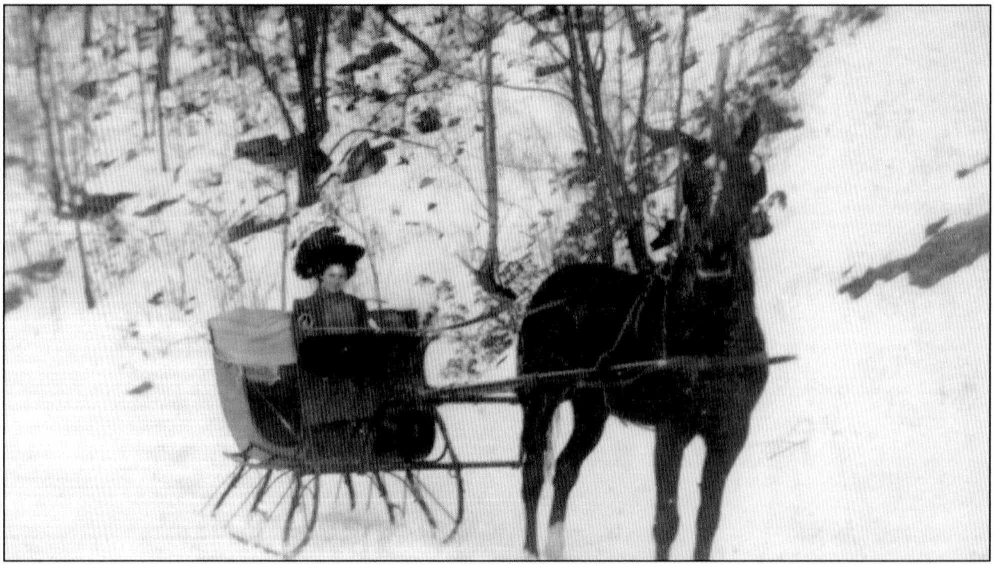

Bertha Wilbur is dashing through the snow on Sanitorium Avenue in her one-horse open sleigh. A sleigh was the only way to travel around town on a blustery winter day in Otisville during the early 1900s. Wilbur was married to Roy Wilbur and had one son, Robert Wilbur.

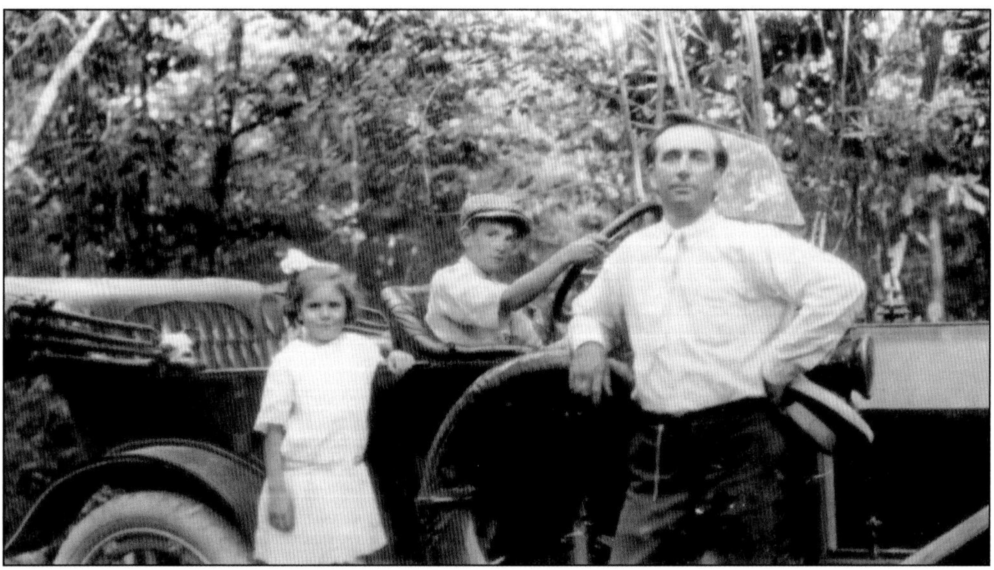

Oscar Benton Greenleaf is steering the car in this photograph from about 1914 taken in front of the Greenleaf Hotel in Otisville. His sister Etta and father, Oscar Shaw Greenleaf, are standing in front of the automobile. In the late 1700s, the Greenleaf family left Coventry, Connecticut, and settled in Mount Hope.

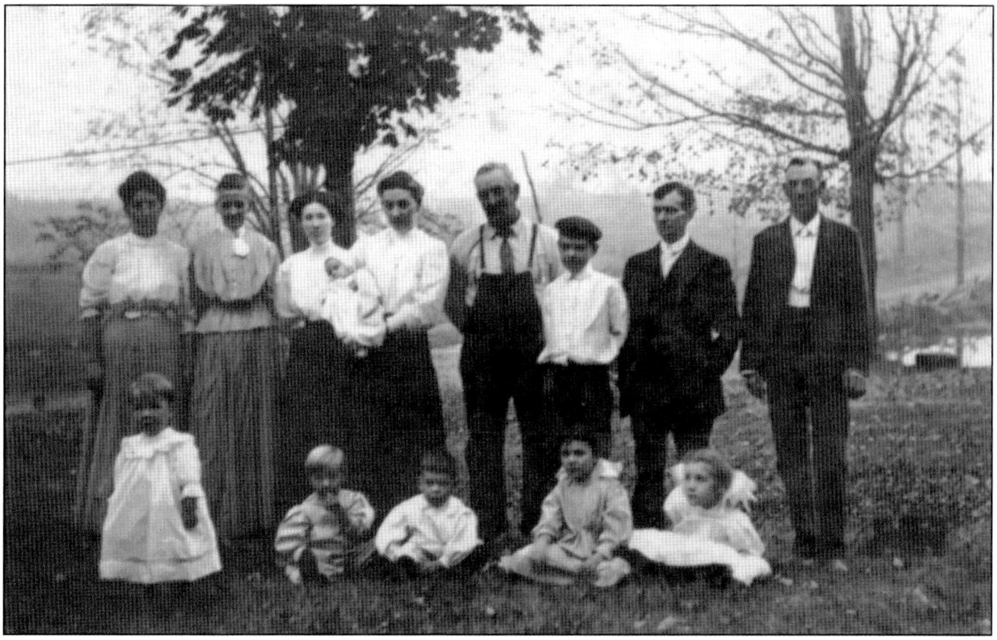

This photograph of the Corwin and Easton family in Mount Hope was taken at a family gathering. Members of the family include Elizabeth Holley at far right in the first row and from left to right in the second row are Nellie Easton Corwin, Francis Easton, Sylvia Easton, Harriet Easton Holley, James Easton, Dutch Holley, Henry A. Holley, and Joseph Knapp Corwin. Others pictured are unidentified.

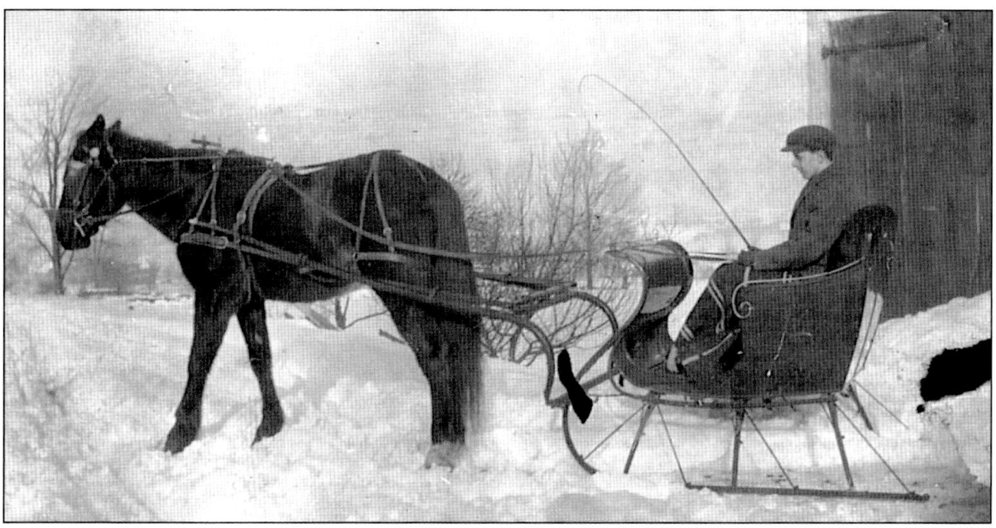

David Vreeland, the son of David and Elizabeth Vreeland, was photographed in his sleigh on a wintry day. The Vreeland farm on Mountain Road was owned by the younger David's brother Rube Vreeland. In the mid-1900s, the house was purchased by the Easkold family.

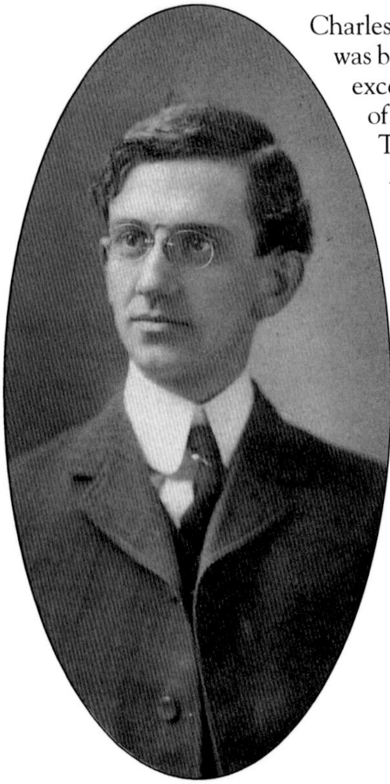

Charles A. Ketcham was the son of Charles C. V. Ketcham, who was born on the Ketcham homestead in Mount Hope. He was an excellent photographer and spent many hours taking pictures of celebrations, parades, and scenic vistas in Orange County. The exceptional photographs by Charles A. Ketcham and Alfred H. Still provide a rich photographic history of the county.

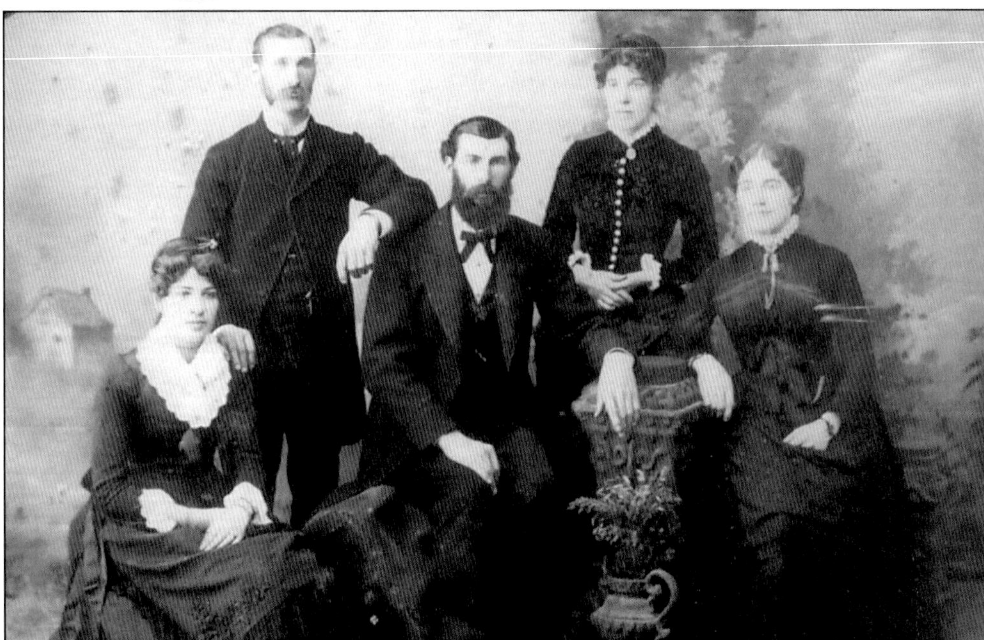

Featured in this photograph are the children of Alsop Woodward and Susan Uptegrove Mapes. They were all born on Tally Ho Road in Mount Hope between 1847 and 1861. The Mapes family members, from left to right, are (first row) Myra Mapes, Hiram Mapes, and Sarah Alice Mapes; (second row) Edson Mapes and Lillian Mapes.

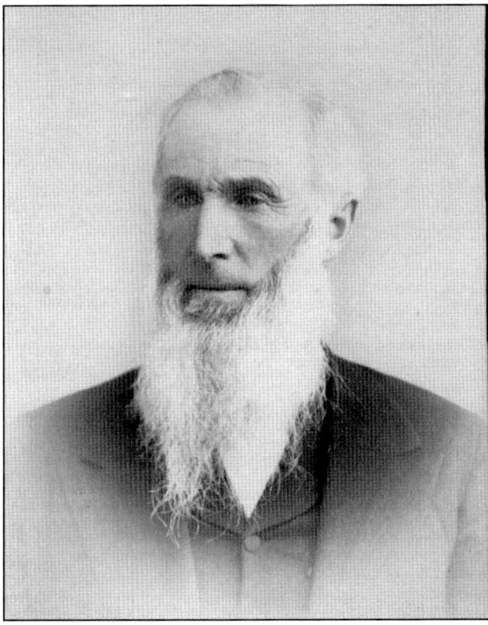

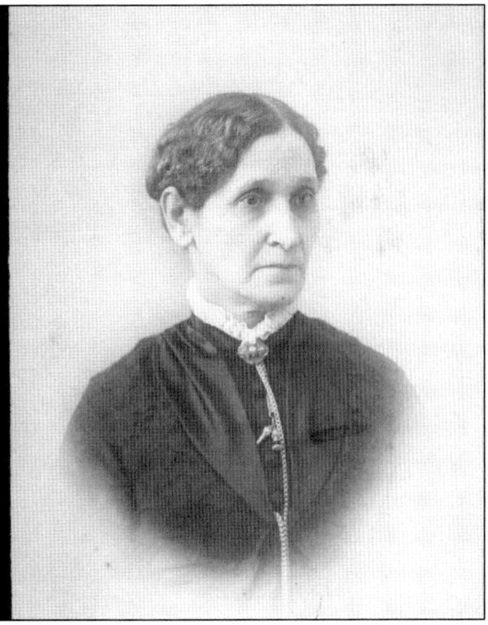

Alsop W. Mapes was born in Mount Hope on April 12, 1823. He married Susan Uptegrove in the Mount Hope Presbyterian Church on October 31, 1846, the same day the first Erie Railroad train arrived at Otisville. The Mapes family lived in the Hezekiah Woodward house on Tally Ho Road in Mount Hope. Susan was a niece of Woodward and a first cousin of Laura Woodward, the Hudson River artist.

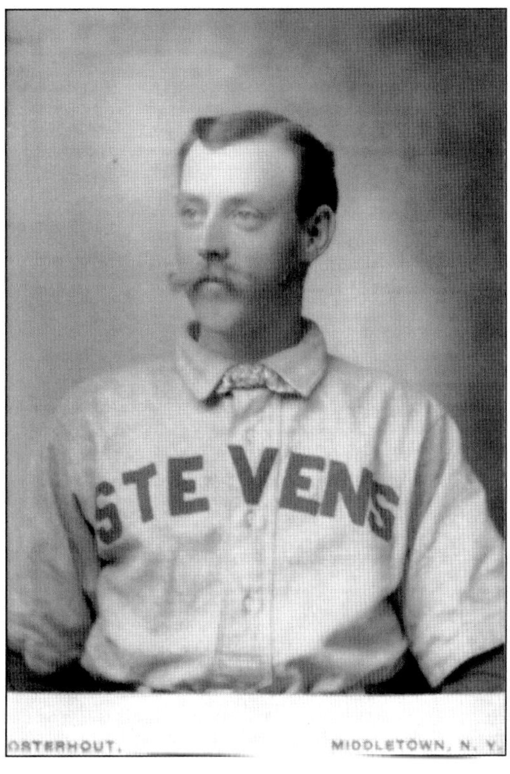

Joseph K. Corwin was born in 1869 in Mount Hope, the son of Silas G. and Charity Corwin. In 1894, he was a pitcher for the Norwich team of the Connecticut State Baseball League. He married Nellie Easton, daughter of T. Horton and Frances Wilkins Easton, in 1900. Corwin served as supervisor for the Town of Mount Hope from 1928 to 1939. He was a descendant of Joshua Corwin, who settled in Mount Hope in the late 1700s.

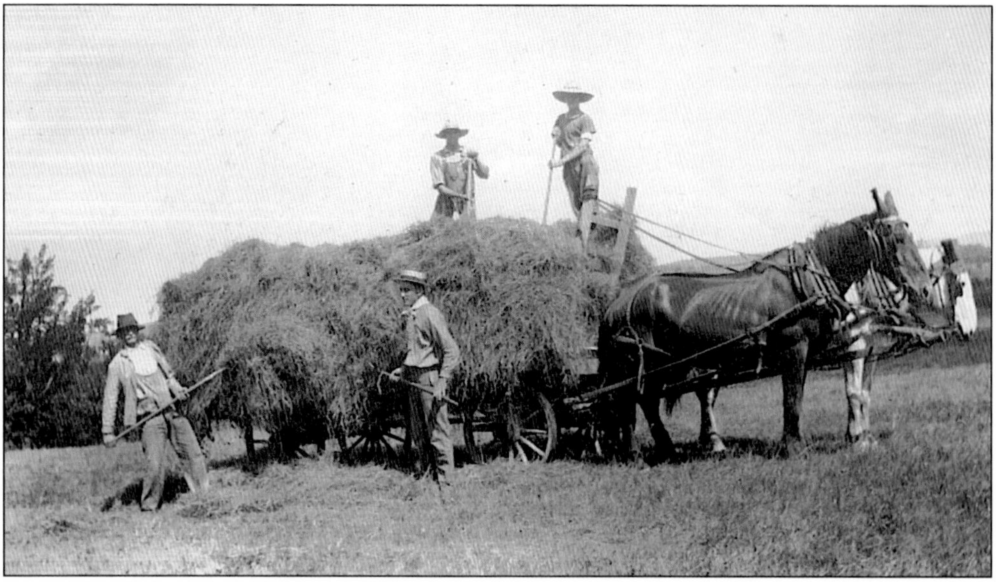

The Vreeland family is harvesting a crop of hay around 1915 in Otisville at the upper farm on Mountain Road. Two workhorses are pulling the massive load of hay. Hay was not baled but was left loose and put in the hayloft by pitchfork. Children loved to go into the hayloft and jump in the mountain of hay.

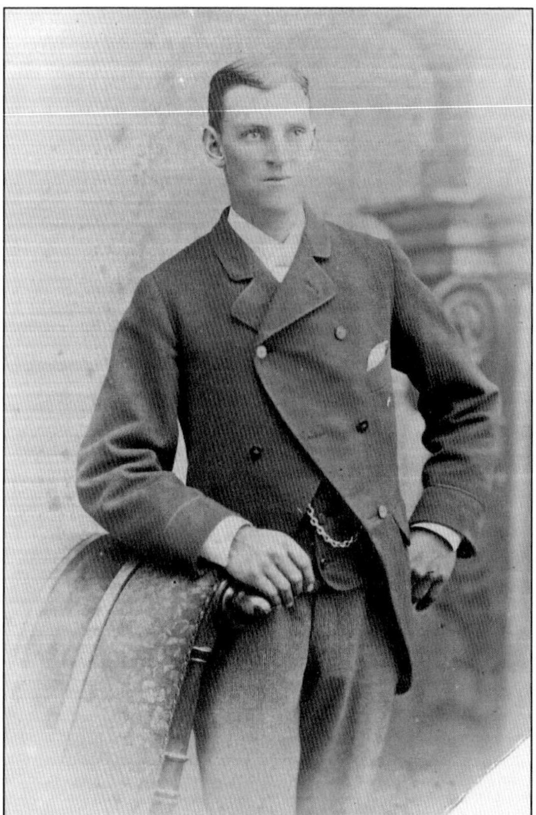

Andrew Mitchell was born in Scotland, and in 1869, he moved to Otisville after purchasing a farm on Shoddy Hollow Road. In 1872, his farmhand discovered a large bone while digging marl from a bog near his farm. It was the first of many bones to be unearthed, and when Mitchell found a pelvic bone, he knew he had discovered a mastodon. In 1875, the mastodon was purchased by Prof. Othniel C. Marsh for the Peabody Museum of Natural History at Yale University.

Charles W. and Nellie Henderson Ketcham pose with their son Robert for this formal family portrait. Charles W. was the last owner of the family homestead in Mount Hope that was located on Guymard Turnpike. His father, Isaac E. Ketcham, and his grandfather Amos Ketcham were both previous operators of Ketcham's mill.

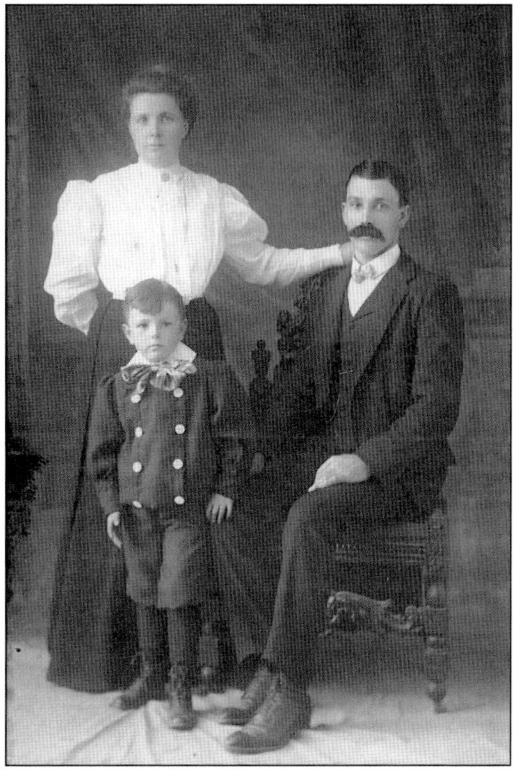

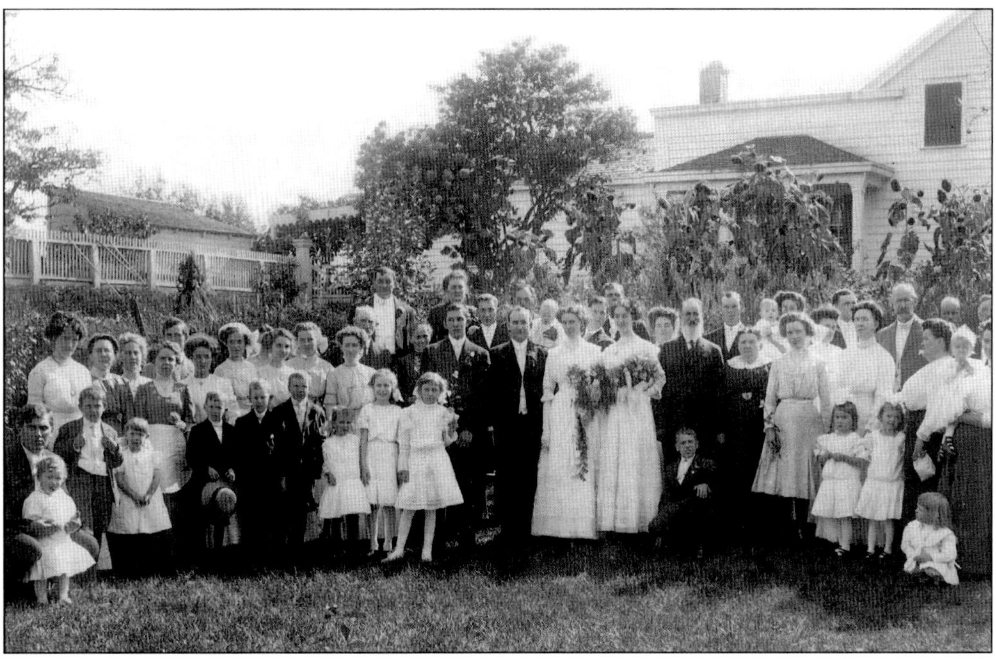

On September 14, 1911, the lovely wedding of Leroy Grant Runnalls and Clara Edna Smith took place at the family home in Otisville. In the center of the photograph is the bride holding her beautiful bouquet of flowers. The groom is standing to the left of the bride. Amy Carwithen, the maid of honor, is to the right of the bride holding her bouquet.

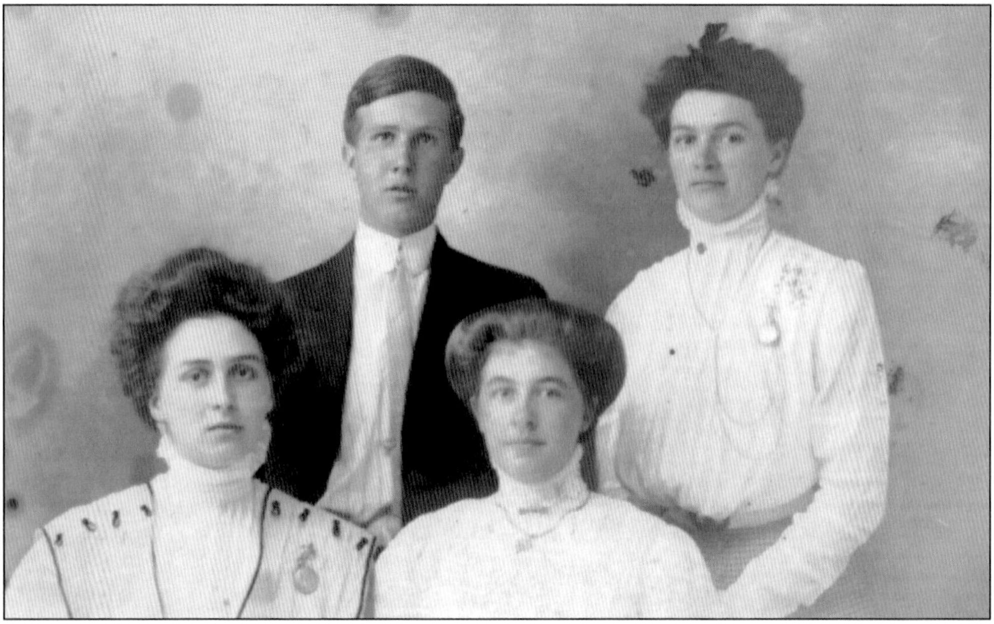

The woman to the far right of this photograph is Mary Ingham, the wife of Harry Stewart Greenleaf. After their marriage, they purchased a large farm on Finchville Turnpike. Their son Harry "Flash" Greenleaf married Gladys Crotty, and they had one daughter, Linda. Linda married John Willis, and their family continues to reside on the farm.

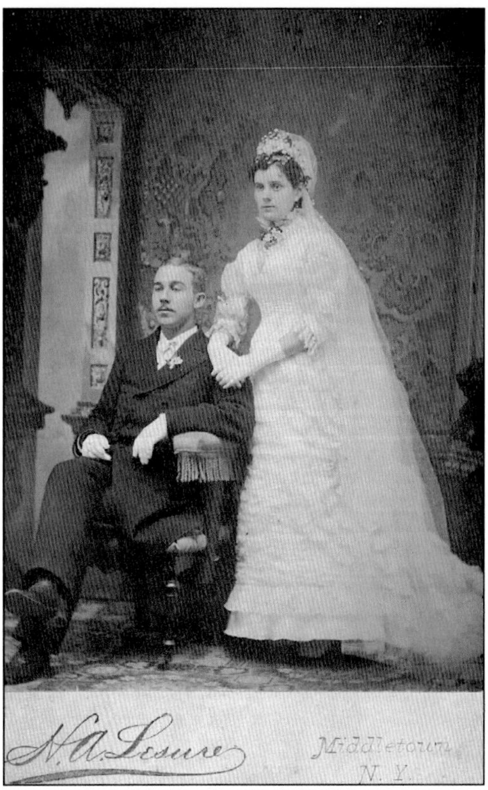

This lovely photograph of Alva Seybolt, born 1859, and Addie Wilkin, born 1859, was taken on their wedding day in 1880 in Otisville. The Seybolts were the parents of five children, Vida, Arthur, Edna, Helen, and Crosby J. Seybolt. Alva was a descendant of Johannes Seybolt, who settled in Otisville in 1789 and for whom Seybolt Avenue is named.

Minnie Field lived in her family's large, white Victorian home on Field Road in Otisville. Field Road was named after her family. After her marriage, she lived next to the Holy Name of Jesus Church on Highland Avenue in a Sears, Roebuck and Company craftsmen-style cottage.

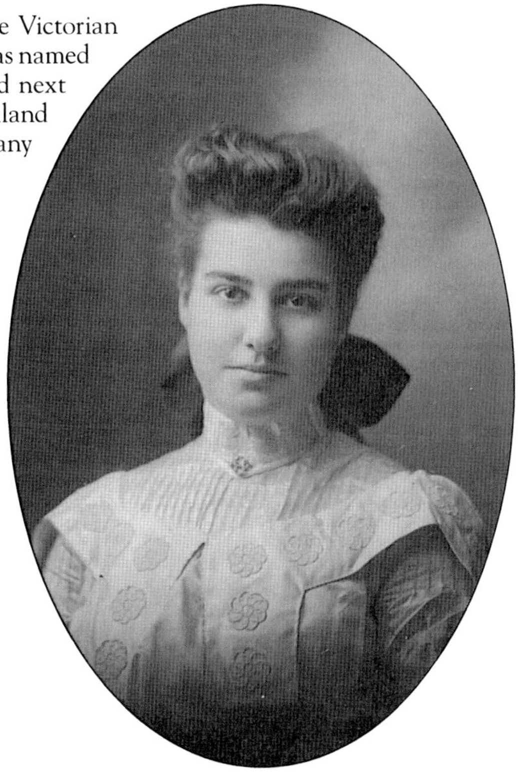

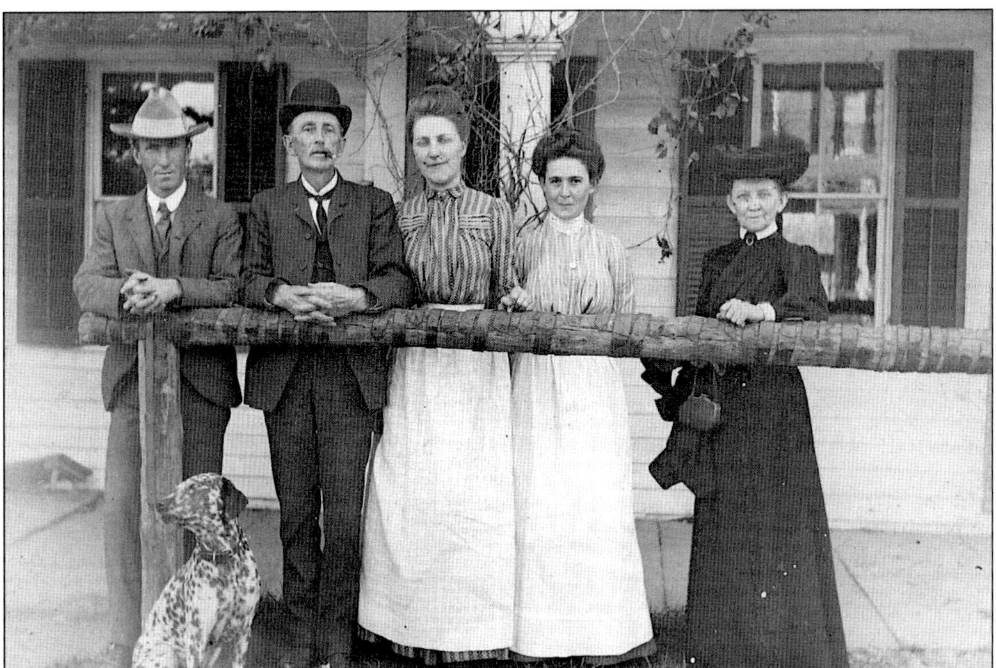

Pictured from left to right in this 1905 photograph outside the Greenleaf Hotel and Livery are Charles Greenleaf, James Hill, Lillian Greenleaf, Mary Greenleaf, and unidentified. The hotel was a popular place for the residents of Otisville to dine in the early 1900s.

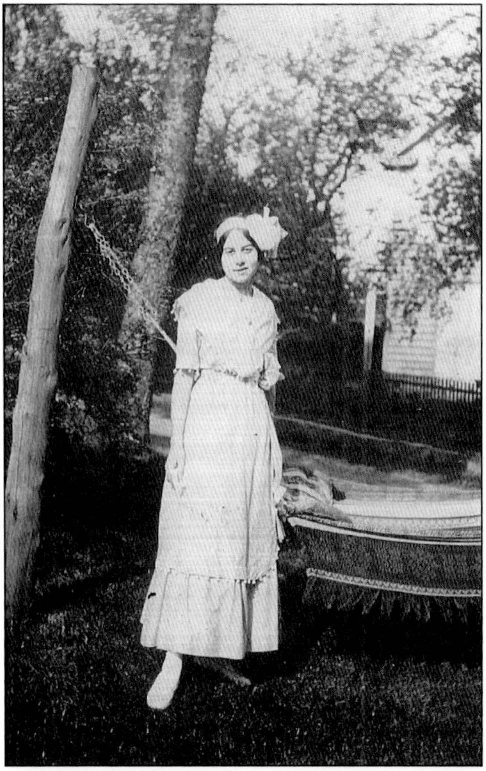

Mary Shepherd Craig was born in Sergeantsville, New Jersey, and came to Otisville as a bride. A craftsmen-style cottage was built for her and her husband, James Craig, next to the family's brick residence on Sanitorium Avenue. She was an organist for the Methodist Episcopal Church in Otisville.

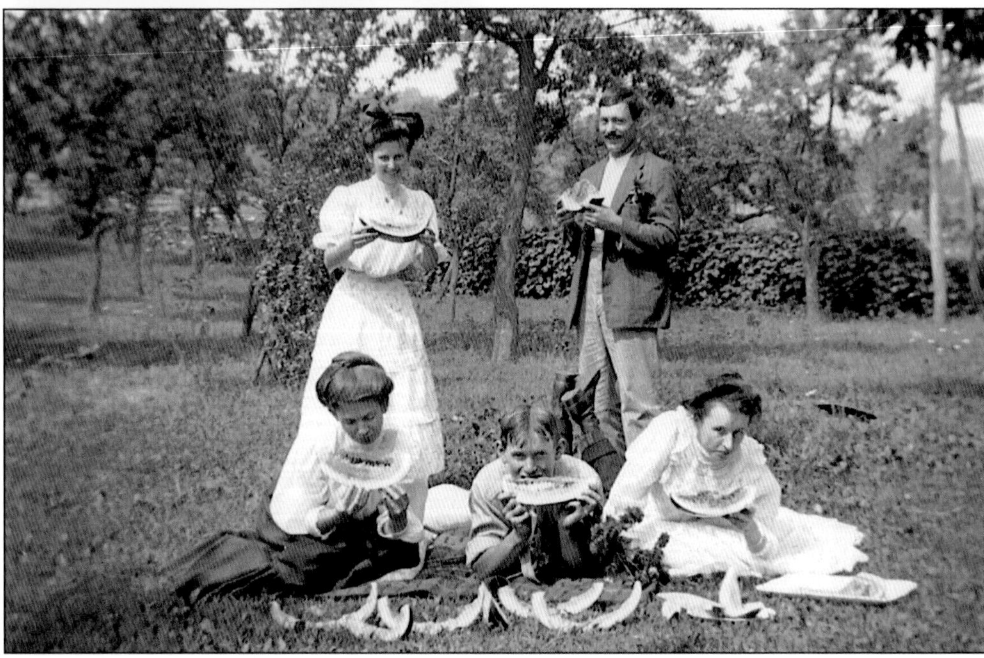

Pictured from left to right enjoying slices of watermelon in front of the Craig house on Sanitorium Avenue are (first row) Ida Craig, James Bailey Craig, and Grace Craig; (second row) Bertha Craig and a doctor from the Otisville Tuberculosis Sanitorium. In the early 1900s, picnics were a popular form of entertainment.

John E. Greenleaf was born in 1852 in Mount Hope. In 1884, he leased the hotel next to the depot formerly known as the Blizzard House. He operated this hotel for two years and then purchased the Washington Hotel, which was located across the street. The hotel then became known as the Greenleaf Hotel and Livery. After his death in 1894, the hotel was operated by his son Oscar Shaw Greenleaf.

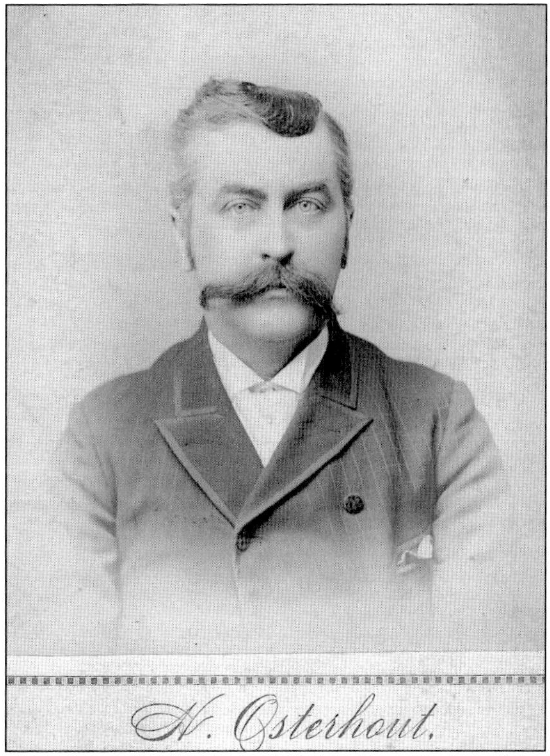

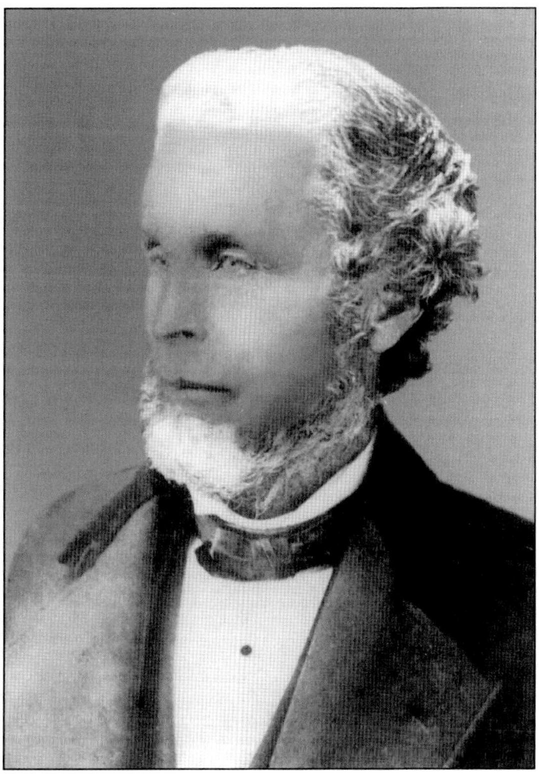

In 1847, James Craig carved a design over the entranceway to Trinity Church in New York during its reconstruction. At the time of his retirement, he was supervising over 100 stonecutters in New York City who were building stone mansions on Fifth Avenue. He purchased the William Brown farm in 1877 and moved to Otisville with his son, Andrew, and his daughter-in-law Etta Craig.

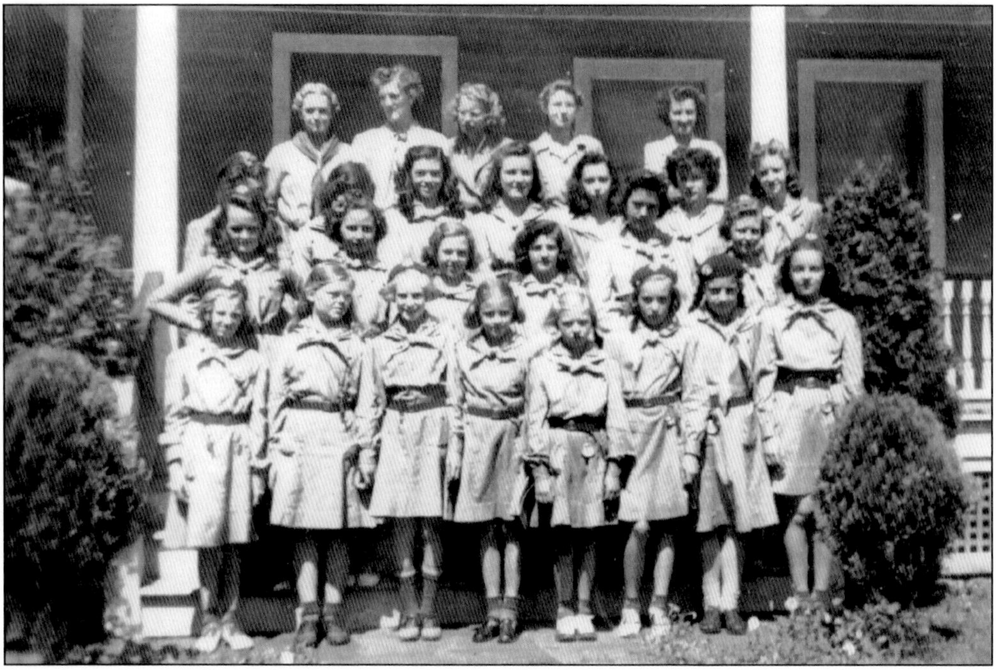

A group of Otisville Girl Scouts posed on Orchard Street in Otisville for this memorable photograph around 1940. They are standing on the porch of the house next to the present-day Presbyterian manse. This group of Girl Scouts enjoyed their summertime excursions to the Patterson camp at Yankee Lake.

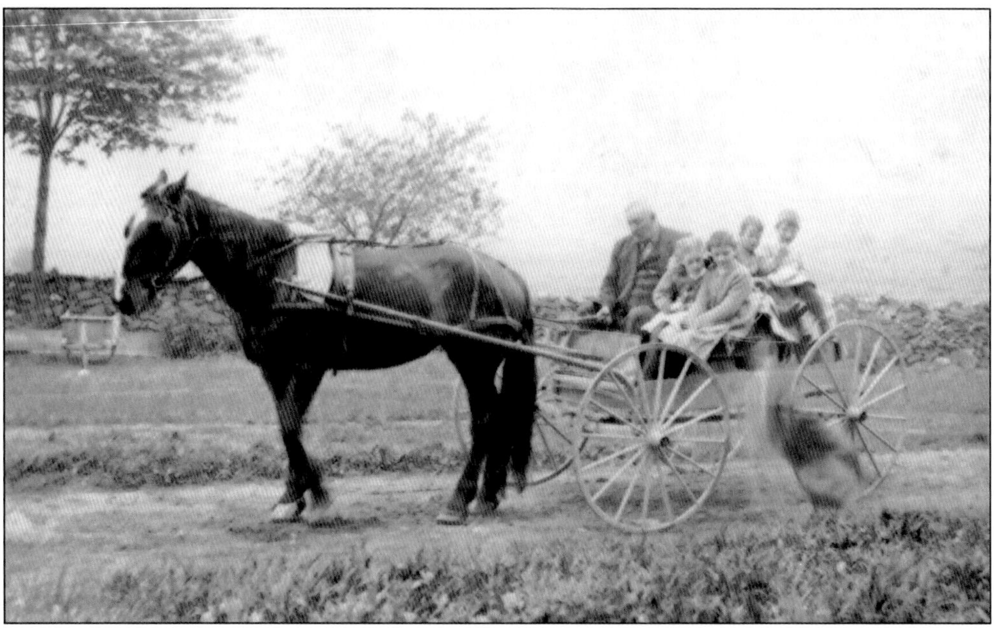

T. Horton Easton is seen is this early photograph transporting a group of children in his horse and wagon in Mount Hope. Easton was the son of James and Rebecca Corwin Easton. He owned the Shady Nook farm that was located on Grange Road. It was operated as a dairy farm for many years.

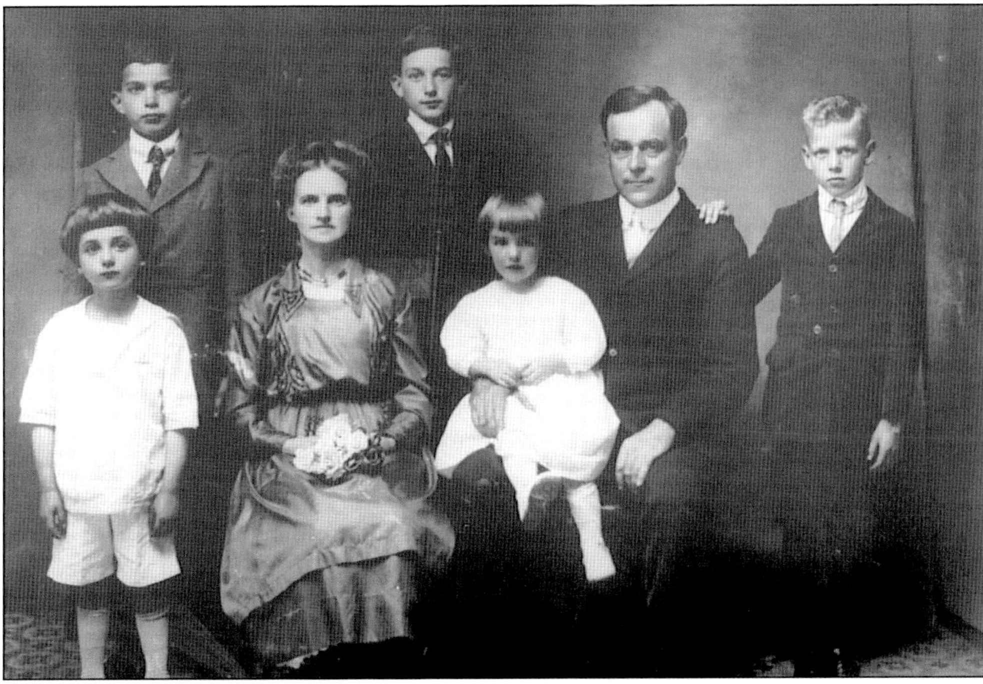

The Horace L. Patterson family lived on Orchard Street in Otisville. The Patterson family, pictured from left to right, includes (first row) Donald, Laura (mother), Lois, and Horace (father); (second row) Maurice, Lindon, and Glen Patterson. The Patterson family was very active in the Mount Hope Presbyterian Church and participated in other civic activities.

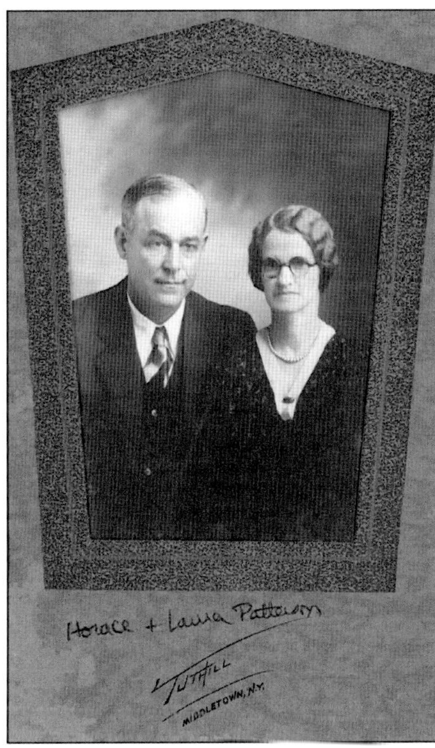

Horace was in the plumbing business and became a master mechanic at the U.S. Army hospital in Otisville. Laura was the first female to be a member of the Otisville Board of Education. Horace played the mandolin, tuba, banjo, and guitar, and he and his wife, Laura, performed in many musicales for the benefit of the church and other charitable organizations in the village.

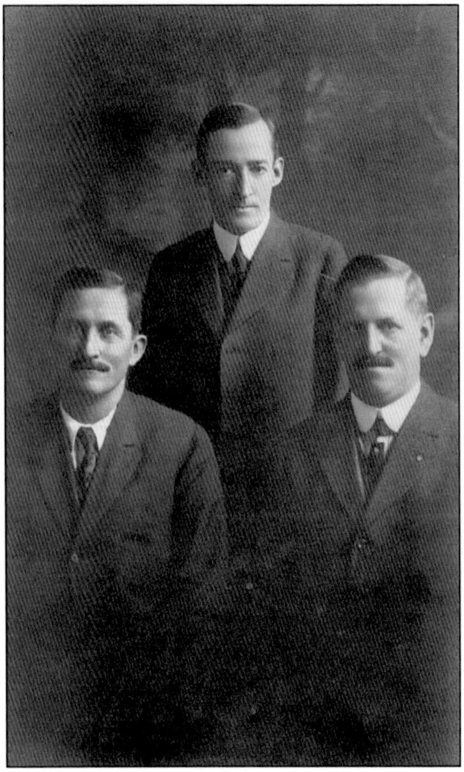

From left to right, the Pierson brothers are Frank, John, and Silas Gilbert. They were the sons of John and Elizabeth Halsey Pierson. Frank was manager of the Pierson farm in Otisville. The younger John moved to Denver and was an employee of the Mine and Smelter Supply Company, and Silas Gilbert was a purchasing agent for the Colorado Fuel and Iron Company in Denver.

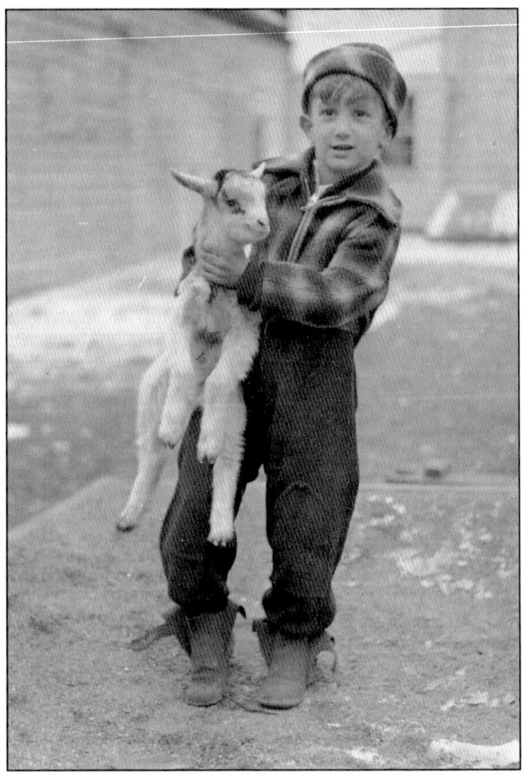

Steve Pierson helps with the goats on the Pierson farm in 1939. In 1930, his father Orrin Pierson, who was born in Denver, attended the Columbia Journalism School, and spent a year in Europe on a Pulitzer fellowship, returned to the Pierson ancestral farm to continue the family tradition. Orrin's column, "The Gleaner" in the *Times Herald*, brought life on the farm to thousands of readers with his unabashed frankness.

Henry A. Holley and his wife, Harriet Easton, were married on October 7, 1896. They were the parents of three children, including Henry Easton, who was born on August 26, 1898, Elizabeth Corwin, who was born on April 30, 1900, and James Easton, who was born on September 20, 1905. In 1905, Henry A. became the owner of a coal and fuel business in Otisville.

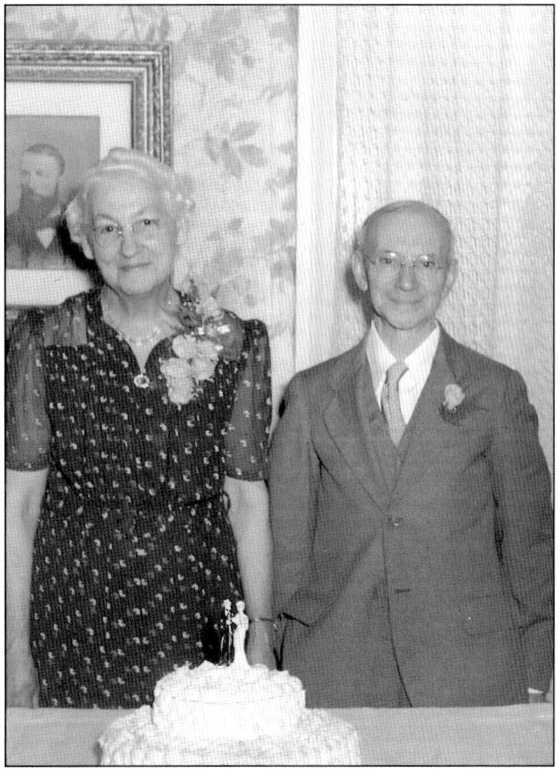

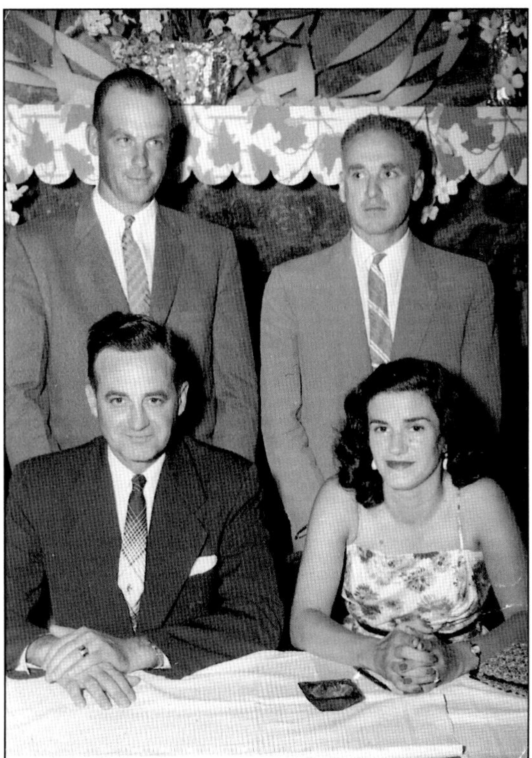

The Otisville alumni dinner is a yearly event that is held in high esteem by citizens who graduated from the brick school in Otisville. This 1950s photograph shows alumni members (first row) Donald Patterson and Audrey Vreeland; (second row) Walt Lang (left) and Art Zimmerman.

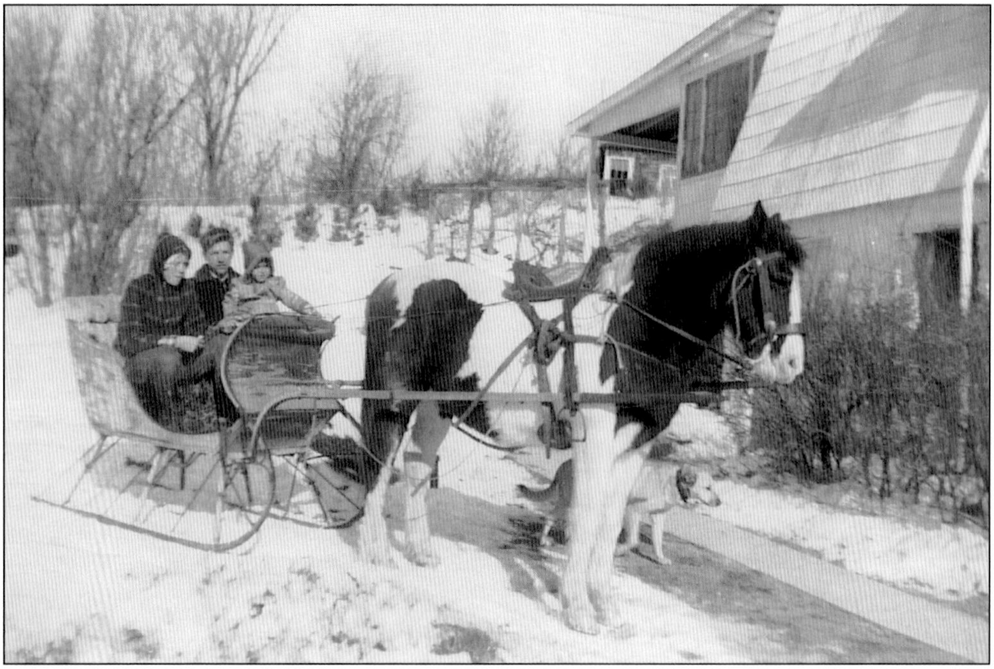

The Wessel family is out for a ride in their horse-drawn sleigh near their home on Bull Road in Otisville. The Wessel family had a large poultry business near Otisville. Today the Wessel family operates a large, wholesale annual and perennial plant business.

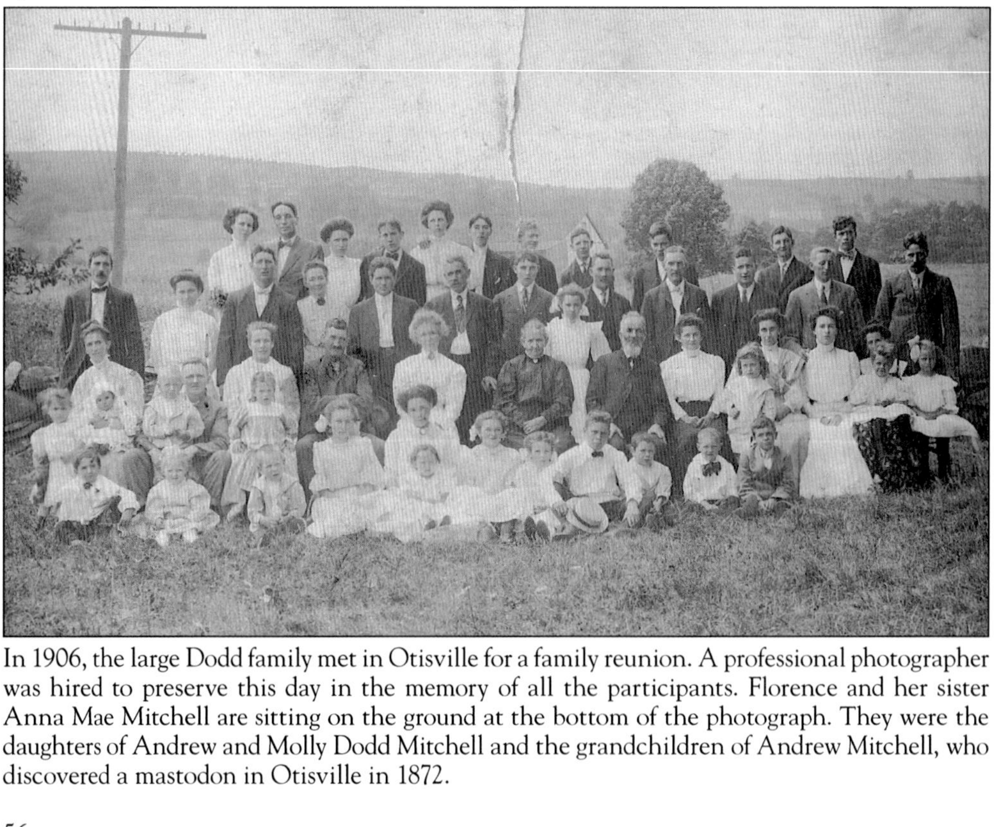

In 1906, the large Dodd family met in Otisville for a family reunion. A professional photographer was hired to preserve this day in the memory of all the participants. Florence and her sister Anna Mae Mitchell are sitting on the ground at the bottom of the photograph. They were the daughters of Andrew and Molly Dodd Mitchell and the grandchildren of Andrew Mitchell, who discovered a mastodon in Otisville in 1872.

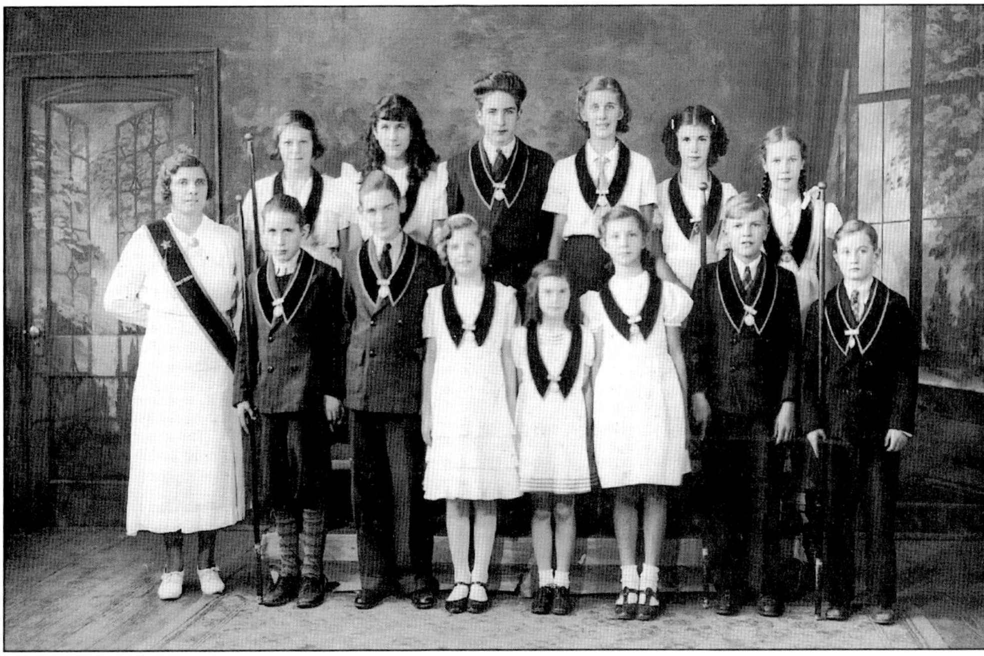

This photograph of youth members was taken at the Otisville Grange in the mid-1930s. Pictured from left to right are (first row) unidentified, Joe McGowan, Don Seely, Louise Wilson, ? Murray, Eleanor Holley, Lloyd Goldsmith, and Pete Hull; (second row) Ruth Simons, Lorraine Regansberger, Curt Dailey, Bessie VanDyne, Audrey Ketcham, and Helen Cady.

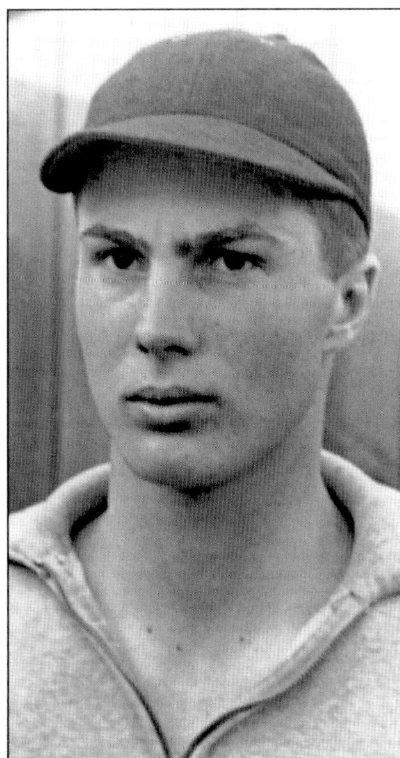

Harry "Flash" Greenleaf, the son of Harry Stewart and Mary Ingham Greenleaf, was an ace right-handed pitcher for the Otisville High School baseball team. On April 29, 1938, he played the best game of his career. He hurled a no-hit, no-run game, beating Walden High School.

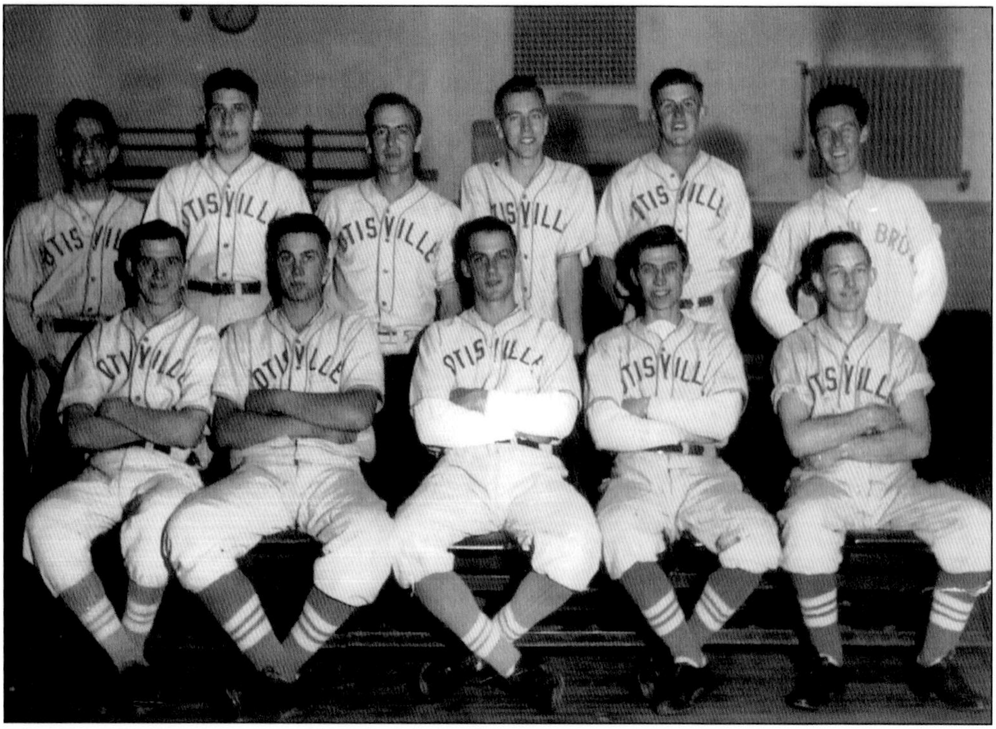

The Otisville Divers was a village baseball team that played in the 1940s. The members from left to right are (first row) Sid Green, Harry "Flash" Greenleaf, Walt Lang, Lou Butzgy, and Carl Penney; (second row) Art Zimmerman, Joe Brant, Chub Wilbur, unidentified, Ed Vreeland, and Billy Stanfield.

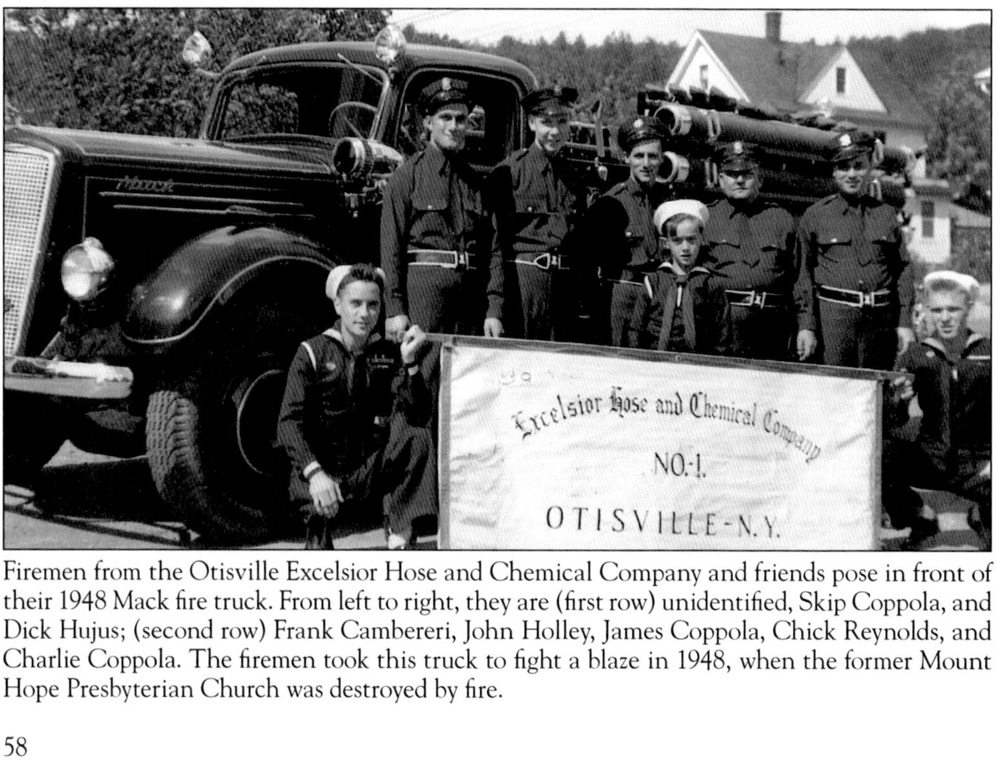

Firemen from the Otisville Excelsior Hose and Chemical Company and friends pose in front of their 1948 Mack fire truck. From left to right, they are (first row) unidentified, Skip Coppola, and Dick Hujus; (second row) Frank Cambereri, John Holley, James Coppola, Chick Reynolds, and Charlie Coppola. The firemen took this truck to fight a blaze in 1948, when the former Mount Hope Presbyterian Church was destroyed by fire.

Four

Schools and Students

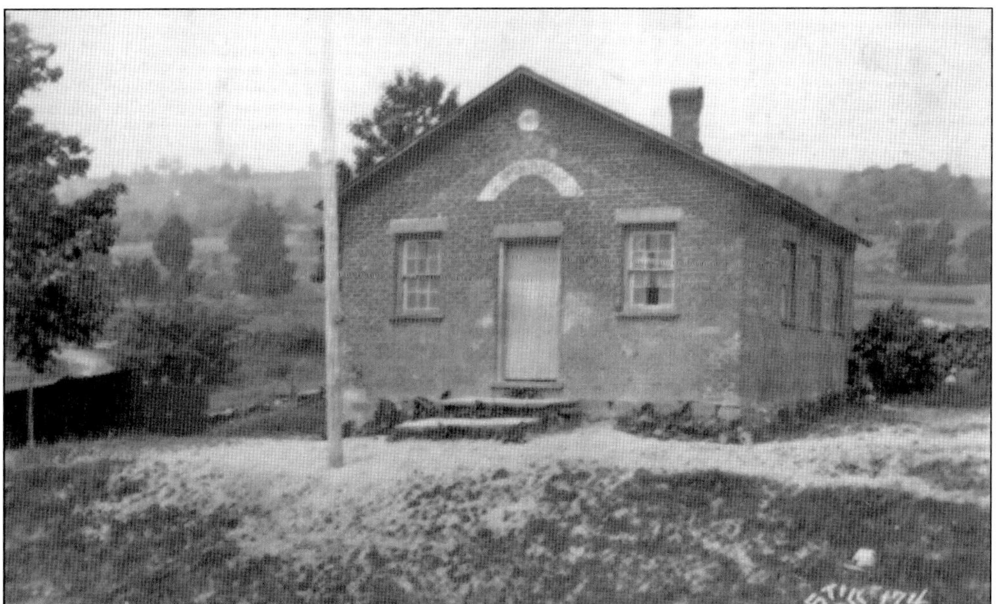

The little brick schoolhouse was built in 1853 on Old Mountain Road near the intersection with Bull Road. Children in the district walked long distances to attend the one-room schoolhouse. The school was constructed with bricks that were made in a kiln on the William Brown farm in Otisville.

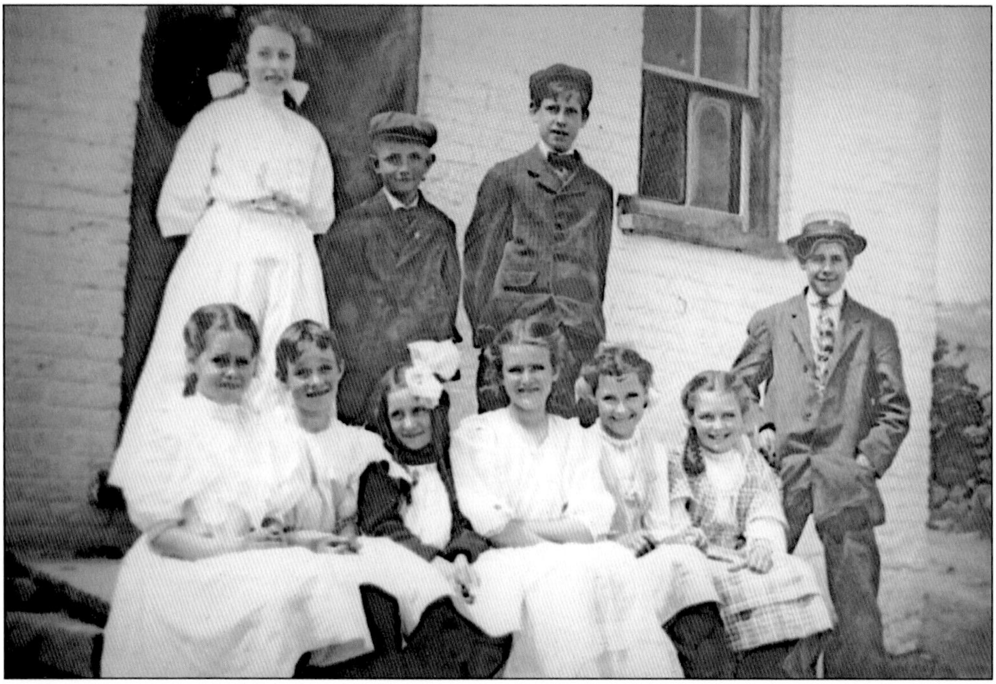

In the early 1900s, the little brick school was painted white. Pictured are a group of students in front of the school during a break from their lessons. The picture was taken by their teacher, Grace Craig Cockrell, who graduated from the Otisville Academy in 1895 and then attended Oneonta Normal School for teacher's training.

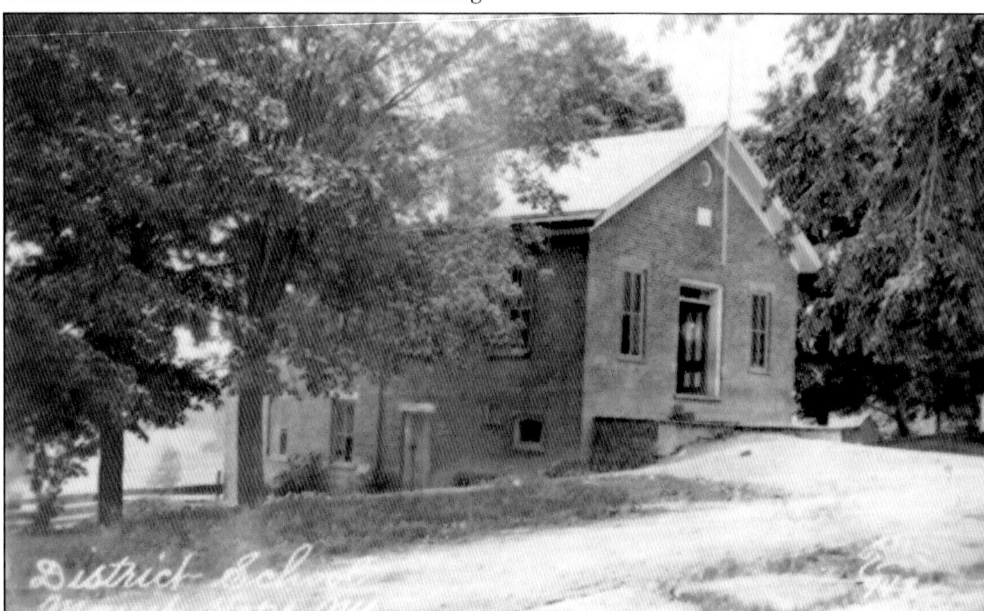

During the mid-1800s, the Mount Hope School was built on Mount Hope Road for the children in that area to attend. It was a one-room school, and children of all ages attended classes when they were not needed on the farm. At the end of the school year, a picnic was held at Waceda Glen in Otisville. The school is currently a private residence.

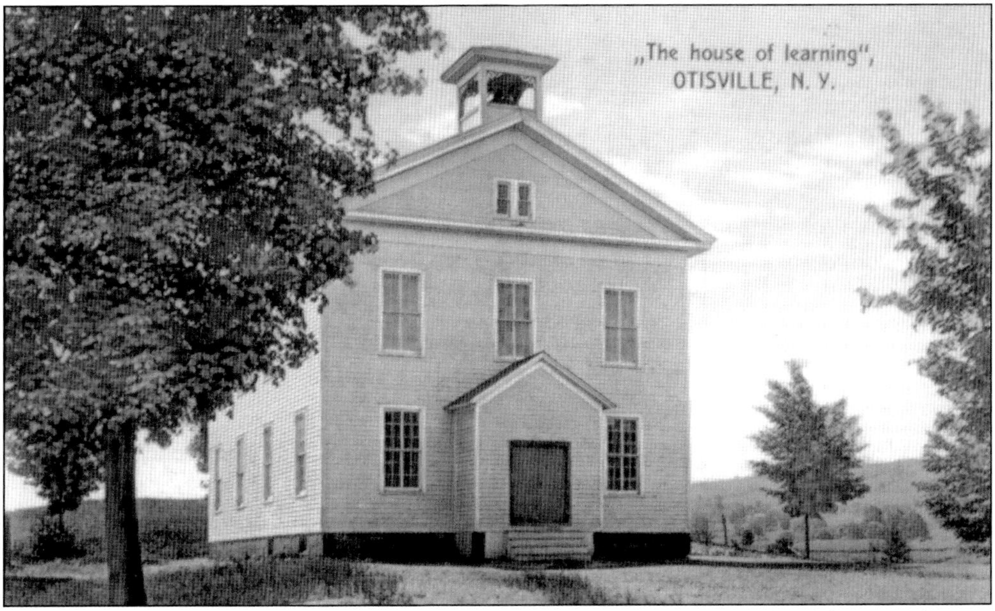

The Otisville Academy was built in 1870 after the village was without a school for several years. The school was located on Academy Avenue, which was later renamed Orchard Street. It was a two-story white frame building, and primary grades were located on the first floor. Land for the school was purchased from the Seybolt family for $600.

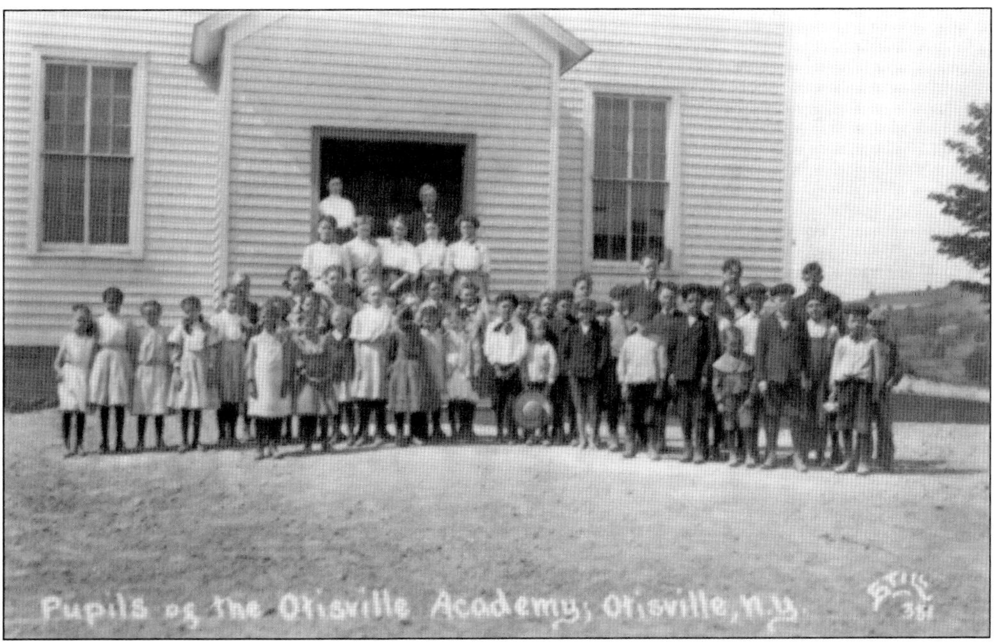

This vintage photograph of students and teachers in front of the Otisville Academy was taken by photographer Alfred H. Still. Taken around 1908, the boys are dressed in their knickers and the girls wear their summer dresses and bonnets. The school was in existence until the brick school was completed in 1914.

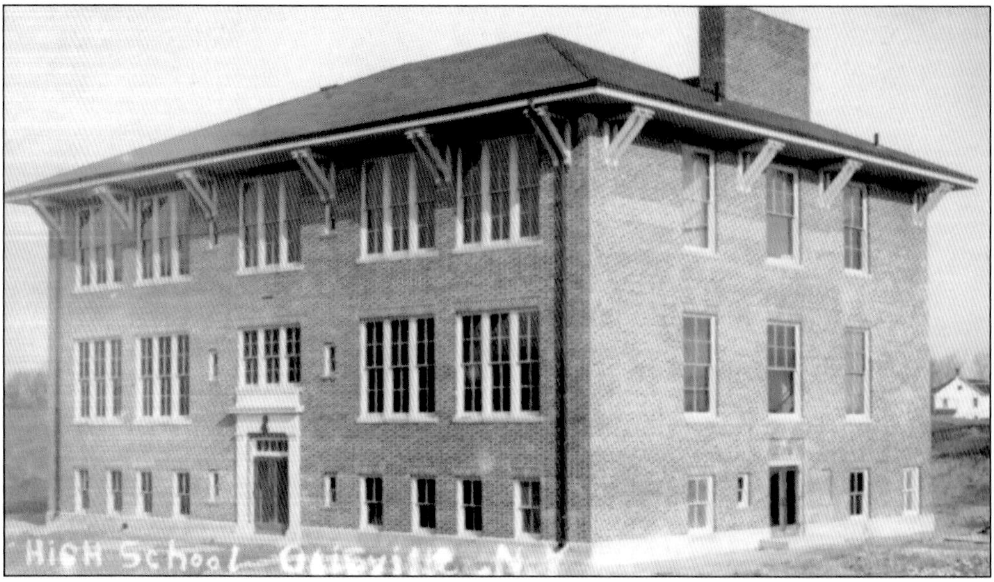

The Otisville Union Free School was completed in 1914 on the corner of School Street and Orchard Street. It served students from elementary through high school. A large addition that included a gymnasium was completed in 1933, and when the new addition was dedicated, the gymnasium was filled with proud townspeople. The last class graduated in 1972. The school will close its doors in June 2008.

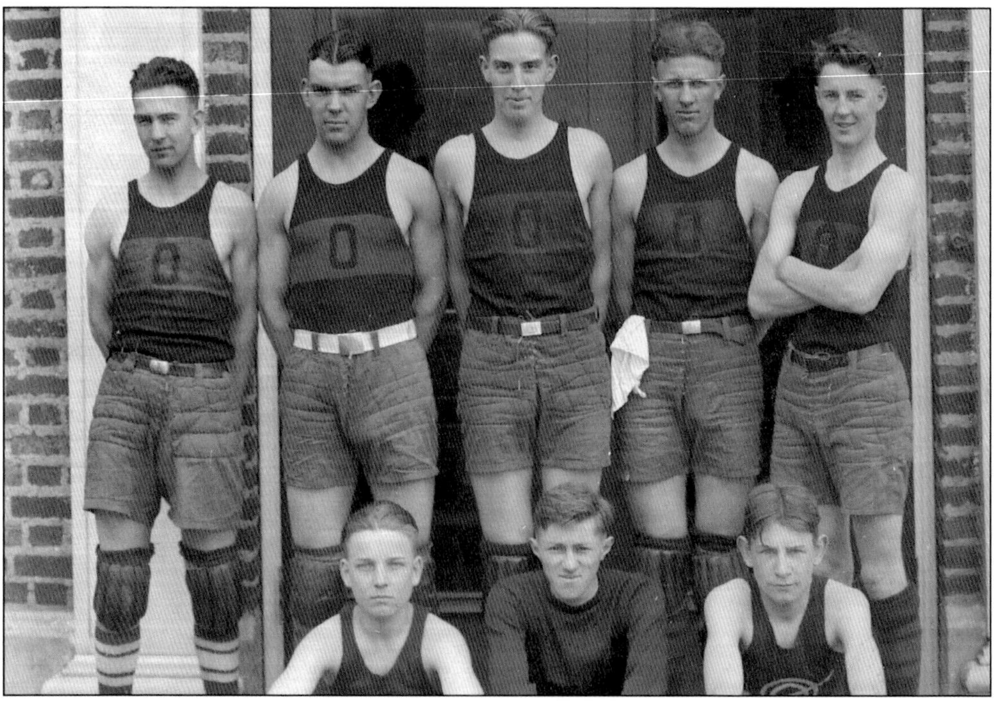

This early photograph shows the 1924 Otisville High School basketball team in front of the school. The first row is unidentified. From left to right in the second row are unidentified, James "Dutch" Holley, Gil Corwin, unidentified, and Eldred Carhart. Upon graduation, Holley attended West Point and was an outstanding player on the West Point lacrosse team.

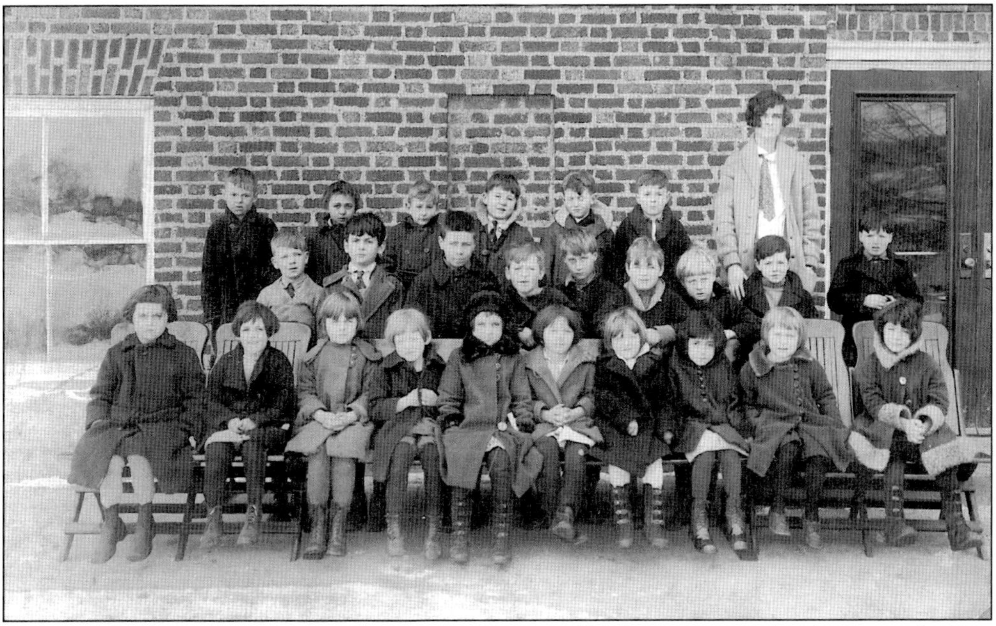

Children from the elementary division of the Otisville Union Free School pose with their teacher outside the brick school. The school was built in 1914 and served its last year as a school in 2008. A new school on Mount Hope Road will replace the brick building on School Street.

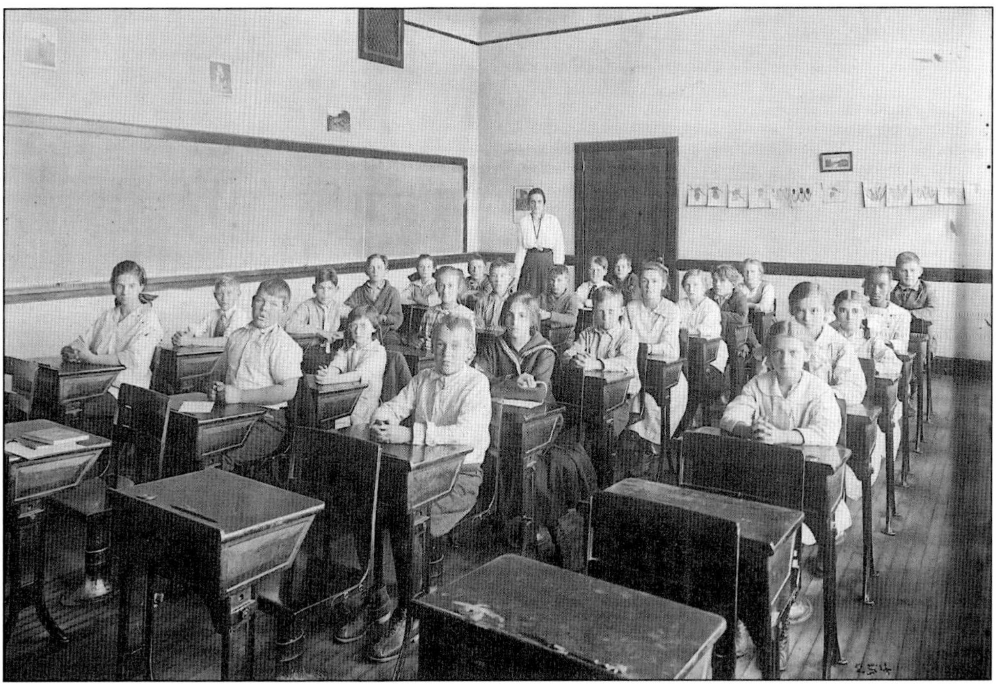

Miss Van Inwegan is photographed with her sixth-grade class at Otisville Union Free School around 1917. Two of her students are Eldred Carhart and James Holley. There is a full-length blackboard in the classroom that was utilized during class instruction. Students wrote their math problems with chalk on the blackboard because paper was expensive.

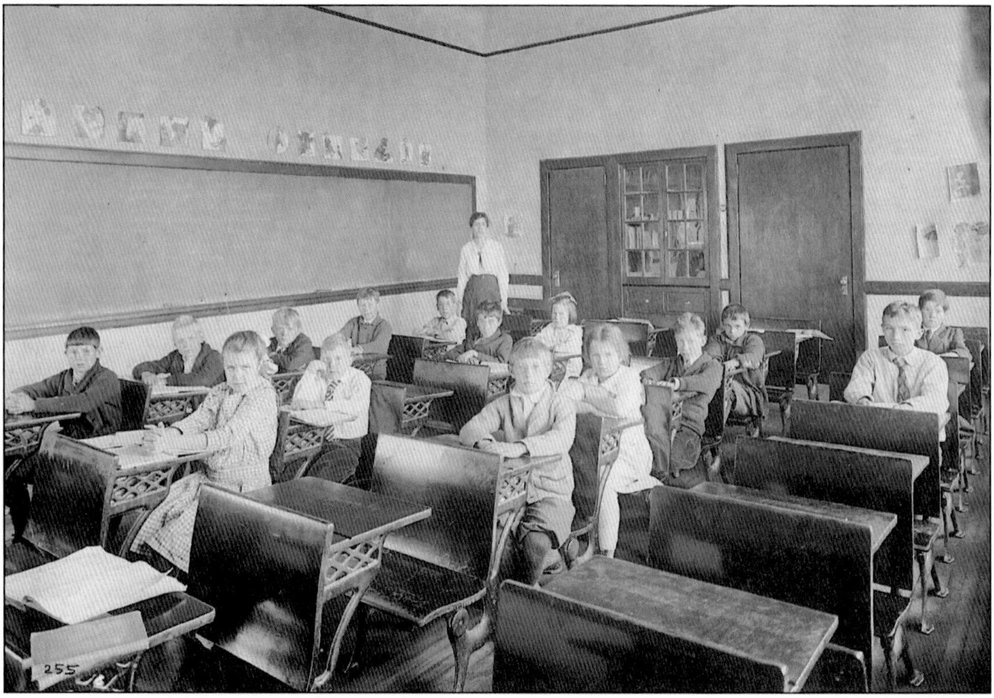

This photograph shows Miss Durant with her fourth-grade class around 1917 at the Otisville Union Free School. Two of her students are Bruce and Ralph Carhart. In the back of the classroom, there is a door that led to a small room where coats and hats were hung. There is also a glass-fronted cabinet in the back of the classroom for supplies.

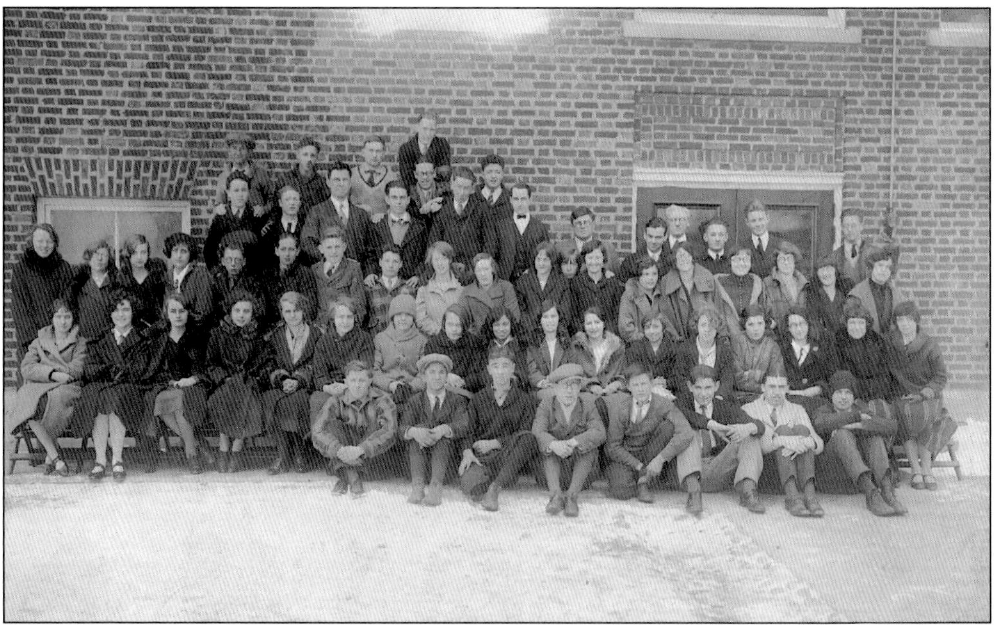

The entire high school is shown in this photograph from the 1924–1925 school year at the Otisville Union Free School on School Street in Otisville. The students and faculty are standing in back of the school for this photograph.

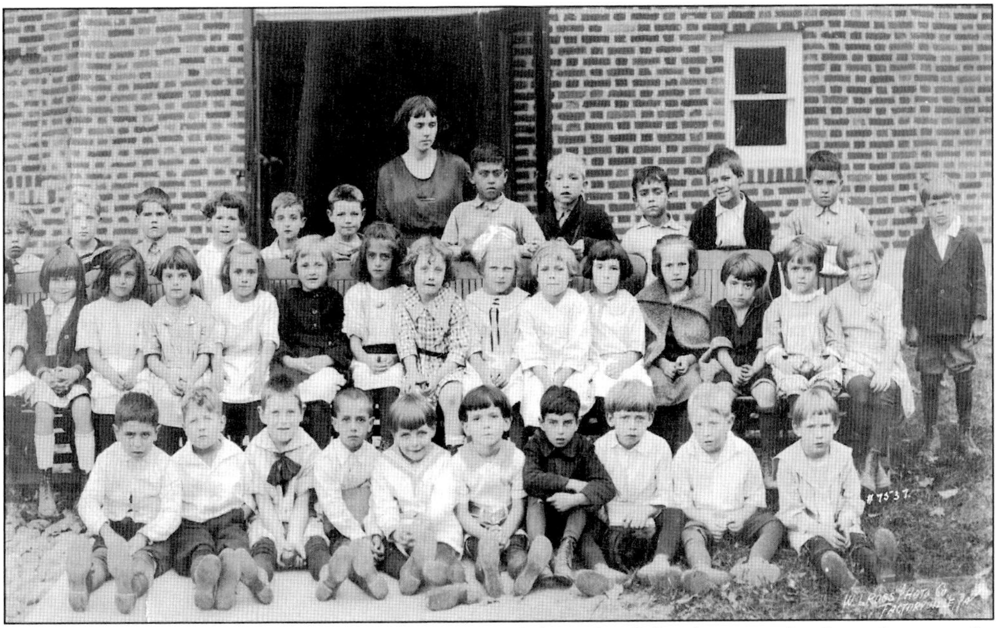

Ethel Breen's second-grade class poses in front of the school for their yearly class photograph. Members of the class are, from left to right, (first row) unidentified, Earnest Runnalls, three unidentified, William Loeven, Fred Jackson and three unidentified; (second row) Catherine Loeven, Catherine Colman, two unidentified, Sarah Horton, two unidentified, Catherine Carboy, Alma Tymeson, Ethel Philhower, Emma Chiswell, Minnie Davis, Honey Carpenteir, Evelyn Hunt, and Bernice Ketcham; (third row) Robert Wilbur (fourth from left), Donald Patterson (fifth from left), and the others are unidentified.

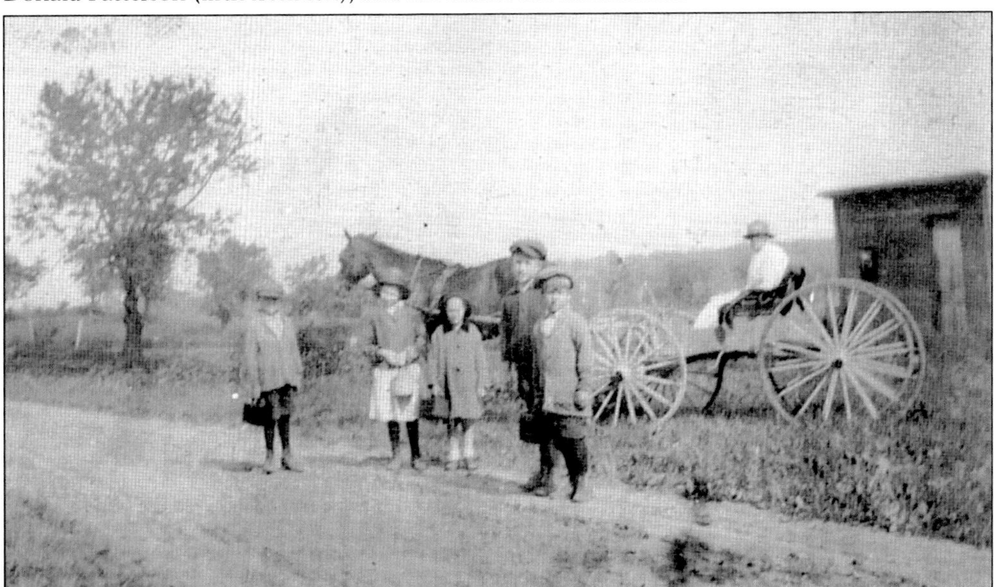

In the 1920s, the children of William and Bertha Goldsmith are seen walking to the Finchville School on Guymard Turnpike in Mount Hope. There were no school buses for students at that time. A horse and buggy sits at the edge of the road. The children from left to right are Herbert Goldsmith, unidentified, Jenny Goldsmith, unidentified, and Dick Goldsmith.

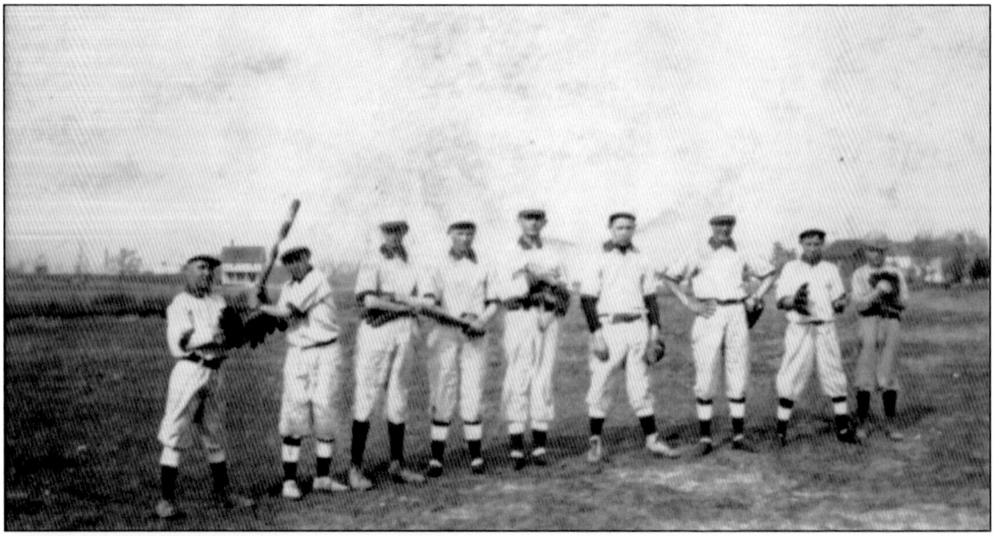

This early Otisville High School baseball team is seen in line for a team photograph at Berger Field in Otisville. Max Berger donated this playing area for the community to enjoy. Many high school baseball and soccer games were played at this location. Today it is primarily used by the little league for its baseball games.

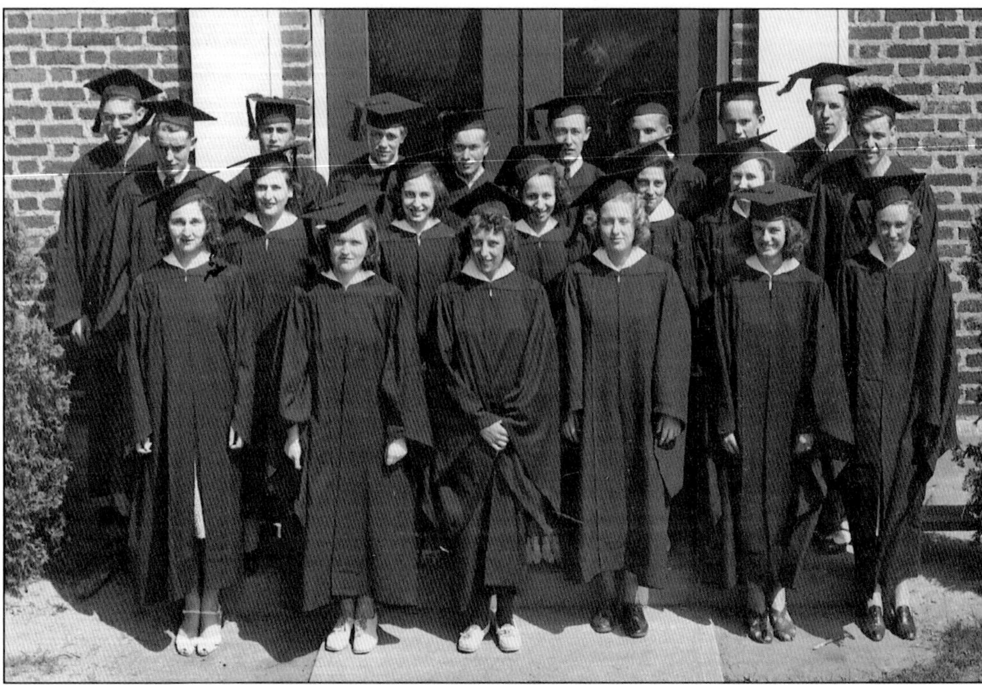

This photograph of the class of 1940 was taken in front of the school. All the graduates are in their caps and gowns. The members of the class from left to right are (first row) Henrietta Klein, Rose McDermott, Pyllis Runnalls, Ruth Van Brunt, Audrey Ketcham, and Evelyn Bimble; (second row) Laurence Doty, Natalie Levine, Madeline McGowan, Marie Coppola, Martha Sangialosi, Norma Elmer, and Leon Cannon; (third row) Coleman Ketcham, Vincent Rooney, Francis Doty, Ralph Flood, William Stanfield, Richard Hosking, Neil Osterdahl, and Ralph Breakell.

The Otisville High School gymnasium is the scene for this photograph of the 1939–1940 basketball cheerleaders performing a pyramid. The cheerleaders from left to right are (first row) Ena Lang; (second row) Dottie Vreeland, Audrey Ketcham, Arline Cannon, and Madeline McGowan; (third row) Kay Crowley.

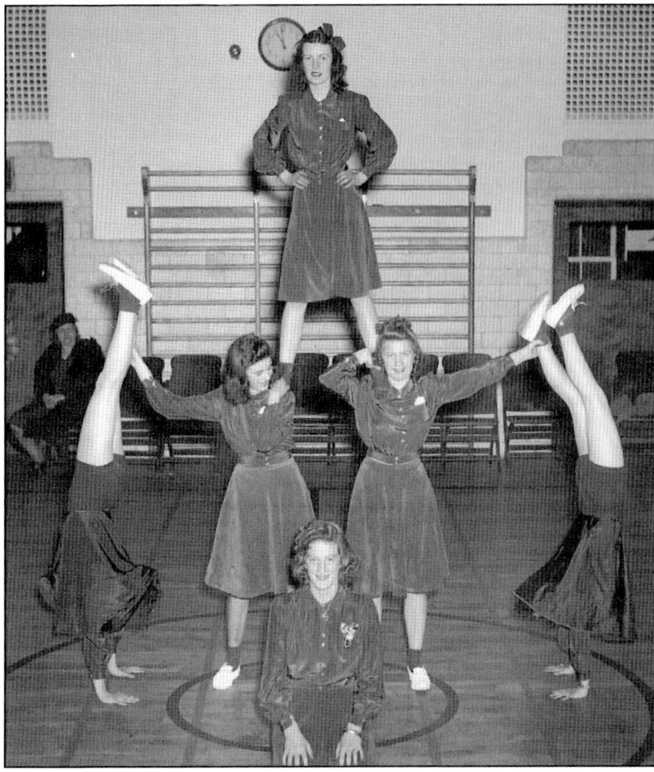

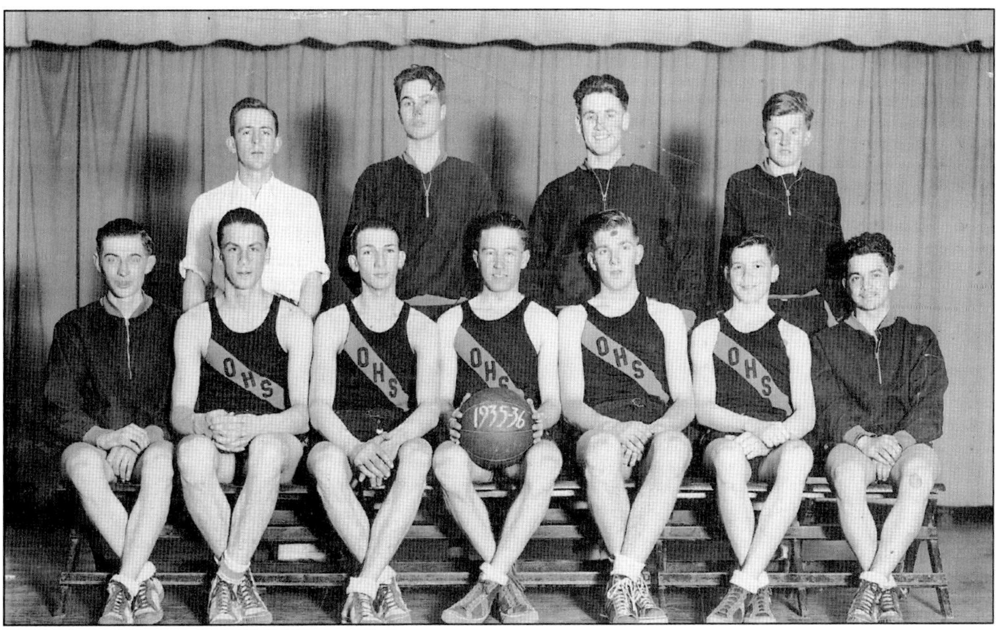

The Otisville High School basketball team from the 1935–1936 school year appears in this photograph taken on the stage at the school. Members from left to right are (first row) Lou Butzgy, Walt Lang, Tony Miceli, Ernie Reynolds, Pop Everly, Sid Green, and Art Zimmerman; (second row) coach Chub Wilbur, Harry "Flash" Greenleaf, Charles "Pete" Thomas, and Ed "Rube" Vreeland.

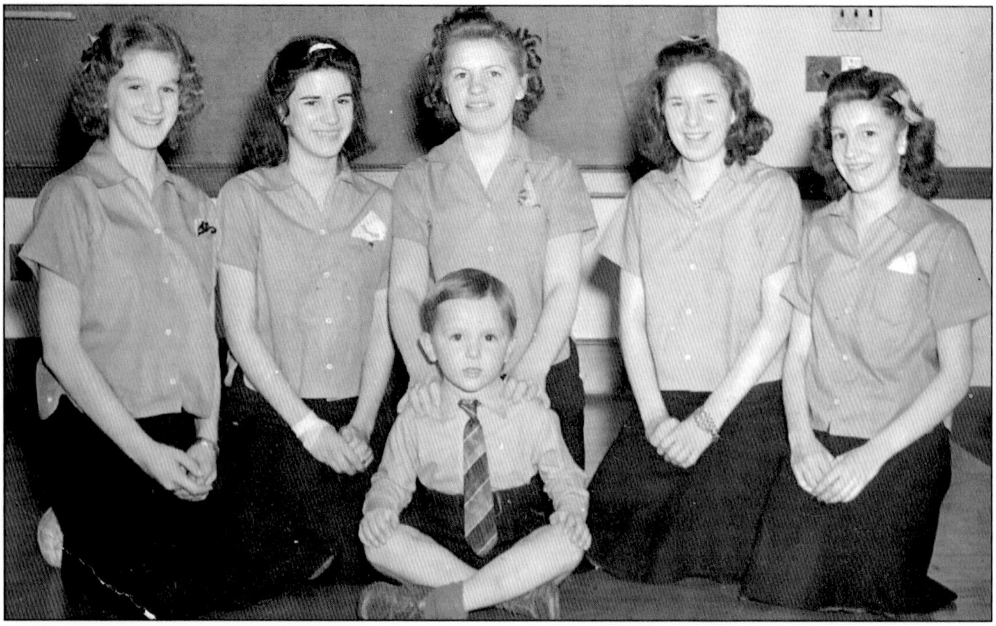

This photograph was taken at Montgomery High School in 1940. Basketball games were well attended at home and away. Townspeople gave their support to the Otisville players and the cheerleaders were always present to cheer them on to victory. The group pictured from left to right includes (first row) Francis Wilbur; (second row) Ena Lang, Audrey Ketcham, Arline Cannon, Sara Budd, and Dottie Vreeland.

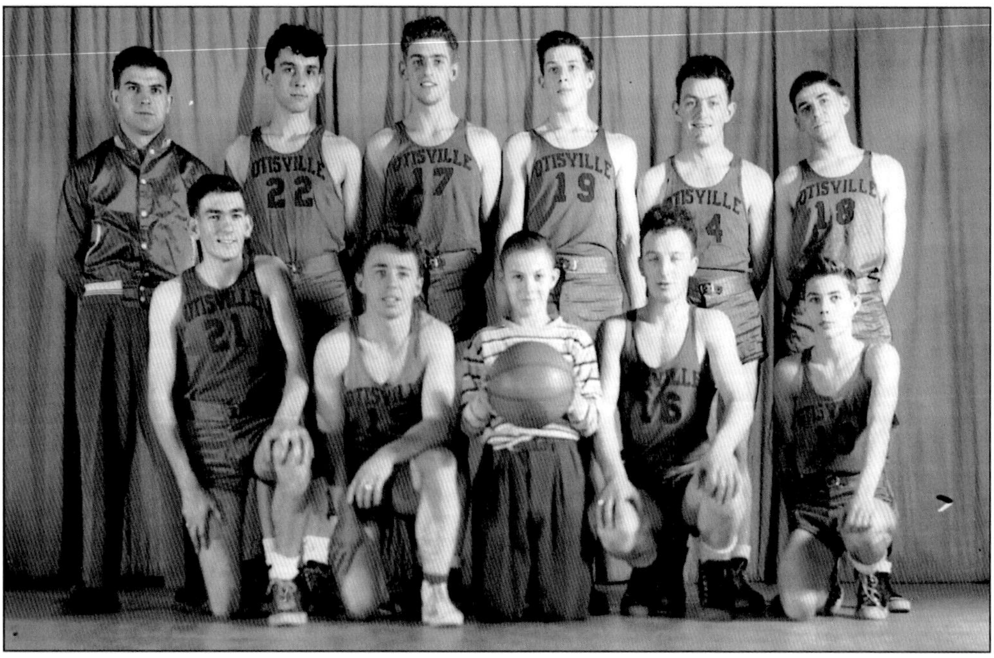

Otisville High School had many fine basketball teams. Pictured here is the team from 1949–1950. From left to right, they are (first row) Joseph Sausville, William Brocket, Walter Cawein, Sam Sangialosi, and Ray Cawein; (second row) coach Wesley Kissel, George Collins, Louis Wilson, Howard Gick, Ray Moran, and Robert Walker.

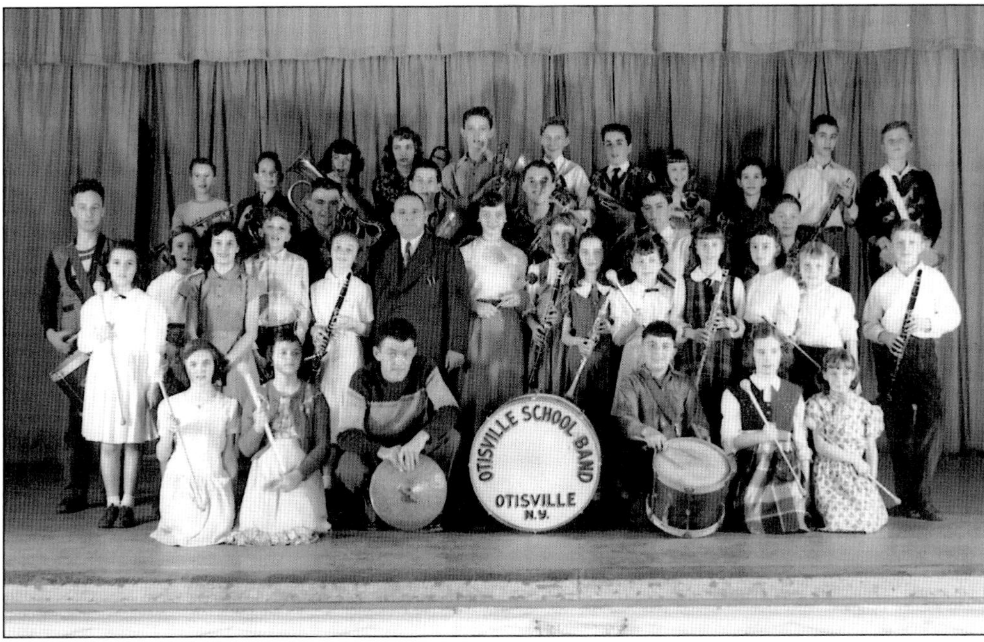

The Otisville band from 1949–1950 is photographed on the stage in the Otisville High School auditorium. The members of the band performed for school functions and parades in the village. In the 1940s and 1950s, Otisville had Memorial Day parades and parades sponsored by the Otisville firemen.

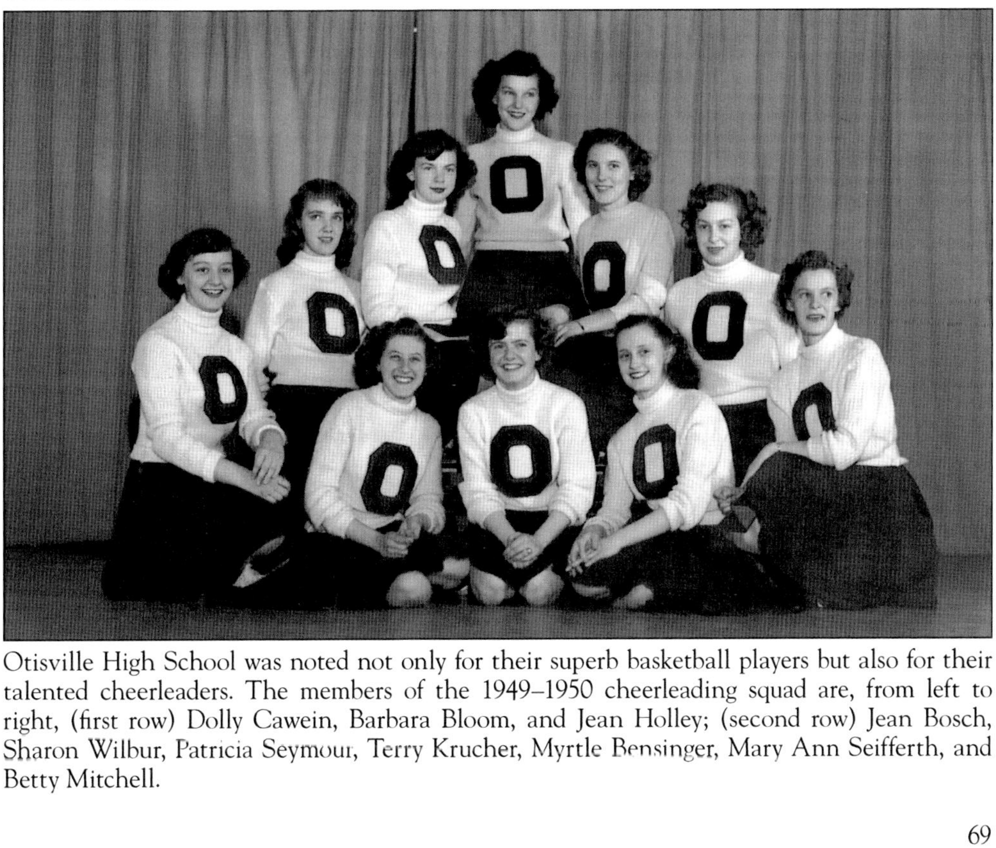

Otisville High School was noted not only for their superb basketball players but also for their talented cheerleaders. The members of the 1949–1950 cheerleading squad are, from left to right, (first row) Dolly Cawein, Barbara Bloom, and Jean Holley; (second row) Jean Bosch, Sharon Wilbur, Patricia Seymour, Terry Krucher, Myrtle Bensinger, Mary Ann Seifferth, and Betty Mitchell.

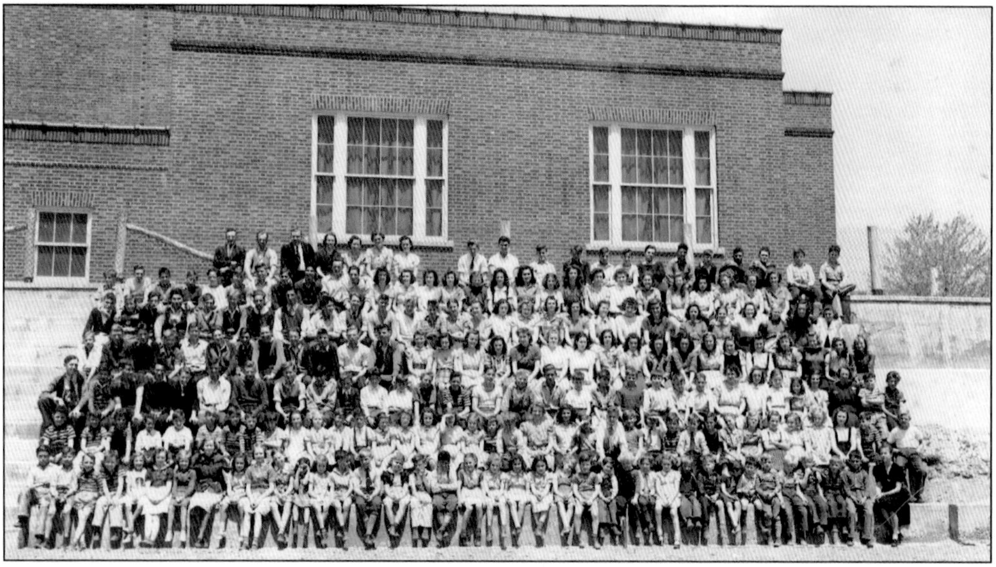

In June 1940, this photograph was taken of the entire student body and members of the faculty on the concrete bleachers at the side of the school .The student body was quite large at that time because the school was still receiving students from the Cuddebackville, Weastbrookville, and Mount Hope districts.

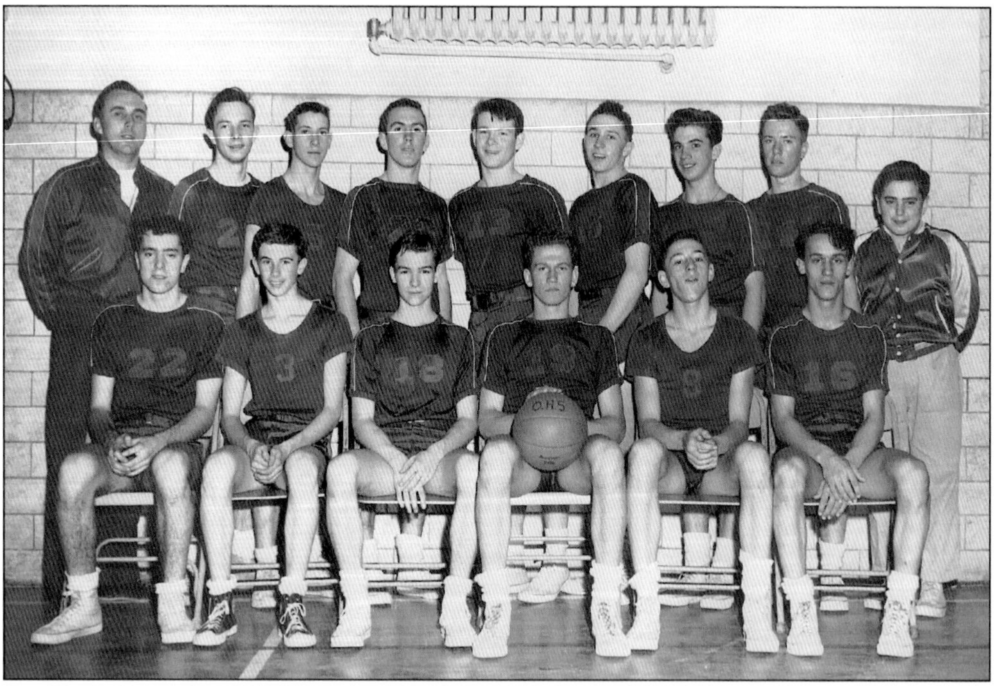

On Thursday night, February 21, 1957, the Otisville High School Mountaineers trounced Montgomery by a score of 59-38 to win the Orange County section B title. The winning team members from left to right are (first row) Ed Budd, Jack Michelitch, Bob Baker, Warren Roda, Andy Pikela, and Skip Coppola; (second row) coach Stan Dean, Allan Ackerson, Cal Runnalls, Kayo Stanfield, Butch Nagy, Gene Ketcham, Greg Garcia, Larry Palmer, and team manager Dave Budd.

Five

Religious Life

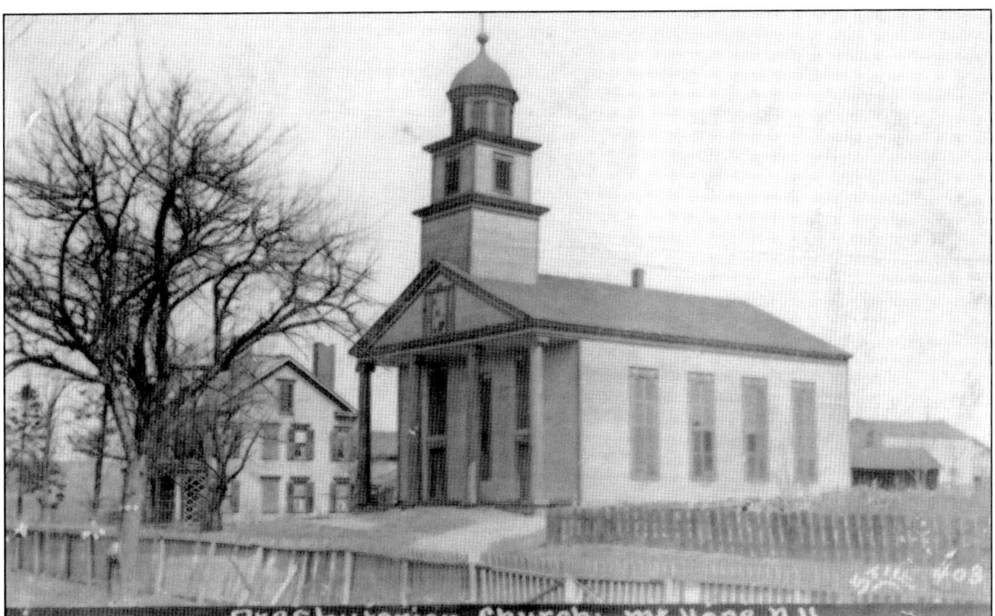

In 1835, Barna Horton and his carpenters built the Mount Hope Presbyterian Church. The church replaced the Deerpark Church, which was located at the present site of the Plains Cemetery in Otisville. The church was erected in Mount Hope because Mount Hope had a larger population than Otisville at that time.

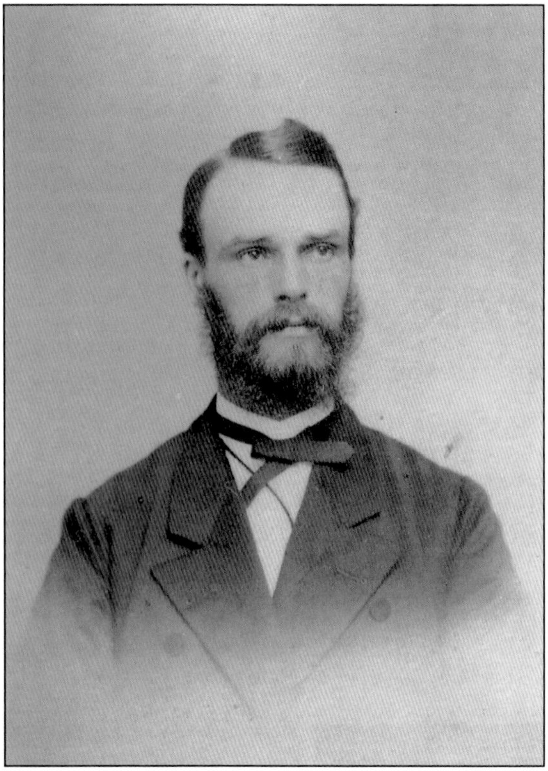

Rev. Robert Houston Craig was a graduate of Princeton Theological Seminary. He was pastor of the Otisville Presbyterian Church from 1871 to 1884. After departing Otisville, he maintained a close relationship with members of his former congregation. Craig often returned to the village to officiate at weddings and funerals. Two of his sons who died in infancy are buried in the Mount Hope Plains Cemetery in Otisville.

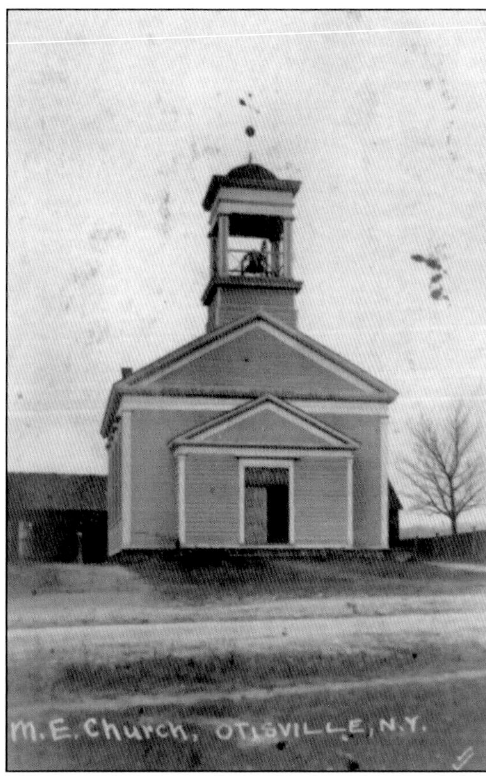

The Otisville Methodist Episcopal Church on Highland Avenue was completed in 1849. The first minister was Rev. Fletcher Lummis. During the pastorate of Lummis, there was a break in the church and many of the female members left the church and were responsible for forming the Otisville Presbyterian Church. In the 1960s, the congregation merged with the Otisville–Mount Hope Presbyterian Church.

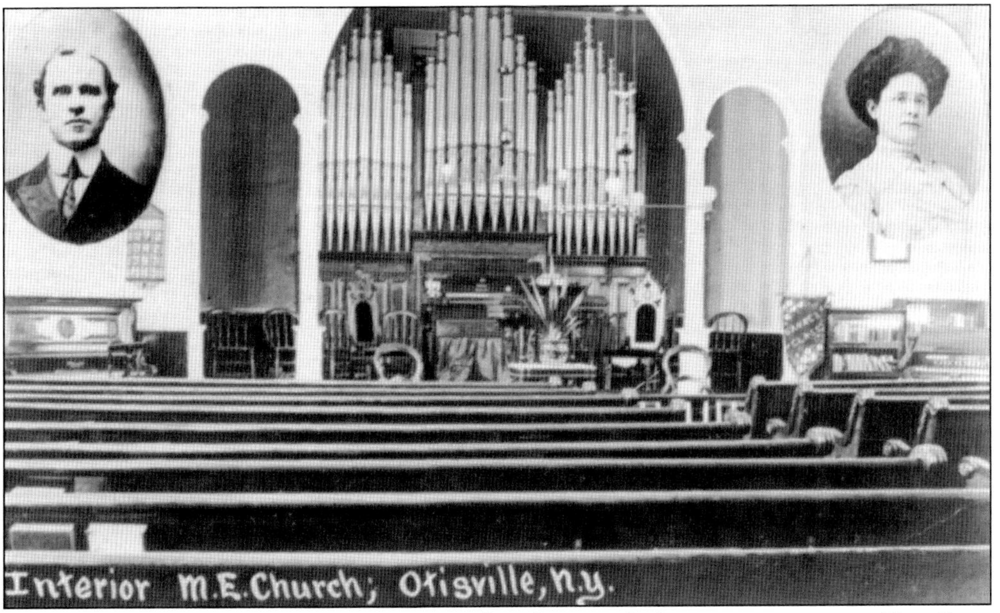

Rev. Robert S. Young and his wife appear in this photograph that was sent out as a New Years greeting in 1907. During the pastorate of Young, a grand pipe organ, pews, a tin ceiling, and gas lamps were installed in the Otisville Methodist Episcopal Church. Young was dedicated to helping not only the members of his congregation but also the many patients who resided at the Otisville Tuberculosis Sanitorium.

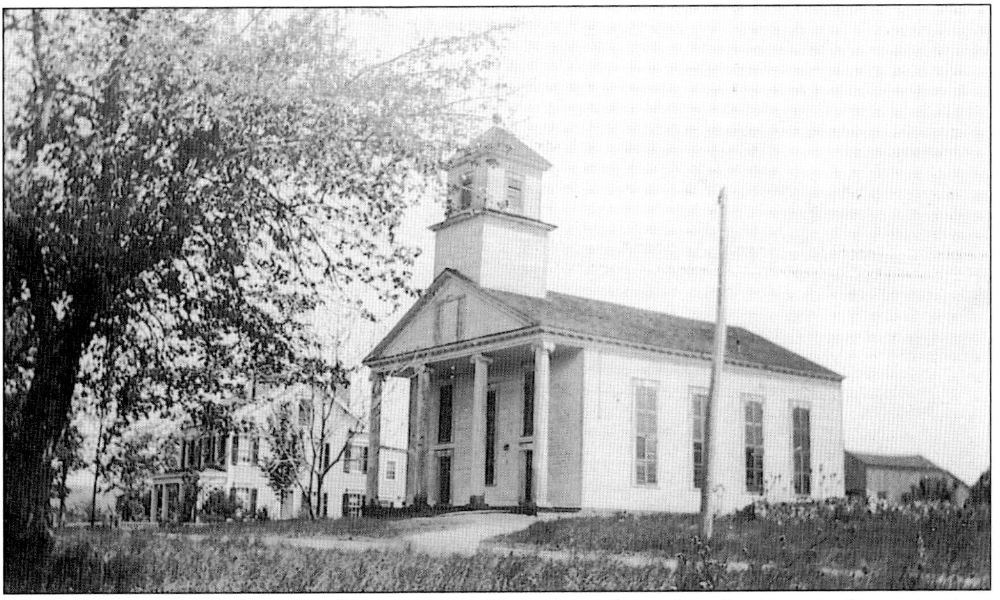

The Mount Hope Presbyterian Church has a shorter steeple in this photograph that was taken in the early 1900s than seen on page 71. The steeple was probably damaged in a storm and was not replaced. To the left of the church is the Charles S. Woodward home. Woodward was a member of the New York State Assembly and did much of the legal work in Mount Hope during the mid-1800s.

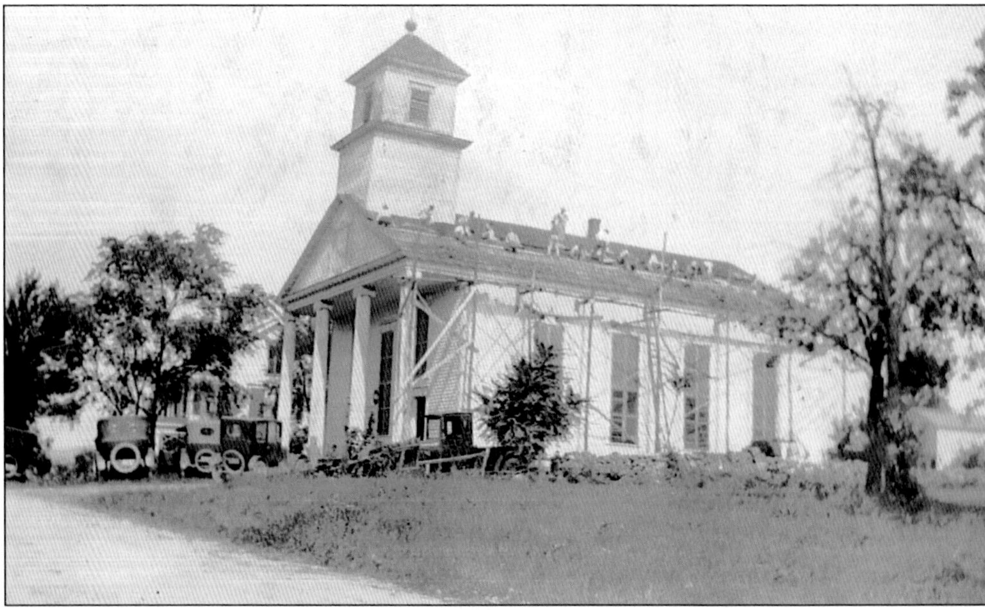

Men are hard at work repairing the roof of the Mount Hope Presbyterian Church in 1921. Members of the congregation spent many hours making repairs on the church in an effort to reduce the cost of maintenance. Several automobiles are parked in front of the church. By this time, the automobile has replaced the horse as a means of transportation.

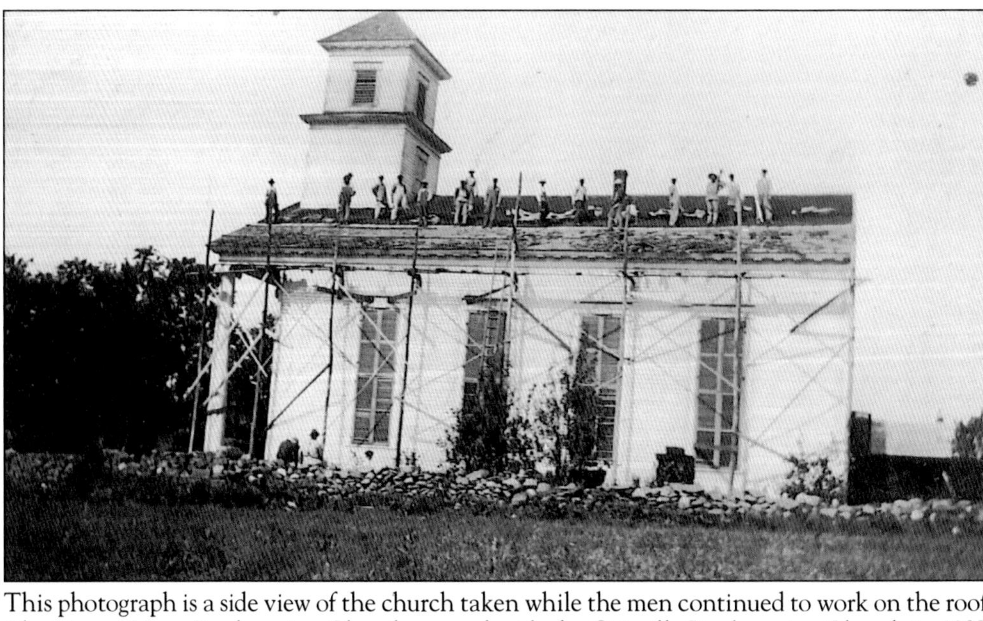

This photograph is a side view of the church taken while the men continued to work on the roof. The Mount Hope Presbyterian Church merged with the Otisville Presbyterian Church in 1935. After that, the Mount Hope church building was purchased by the Grange. Many local people remember attending square dances at the Mount Hope Grange. The building was destroyed by fire in 1948 despite valiant efforts by local firemen.

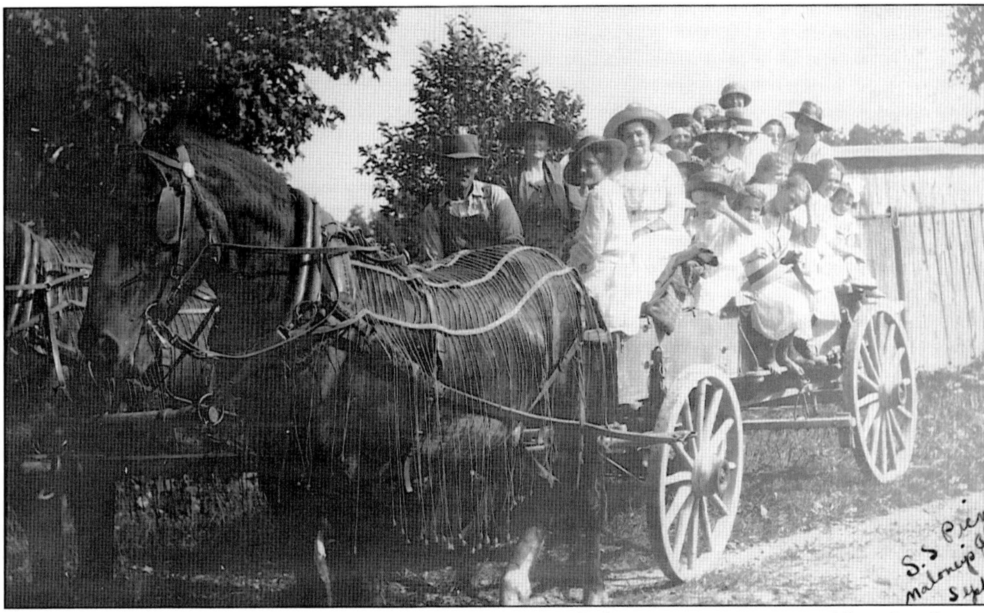

Members of the Mount Hope Presbyterian Church, including Nettie Writer and her family, are on their way to a Sunday school picnic at Maloney's Glen on a lovely day in September 1922. Church suppers, strawberry socials, and picnics at a cool and shady spot were all part of village life, which revolved around the church. The long leather straps on the horses swished back and forth to keep the flies away.

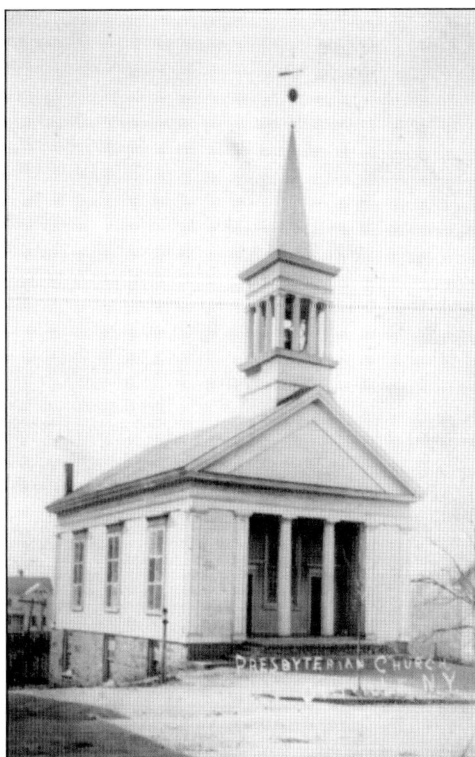

The Otisville Presbyterian congregation was formed in 1855. The Loomis family donated land for a church and the stately building was completed in 1856. During the 1800s and early 1900s, church suppers at the Methodist and Presbyterian churches were almost a weekly event. Frequent fund-raisers were necessary in order to pay for the upkeep of the churches.

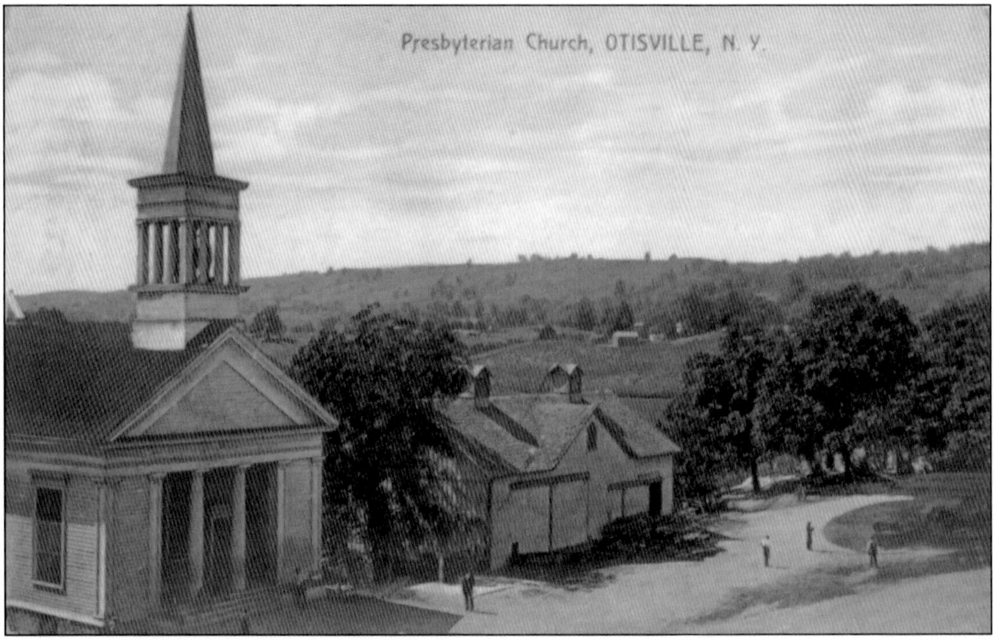

This view of the Otisville Presbyterian Church shows its close proximity to the Loomis barn. When the Loomis barn was destroyed by fire in 1875, the citizens of Otisville feared that the church would be a casualty. However, quick thinking and valiant efforts by the villagers saved the church. The Loomis barn was rebuilt at the same site after the fire.

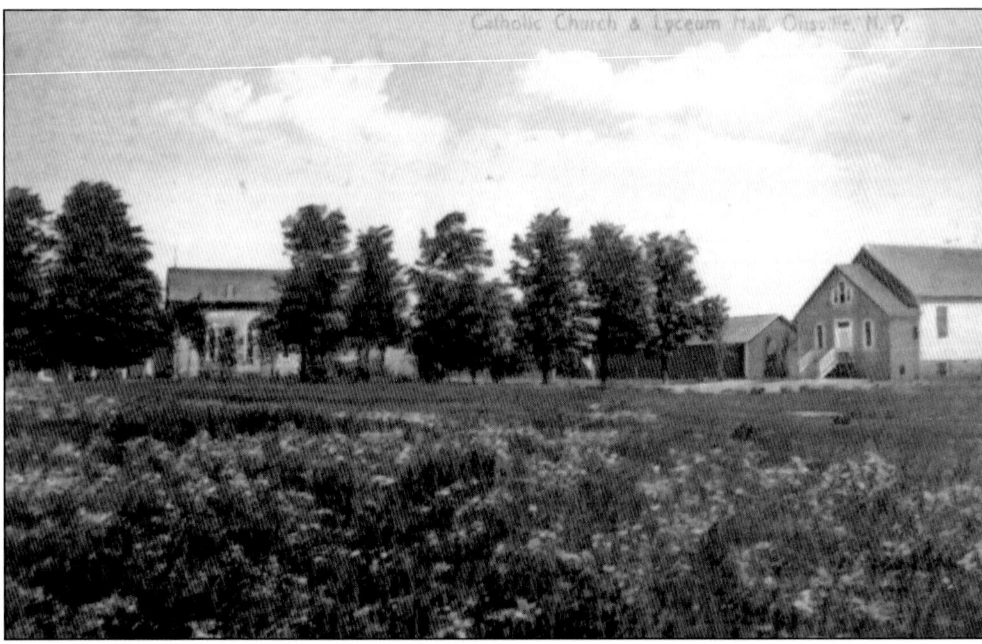

The Holy Name of Jesus Church on Highland Avenue was completed in 1866 due to the efforts of Father Brennan, pastor of St. Mary's Church in Port Jervis. On the day the church was dedicated, 1,200 people were present on the grounds to witness the event. Lyceum Hall, which appears on the right of the photograph, was built in 1912 and was used for church suppers and other functions.

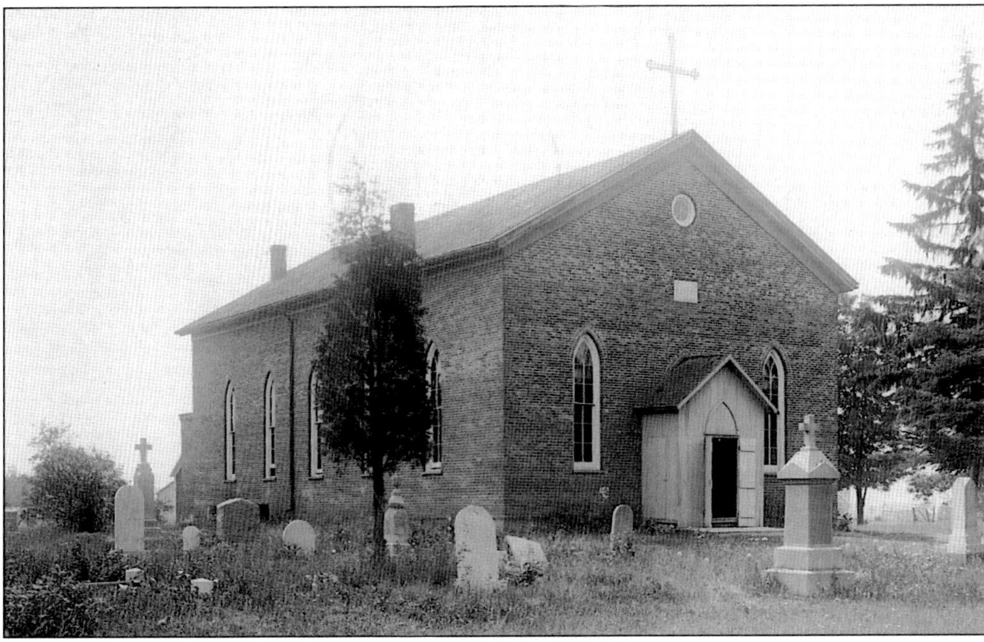

Father Flanagan was the first resident pastor of the Holy Name Church. Prior to that time, priests from other parishes administered the sacraments. Two of the traveling priests were Father Aylward and Father Basset. Flanagan was responsible for constructing an open-air dance pavilion behind the church. Dances were open to the public and proceeds were used for church purposes. These dances were advertised in the newspaper and were popular village events.

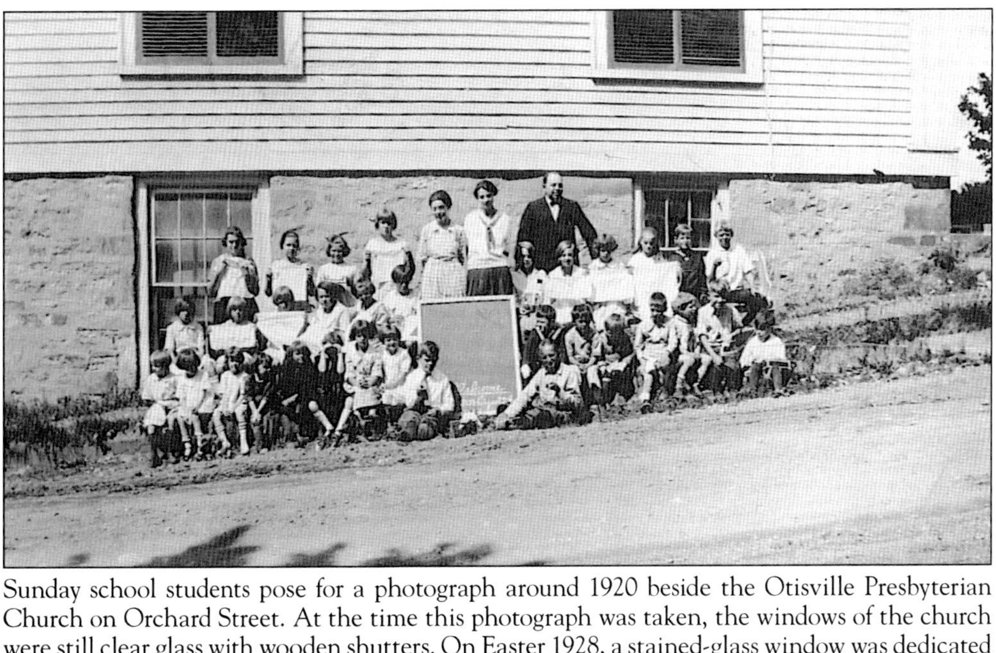

Sunday school students pose for a photograph around 1920 beside the Otisville Presbyterian Church on Orchard Street. At the time this photograph was taken, the windows of the church were still clear glass with wooden shutters. On Easter 1928, a stained-glass window was dedicated in memory of Ezra and Sarah Gray Reed by their daughter Laura Reed Patterson and her family, who were active church members.

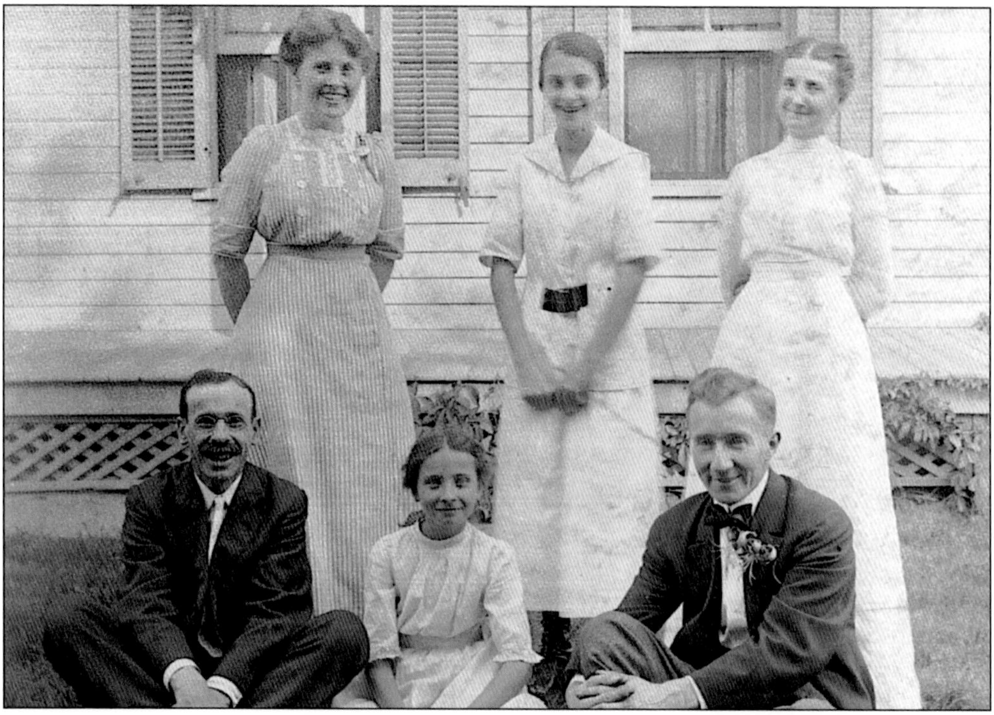

Rev. J. S. Laing and family are seen in this photograph outside their home in Otisville. Laing was once minister of the Otisville Presbyterian Church. The people in the photograph are, from left to right, (first row) unidentified, Alison Laing, and J. S.; (second row) Ruth Lamb, Esther Laing, and Mrs. Laing.

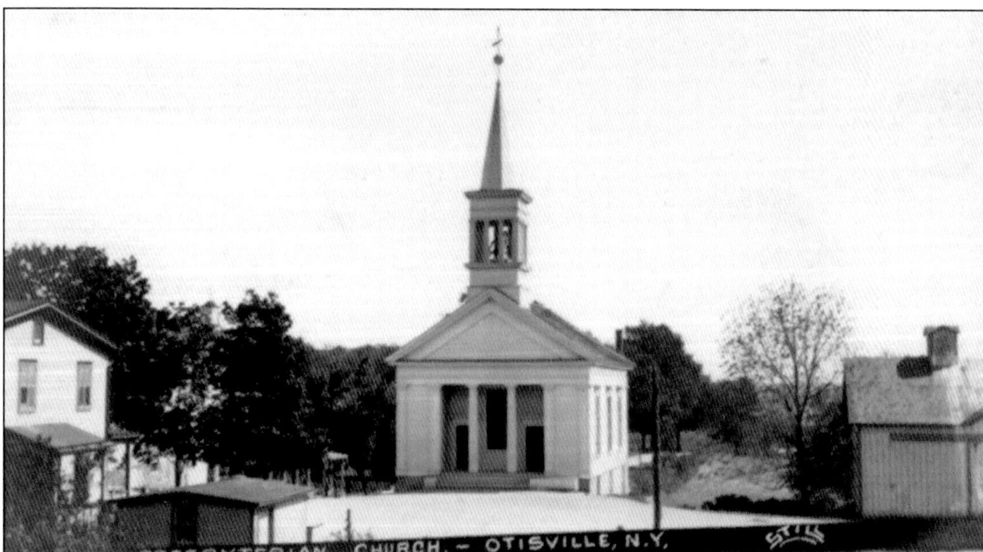

The Otisville Presbyterian Church built a new manse in 1875, and in June of that year, Rev. Robert H. Craig and his family moved into their new home that was located on the property next to the east portal of the Erie tunnel. During the summer of 1886, the choir area was raised and a fine railing was placed around it. The church is now known as the Otisville–Mount Hope Presbyterian Church, and Rev. Jeffrey Farley is the pastor.

Six

The Erie Railroad and Tunnel

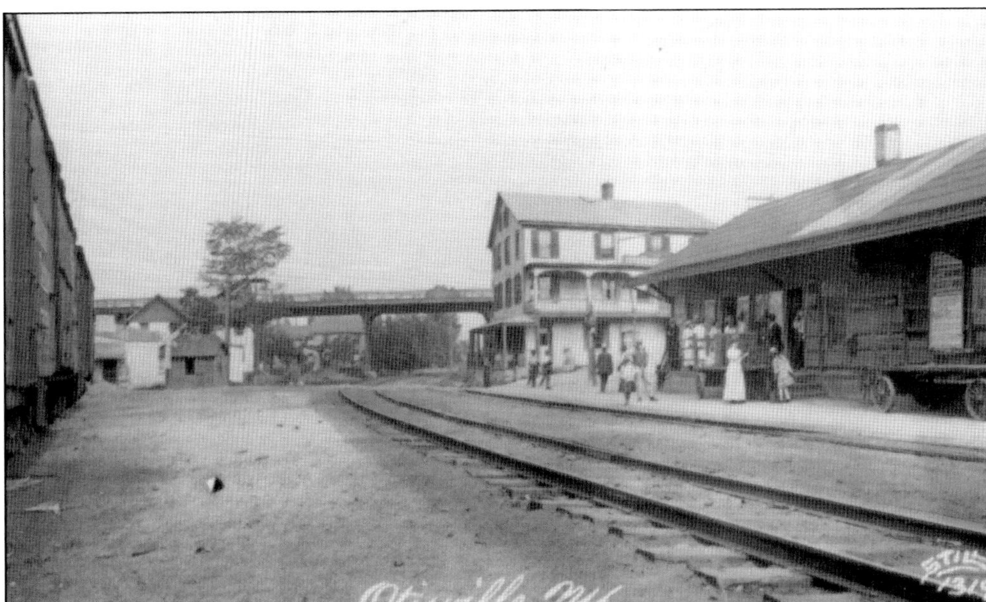

The first Erie Railroad train arrived in Otisville in October 1846. After the arrival of the railroad, the sleepy town of Otisville was transformed. Almost overnight, it became a center of commerce for the surrounding rural area. In this photograph taken around 1908, a group of people is waiting at the depot for the train to arrive. A little girl in a plaid dress and a straw hat waits for the train with her mother, while others are seen purchasing their tickets.

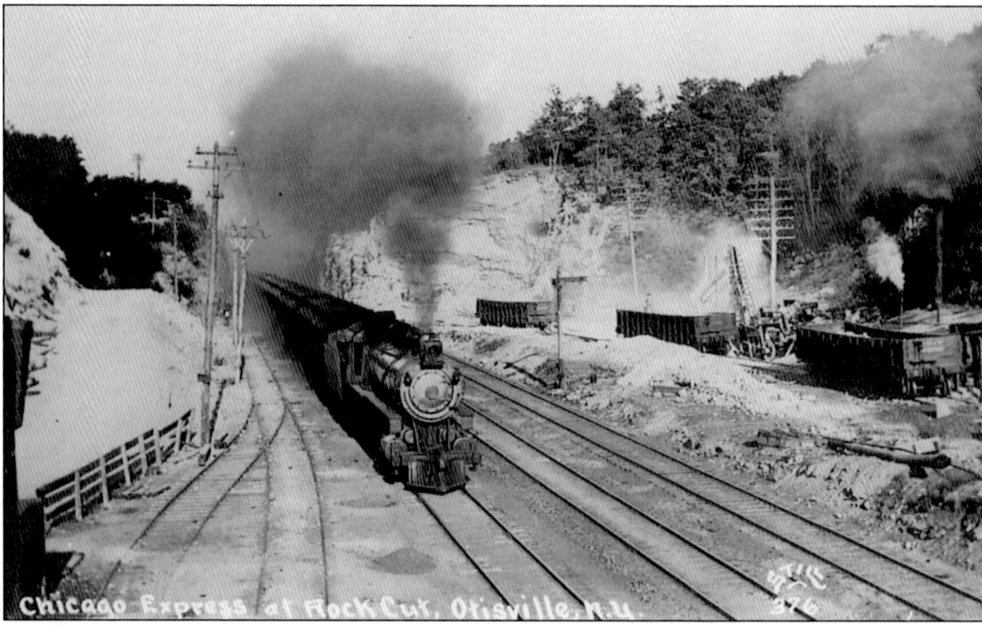

The Chicago Express passes through the rock cut on its way to the Otisville depot. The rock cut is located on the outskirts of Otisville down the mountain toward Cuddebackville. All of the railroad ties for the track running from Otisville to Port Jervis were purchased from Otisville merchant Algernon S. Dodge, who owned 12 sawmills in Sullivan County.

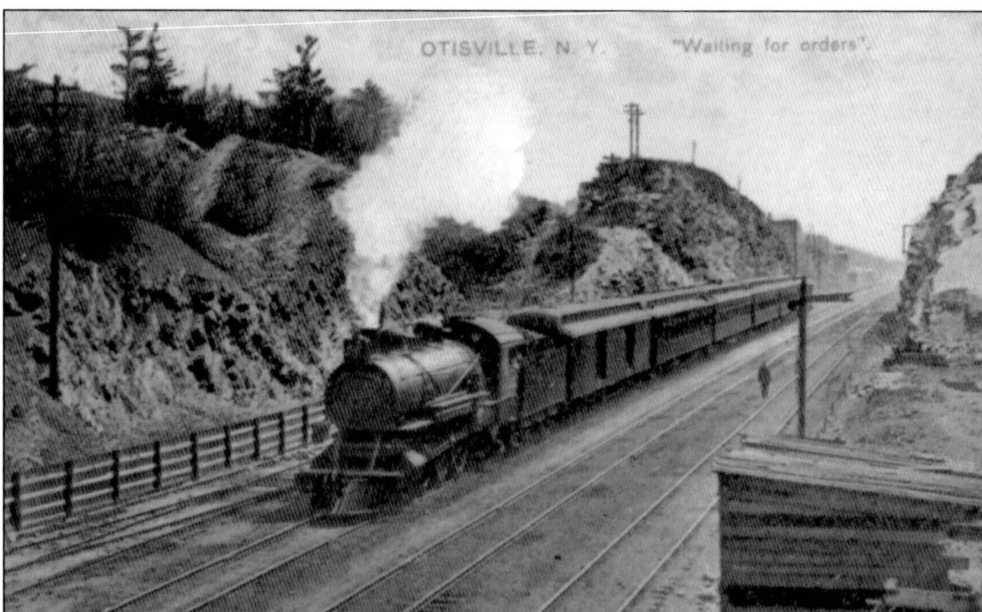

After the arrival of the Erie Railroad in 1846, Otisville and Mount Hope farmers could easily ship their milk and produce to New York City. Before the train ran its tracks to Otisville, farmers had to take their produce by cart to Newburgh and then ship it by sloop down the Hudson River to New York. In this photograph, a steam locomotive barrels down the track near Otisville.

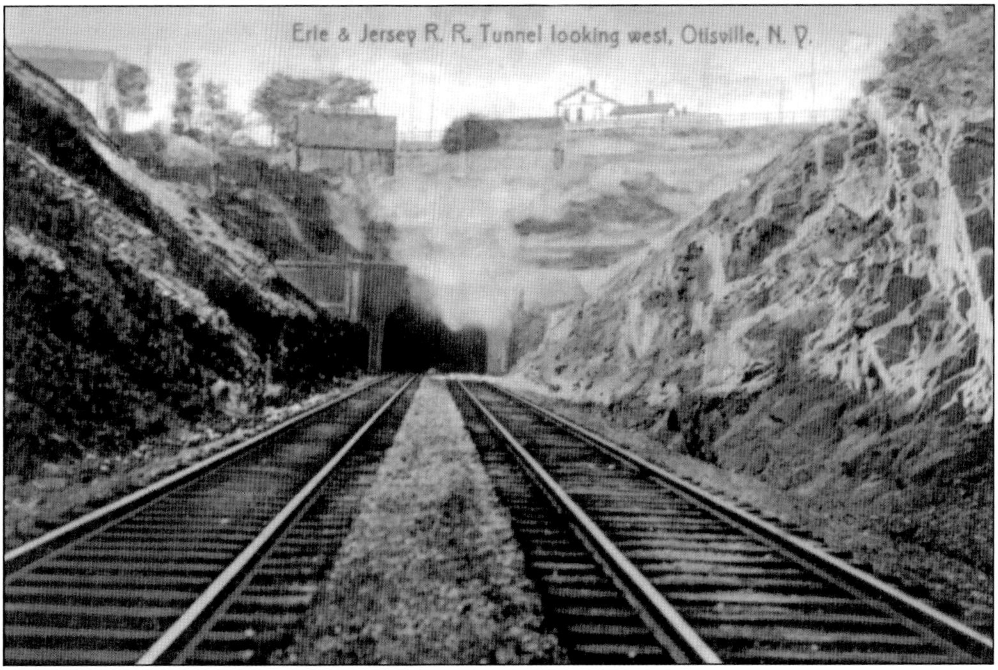

This photograph shows the double track of the Erie Railroad approaching the east portal of the tunnel heading toward the depot in Otisville. After the tunnel was constructed, freight trains could pass under the village of Otisville on their way west.

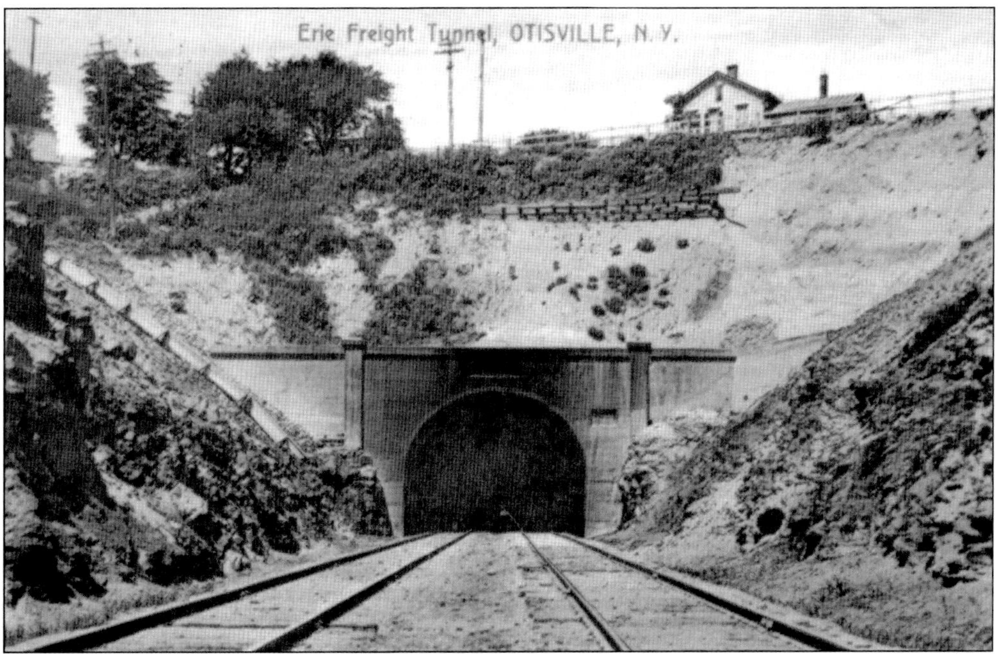

This photograph is a view of the east portal of the Erie Railroad freight tunnel. Route 211 is located above the tunnel, and Kelly Hill is to the left. During the construction of the tunnel, several houses had to be removed, including the Methodist parsonage that was located near the brick house at the head of Kelly Hill.

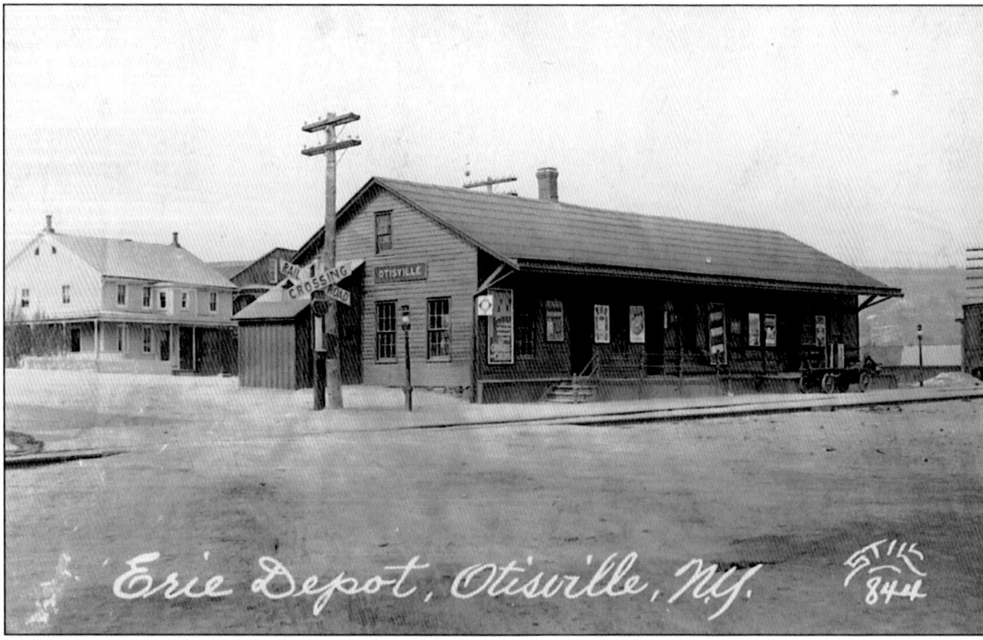

Alfred H. Still took this photograph of the Erie Railroad depot in the early 1900s. The depot began to fall into disrepair during the mid-1900s after all trains were rerouted and there was no longer a use for the depot. The parking lot of the depot was used in the 1950s for an annual bazaar sponsored by the Otisville firemen, which was a highlight of the summer for Otisville children.

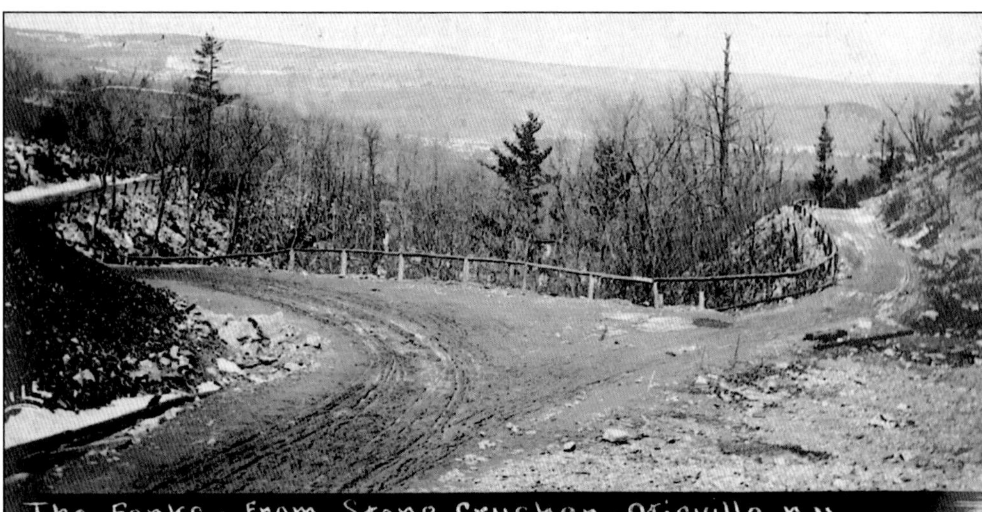

The fork in the road at the stone crusher is located near the rock cut on the border of Otisville. The road on the left goes to Cuddebackville and the road on the right heads toward Westbrookville. The Erie stone crusher was located near this point. Most early residents of Otisville will recognize the locale as the former site of the town dump.

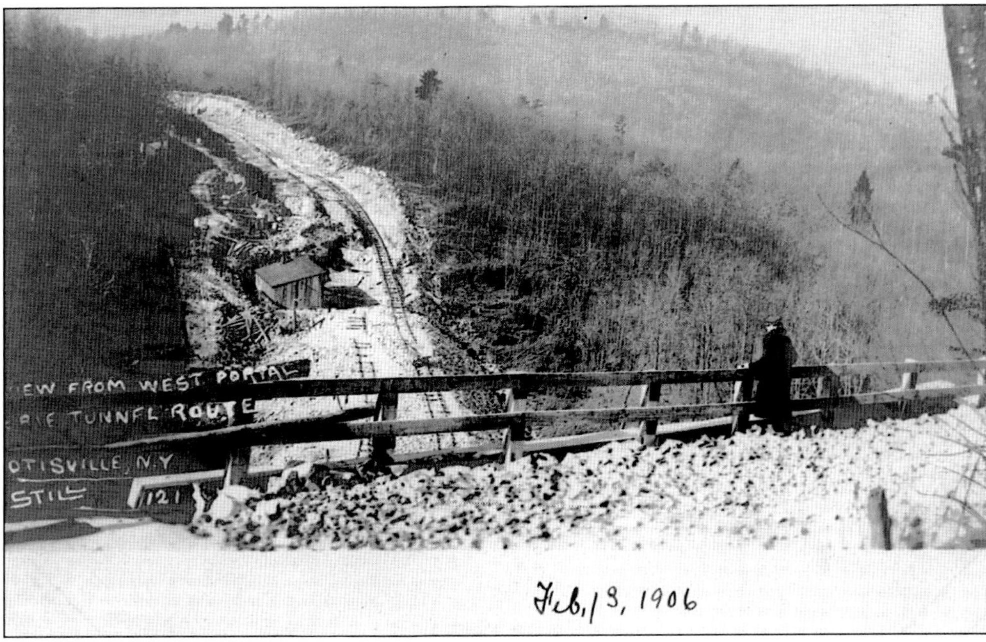

This interesting view from the west portal of the Erie tunnel was taken on February 13, 1906, during the construction of the tunnel. This location is found on Route 211 heading down the mountain toward Cuddebackville. It was the ideal spot to view workers below, who were laboring on the construction of the tunnel.

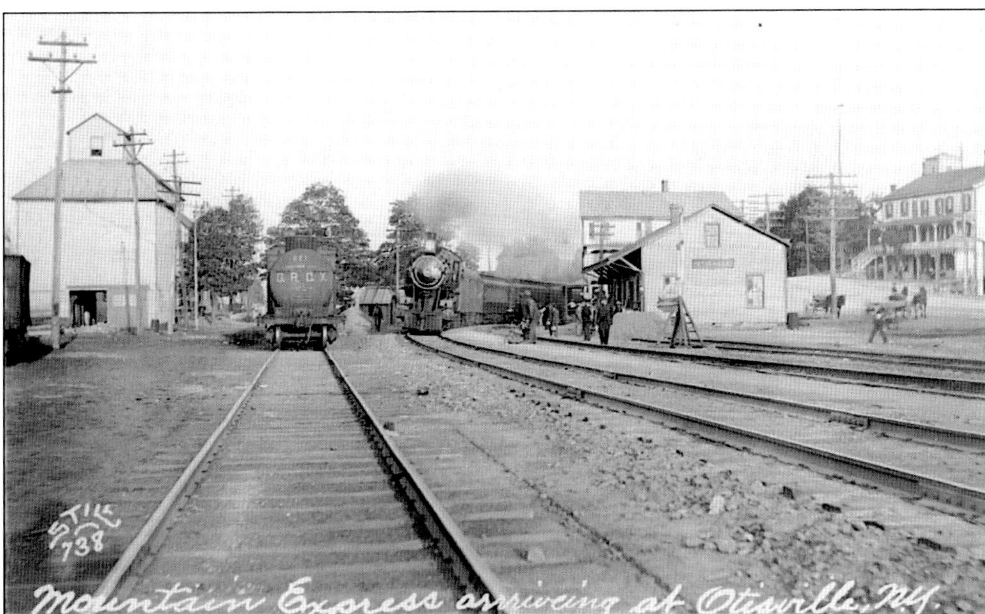

The mountain express arrives at the Otisville depot in this early 1900s photograph. In this view are the double tracks that originally ran through the village. The white building on the left was used to store coal. It was located next to the Wallace feed store.

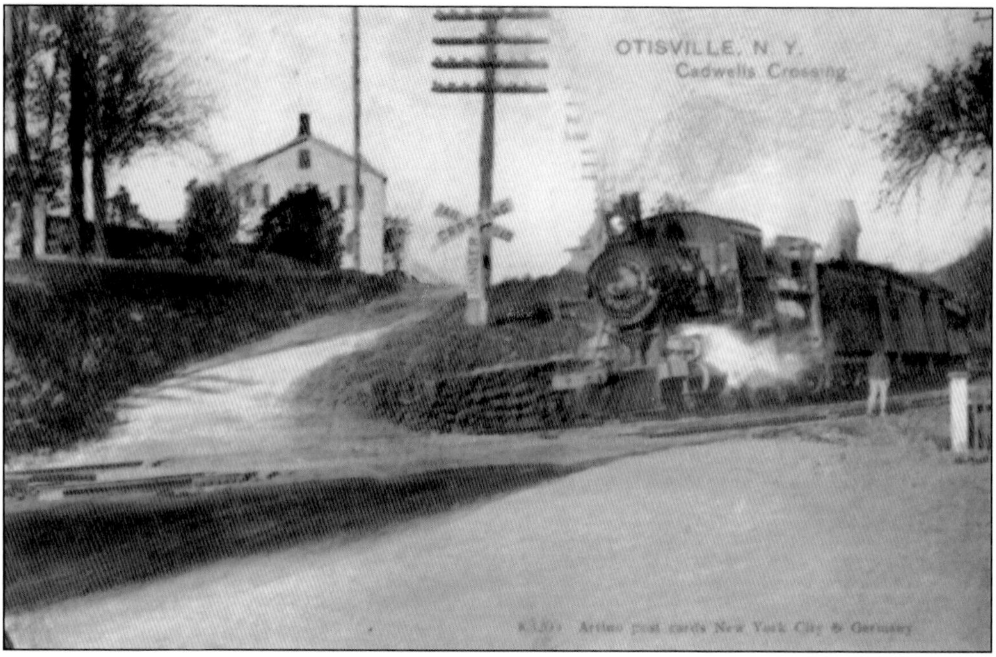

The Erie locomotive is at rest and blowing steam as it awaits a signal from the crossing guard at Cadwell's Crossing in Otisville. Cadwell's Crossing was located at the head of Kelly Hill. It was named after the Cadwell family that once owned a large farm near the crossing. Throughout the years, unmanned railroad crossings resulted in numerous fatal accidents in and around Otisville. Horses and buggies could not outrun trains.

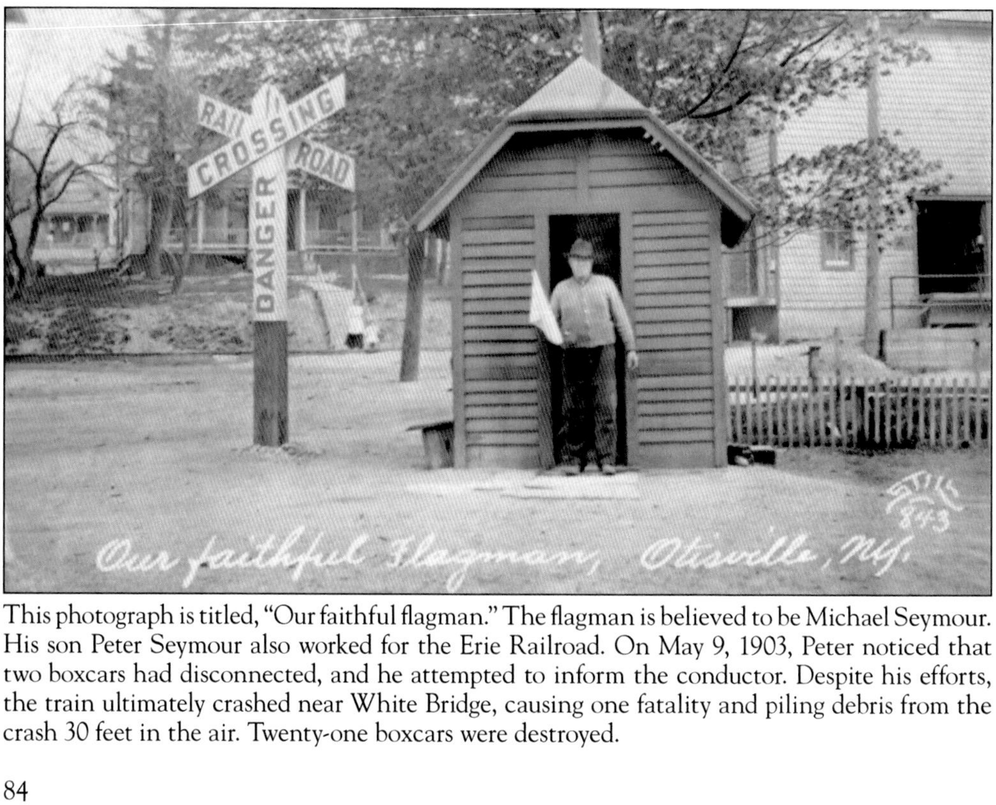

This photograph is titled, "Our faithful flagman." The flagman is believed to be Michael Seymour. His son Peter Seymour also worked for the Erie Railroad. On May 9, 1903, Peter noticed that two boxcars had disconnected, and he attempted to inform the conductor. Despite his efforts, the train ultimately crashed near White Bridge, causing one fatality and piling debris from the crash 30 feet in the air. Twenty-one boxcars were destroyed.

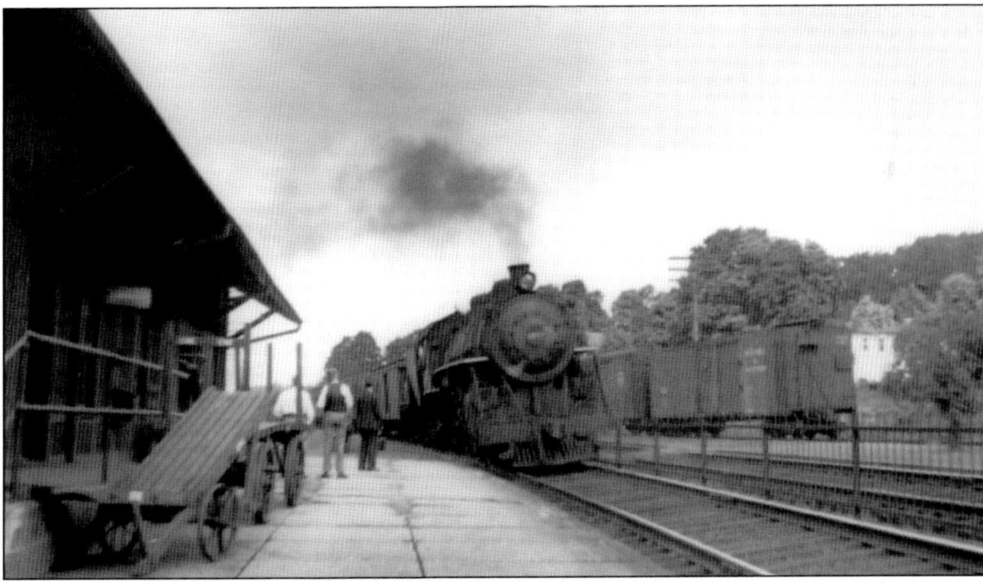

An Erie Railroad steam locomotive approaches the Otisville depot from the west. The baggage and freight carts are lined up outside the depot ready to be loaded with incoming freight. This photograph was taken around 1908, when the Erie Railroad was largely responsible for the economy of many small communities such as Otisville.

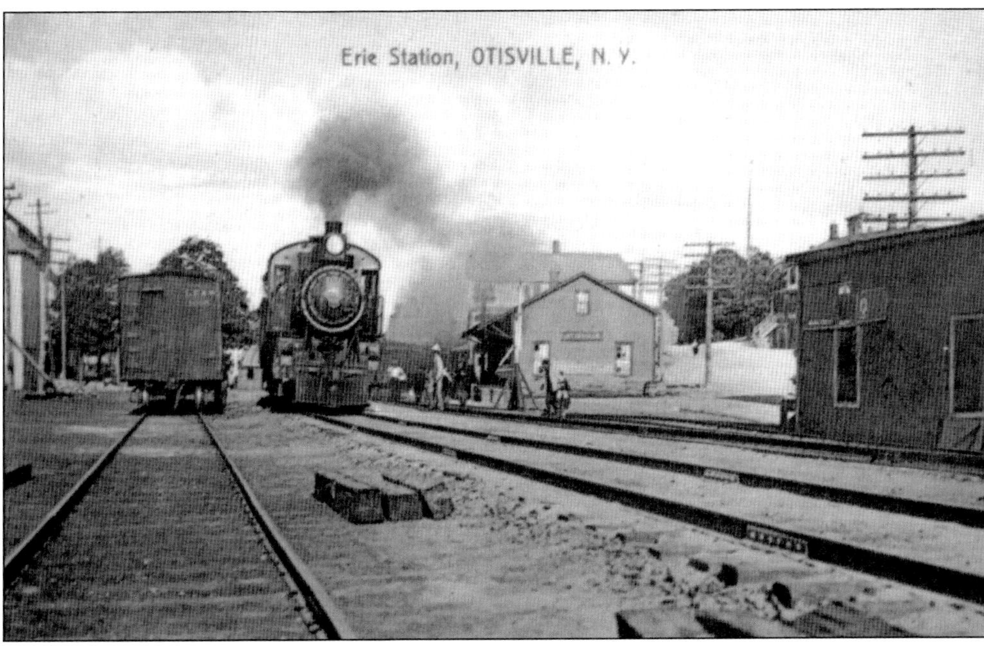

In this photograph, an Erie Railroad locomotive approaches the village of Otisville from the east. On the far right is the back of a general mercantile store, which was built by Harry Reed and George Smith in 1884 after a fire destroyed their previous store. Above the store is a power line. Electric lights came to the village business center in 1915. The night they were turned on, everyone paraded up and down Main Street enjoying the illumination.

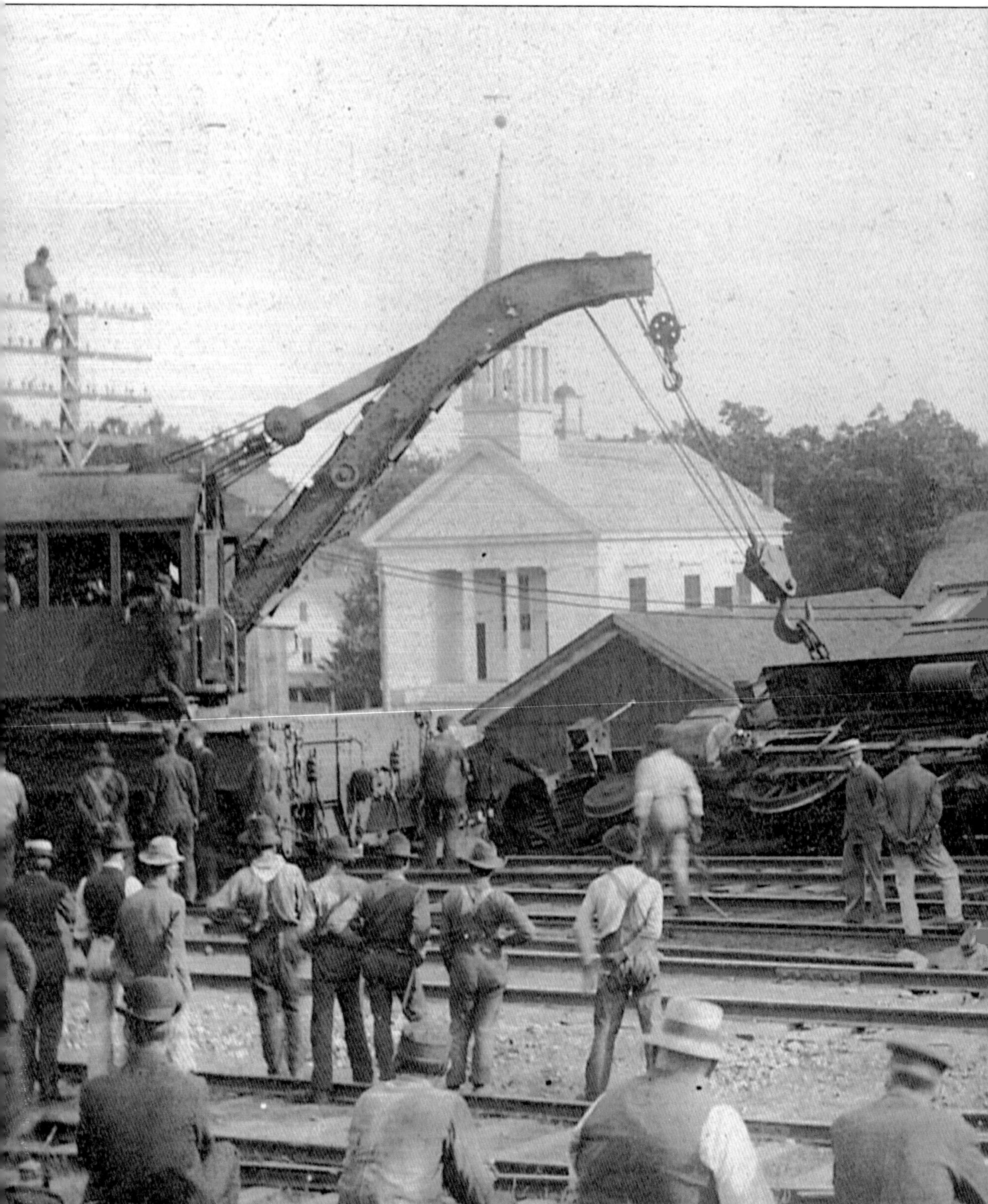

There were many train accidents and derailments in and around Otisville after the Erie Railroad arrived in the village in 1846. This derailment in front of the Otisville Presbyterian Church occurred during the early 1900s, probably while switching tracks. Two large and powerful derricks are attempting to hoist the locomotive that is turned on its side. The train slipped down

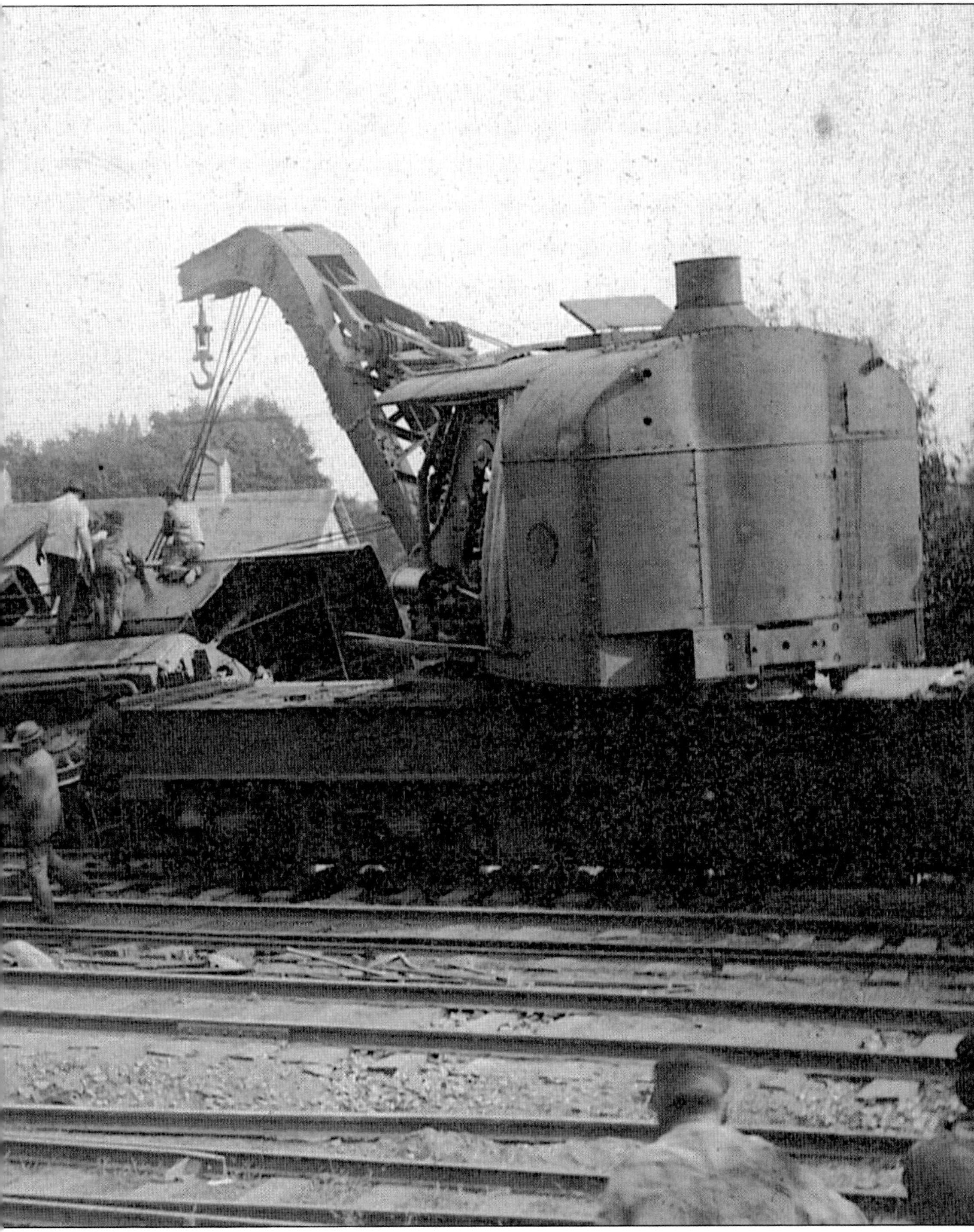

the embankment next to the railroad bed. Town supervisor Gideon C. Harding, in a white straw hat, is seen observing the event in the foreground of the photograph. Many other townspeople are also captivated by this event, including the man perched on the pole.

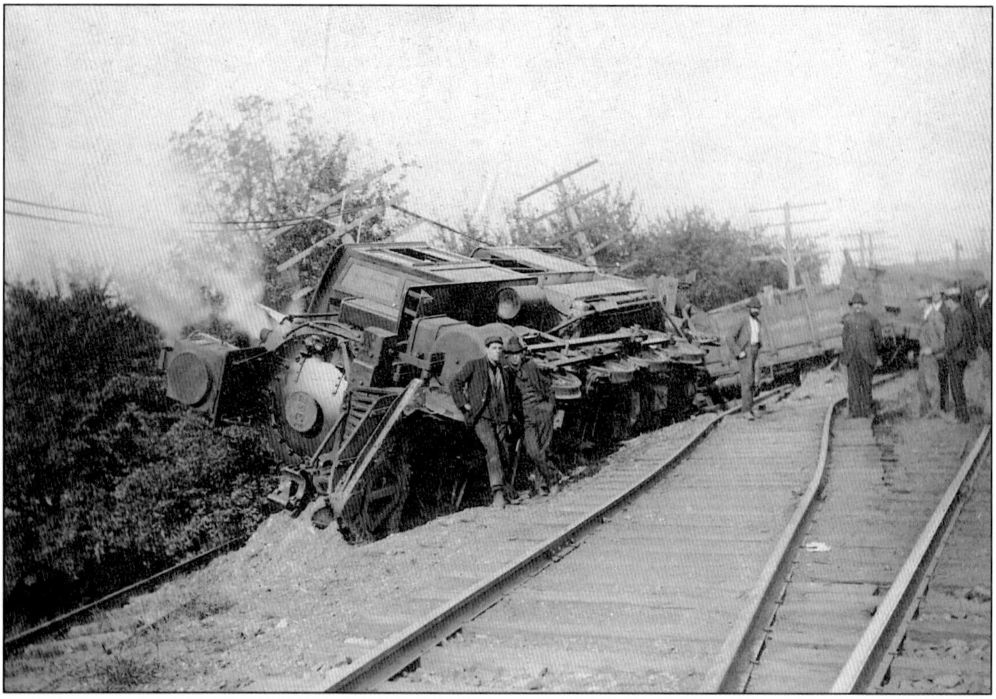

A train is overturned in this vintage photograph, which was owned by an Otisville family. The site of the accident or derailment is unknown but it was located near Otisville and took place during the early 1900s. Research is currently being conducted on train accidents that took place near Otisville.

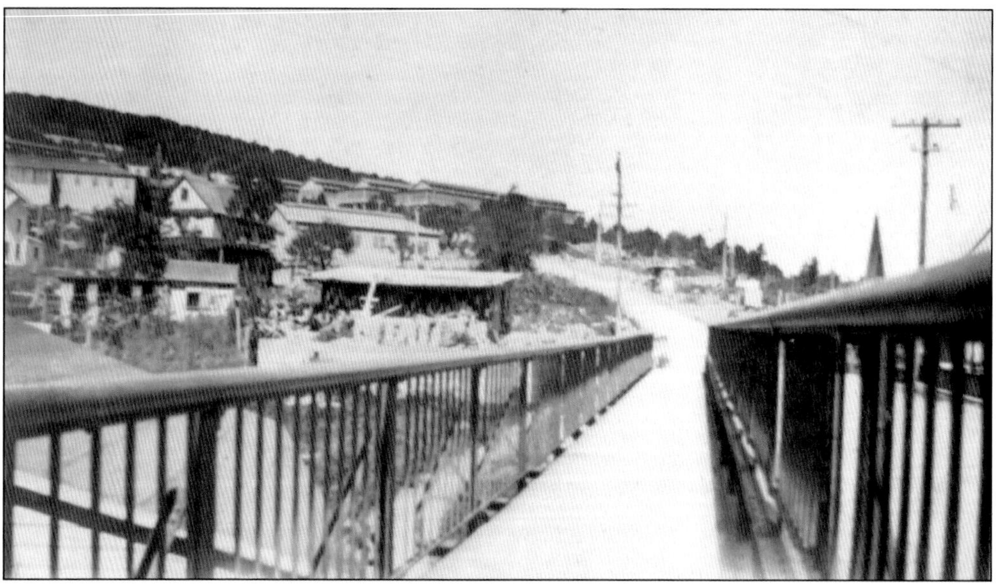

The walkway on the bridge over the Erie Railroad tracks is shown in this photograph looking from the junction of Main Street and Highland Avenue in Otisville. People who lived on the other end of the village used this walkway when walking to the post office or businesses on Main Street. There was also a flight of stairs that led from the walkway to the lower road. The walkway is now closed.

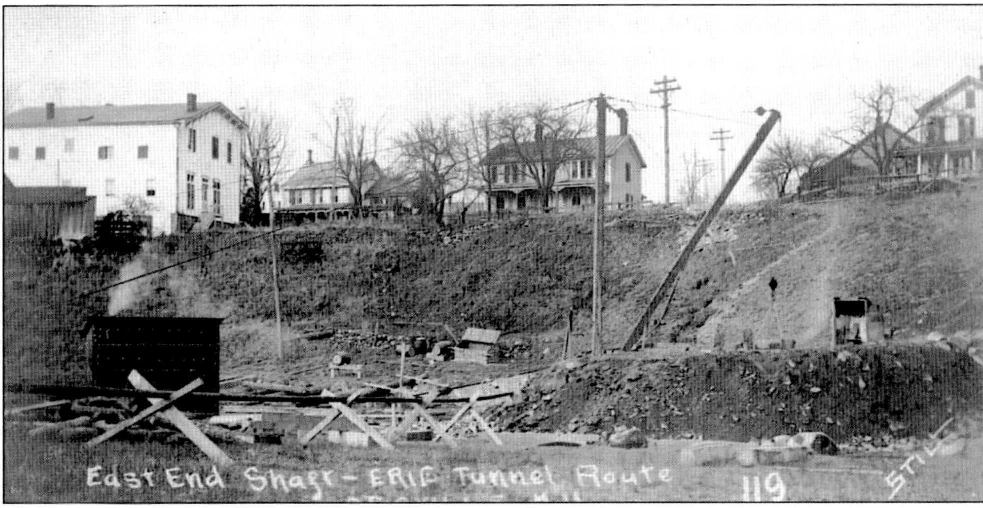

On September 4, 1905, work was begun by the engineering firm Bennett and Talbot on a huge undertaking in Otisville. Work began midway between the east and west ends of the tunnel. At the center, a shaft was sunk about 125 feet deep through solid stone. From this point, two crews of men began forging their ways east and west. In this photograph, work is starting at the east end of the tunnel.

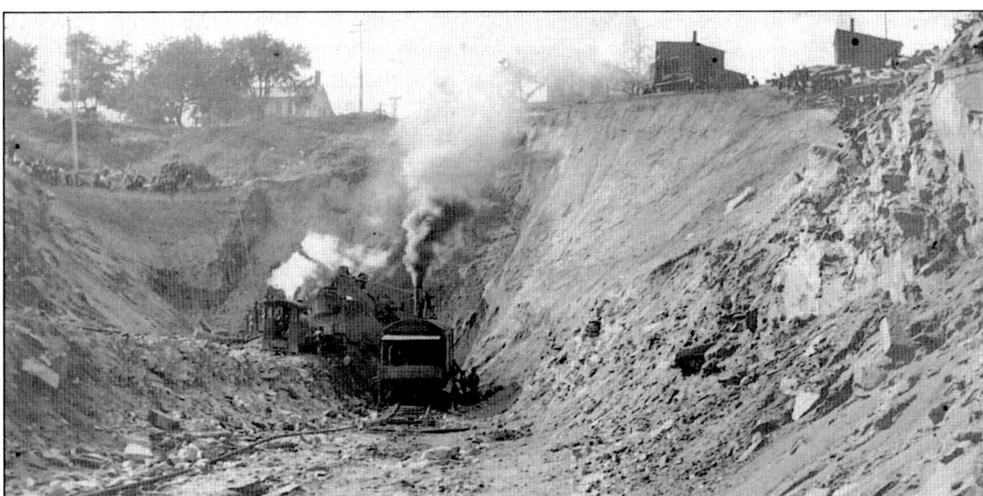

As crews were burrowing through solid stone from the center shaft, a steam shovel was digging through the tunnel from the east portal. In this photograph, a steam shovel is moving dirt from a cave-in at the tunnel site. An immense mine of quicksand at the east portal was encountered, causing work to be slowed for three months while engineer Albert Norton dealt with the obstacle.

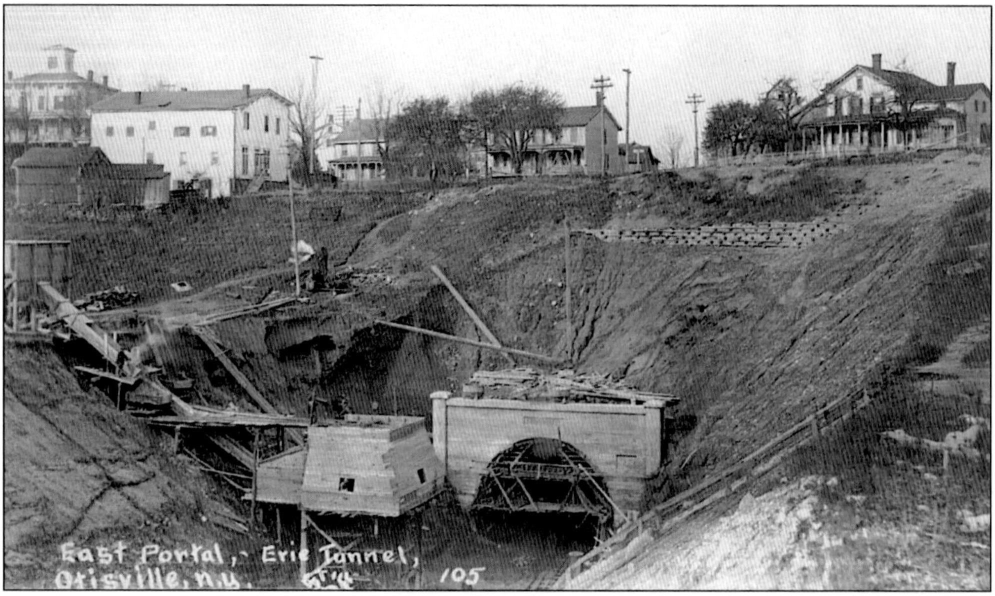

During the excavation of the Erie tunnel at Otisville, six million cubic feet of material, such as shale, dirt, adamant slate, and grey stone, was removed. In this photograph of the east portal of the tunnel, the concrete exterior has been completed. The masonry company that was hired by the Erie Railroad to do the concrete construction for the tunnel was the firm of Bennett and Cavanaugh.

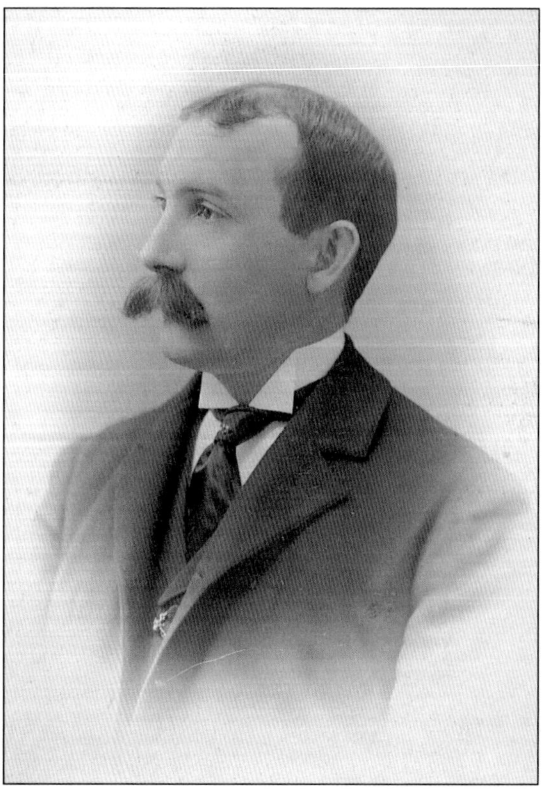

When the tunnel work was completed, Frank J. Cavanaugh presented this photograph to the Oscar S. Greenleaf family as a remembrance. Cavanaugh was a skillful engineer. In the early 1900s, concrete was a relatively new building material. During the construction of the Erie tunnel, 729,000 cubic feet of concrete was used in the 10-foot-high walls that ran the length of the mile-long tunnel.

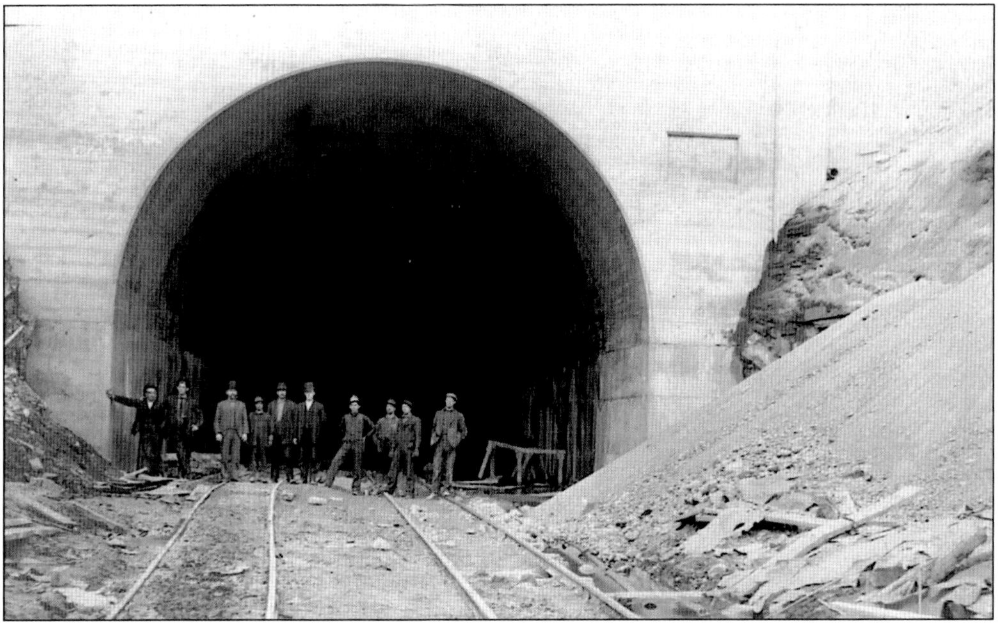

In this photograph from about 1907, a group of laborers is standing outside the tunnel. During the construction, two crews of men worked around the clock. Generators provided electricity for lighting in the tunnel. Sundays were strictly observed and no work was done from 11:00 p.m. on Saturday until 1:00 a.m. on Monday. Six men were killed during the construction of the Erie tunnel, and two were buried in the Holy Name Cemetery in Otisville.

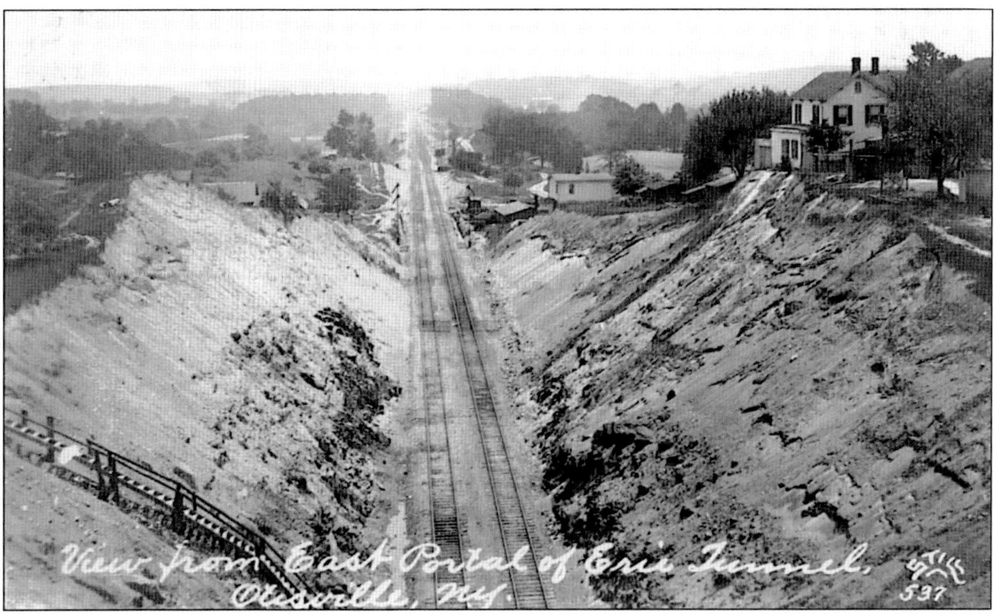

A view of the railroad track is seen in this photograph, which was taken at the head of Kelly Hill. The tunnel was initially built so that freight trains would not have to climb the steep grade on its approach to Otisville. Nine steam shovels and several trains of dinkies were used during the excavation. A power plant consisting of Ingersol machines furnished 3,600 feet of free air per minute for raising drills and shovels.

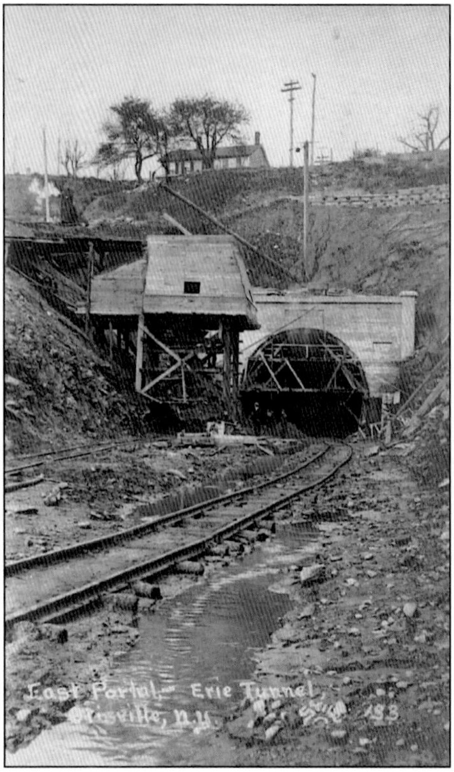

The tunnel is nearing completion in this early photograph. Albert Norton, who was one of the engineers in charge of the tunnel construction, was well known in his field of employment. When the east and west cuttings met at the center of the tunnel, there was an error of only three eighths of an inch. This was a remarkable accomplishment, which was due to Norton's skill as an engineer.

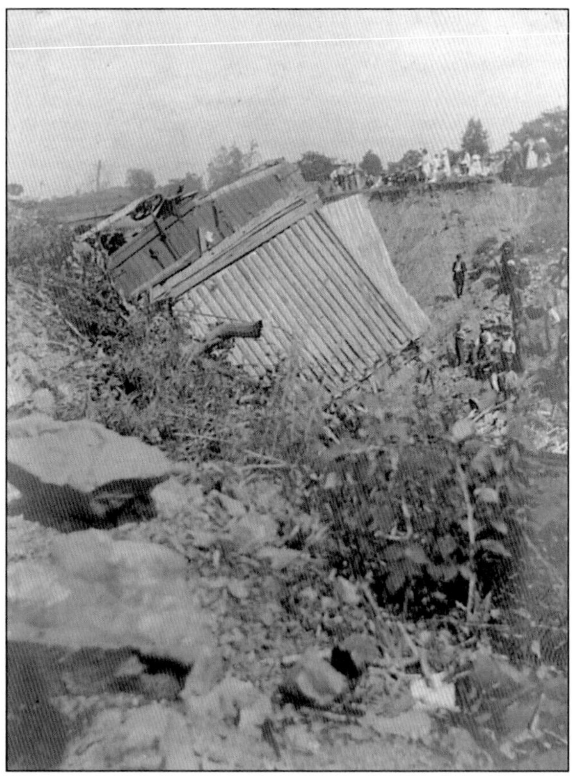

This train derailment happened near Otisville in the early 1900s. Quite often the accidents were caused by human error, and it was difficult for rescuers to reach an area when a derailment did occur.

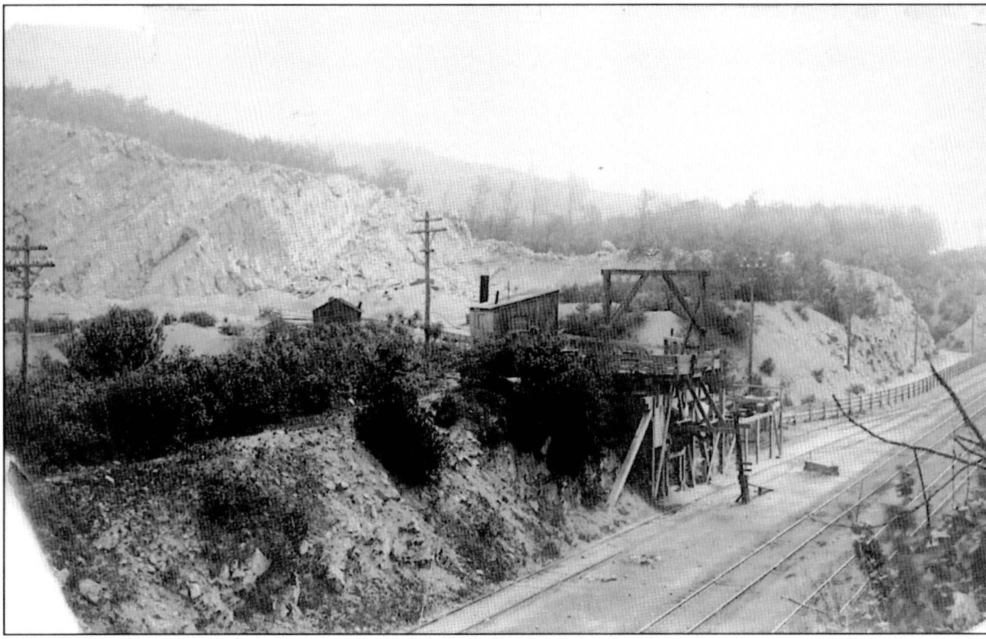

The Erie stone crusher was located at the rock cut just outside of Otisville. The massive crushing machine crushed the rock that became ballast. The ballast was used along the railroad track.

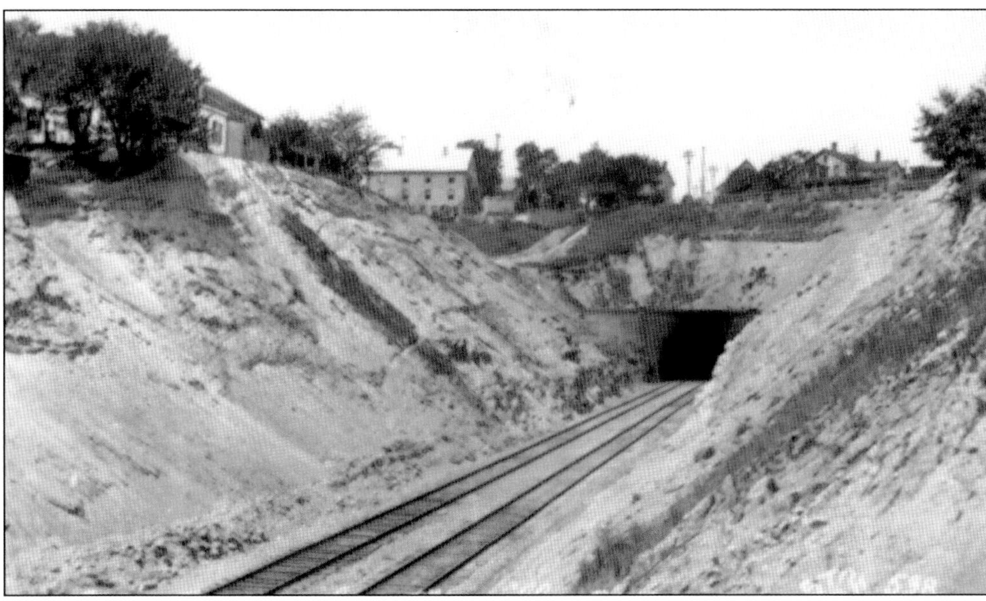

The Erie tunnel was completed in three years despite various obstacles that had to be overcome. A small hospital nearby dealt not only with the injuries that occurred but also cases of "tunnel cramps," which some of the workers experienced. Over 1,000 workers were employed during the excavation and construction of the tunnel in Otisville. It was a very profitable three years for local merchants.

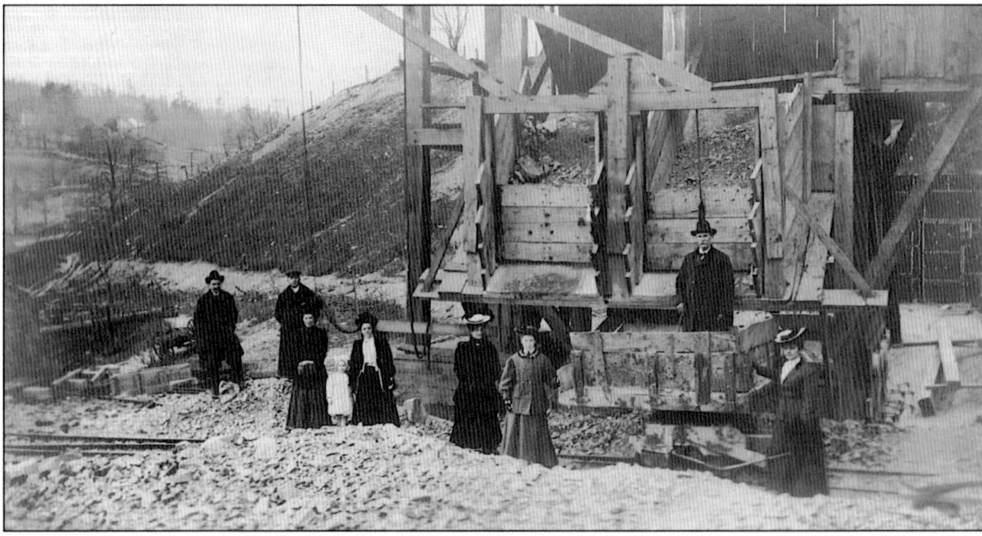

In this photograph, citizens of Otisville stop by to look at the Erie stone crusher and to have their photograph taken beside the huge and powerful machine. The villagers had never experienced such an influx of people into their village. All aspects of the tunnel construction were of interest to the villagers, including the Erie stone crusher.

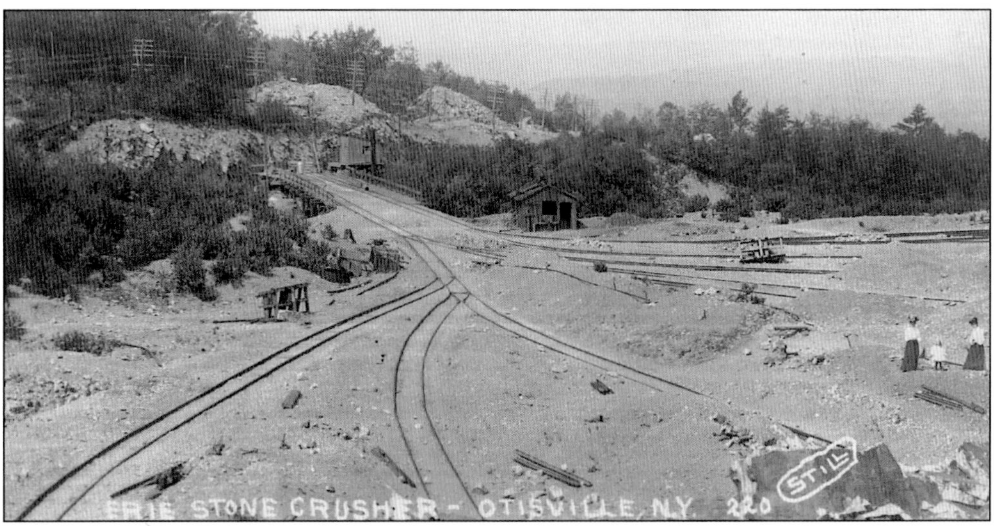

Several narrow-gauge tracks are seen in this photograph, which was taken at the Erie crusher near Otisville. The narrow tracks were used for carts that transported the crushed rock to a nearby holding area. Italian laborers were hired in New York City to work on the tunnel project. Many workers only spoke Italian, and they were assigned numbers because the bookkeepers could not understand their names.

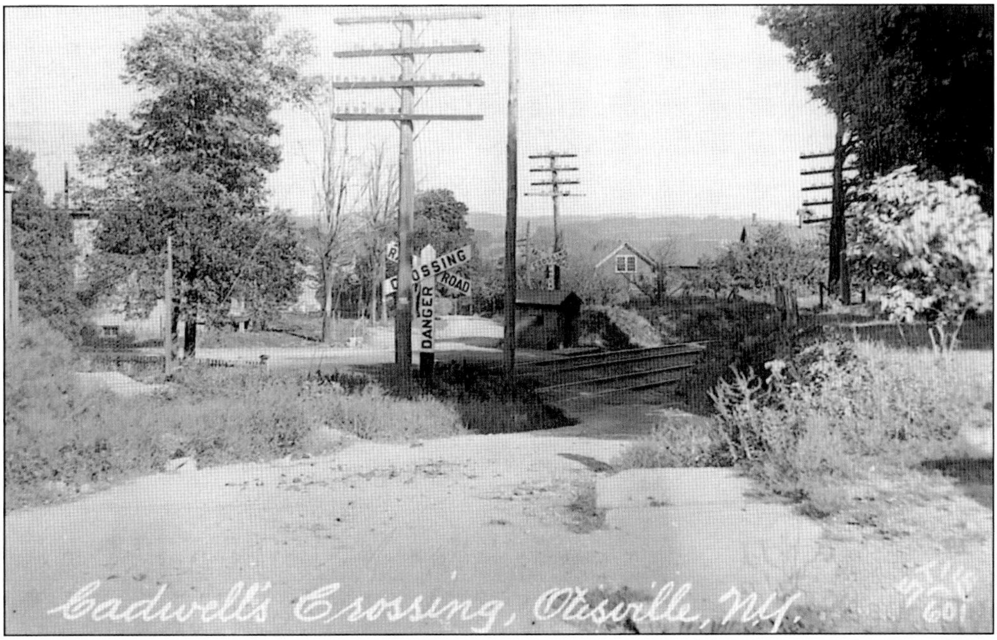

This photograph is a view of Cadwell's Crossing as seen from Highland Avenue looking down to Kelly Hill Road. A flagman was stationed at Cadwell's Crossing during the early 1900s. A railroad sign located at the crossing warns of danger.

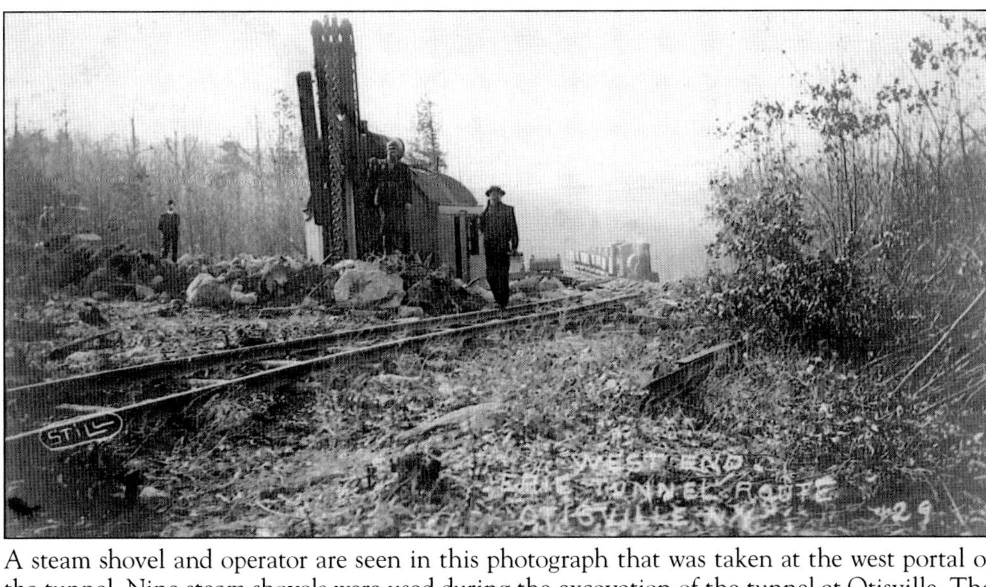

A steam shovel and operator are seen in this photograph that was taken at the west portal of the tunnel. Nine steam shovels were used during the excavation of the tunnel at Otisville. The firm of Bennett and Talbot expended $200,000 on machinery and repairs during the tunnel construction. A dinkey engine is pulling a row of cars in the middle section of the photograph.

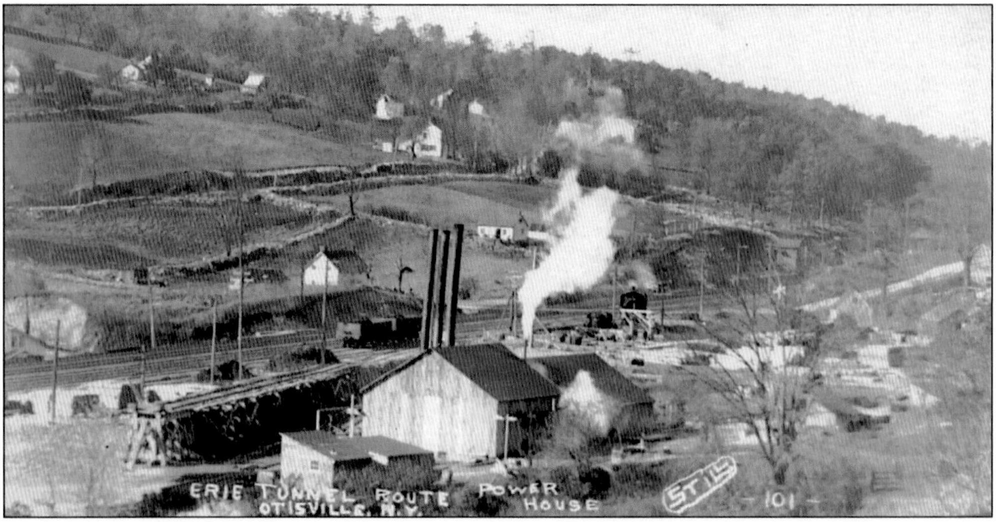

This photograph shows the area known as Hungry Hill. Today the land around Hungry Hill is heavily wooded, but at the time of this photograph, the area was open pastureland. The stacks from the Erie powerhouse are in the foreground. Hungry Hill is located near Field Road in Otisville.

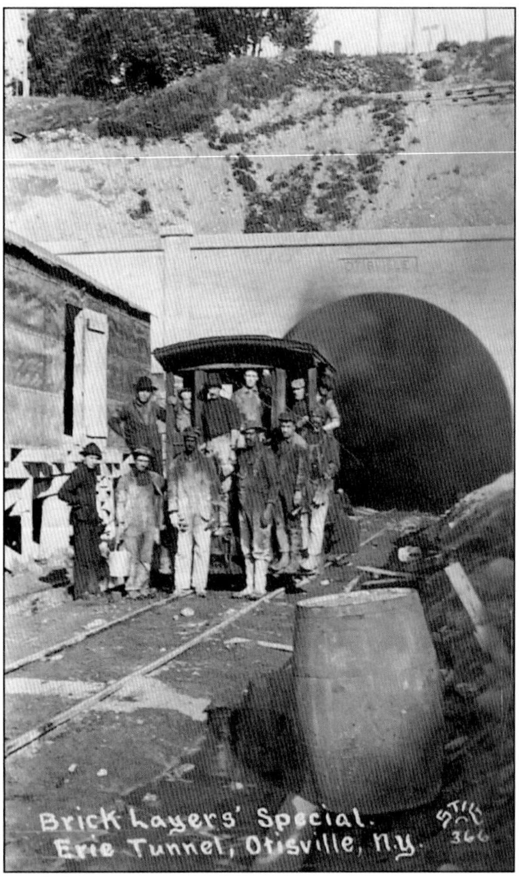

Masonry contractor Frank J. Cavanaugh was the engineer in charge of all the concrete and brick work that was done in the tunnel. About seven million vitrified shale bricks were laid in the tunnel interior. To place the concrete and bricks, it required 140 men working six days a week, day and night for seven months to complete the installation. This photograph shows a group of bricklayers standing outside of the Erie tunnel.

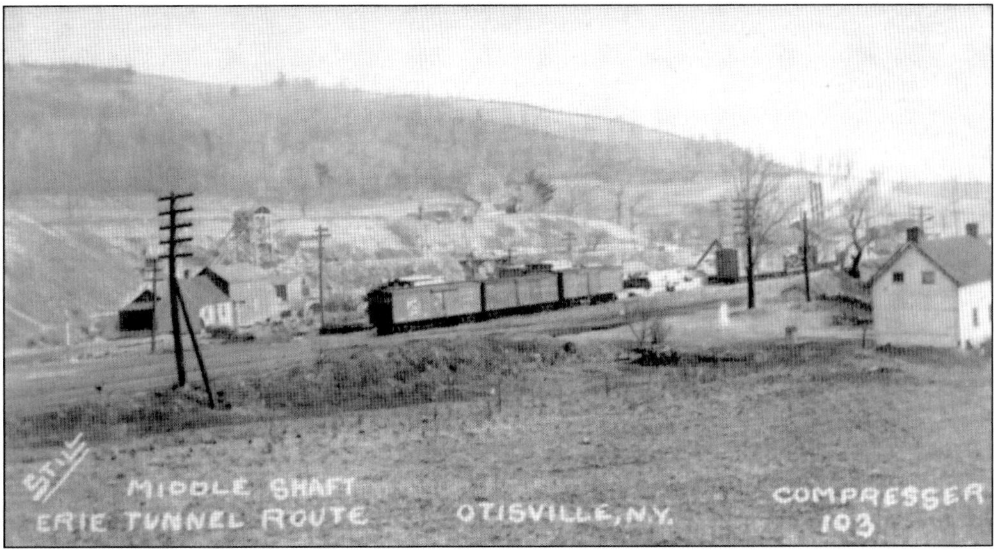

The middle shaft of the Otisville tunnel was drilled to a depth of about 125 feet through solid stone in September 1905. The first shovel of dirt was removed by H. R. Davey of New York City. It was the first major step in the construction of the Erie tunnel at Otisville. The tunnel was completed in the fall of 1908.

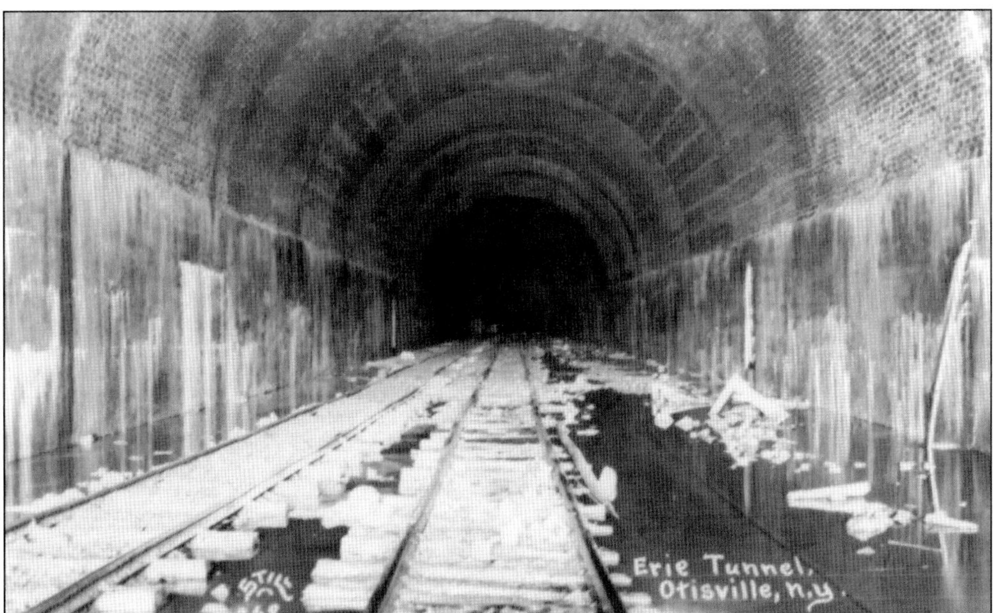

The brick and concrete lining of the Otisville tunnel is shown in this picture taken around 1908 by postcard photographer Alfred H. Still. It was a backbreaking task for the bricklayers to lay brick in the arched ceiling of the tunnel interior. The tunnel laborers lived in makeshift shacks on Walker Street during the tunnel construction.

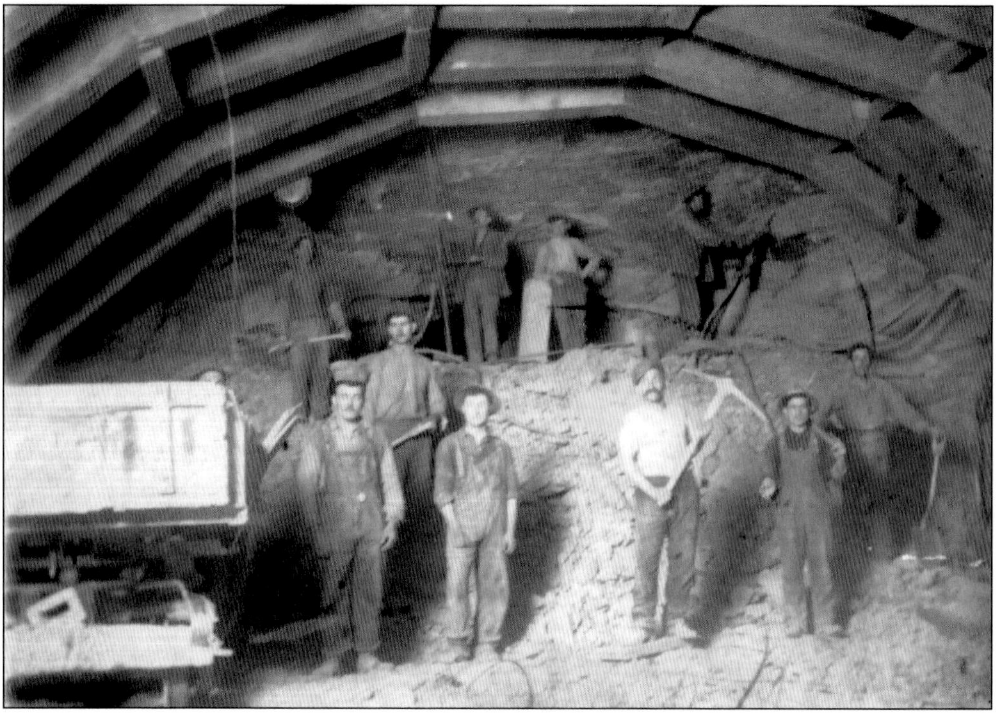

Laborers in the tunnel are using picks and shovels to excavate this area of the tunnel. Wood framing is in place on the tunnel ceiling. Dinkey engines were used to carry the stone and dirt out of the tunnel. It was a very long and exhausting workday for tunnel laborers.

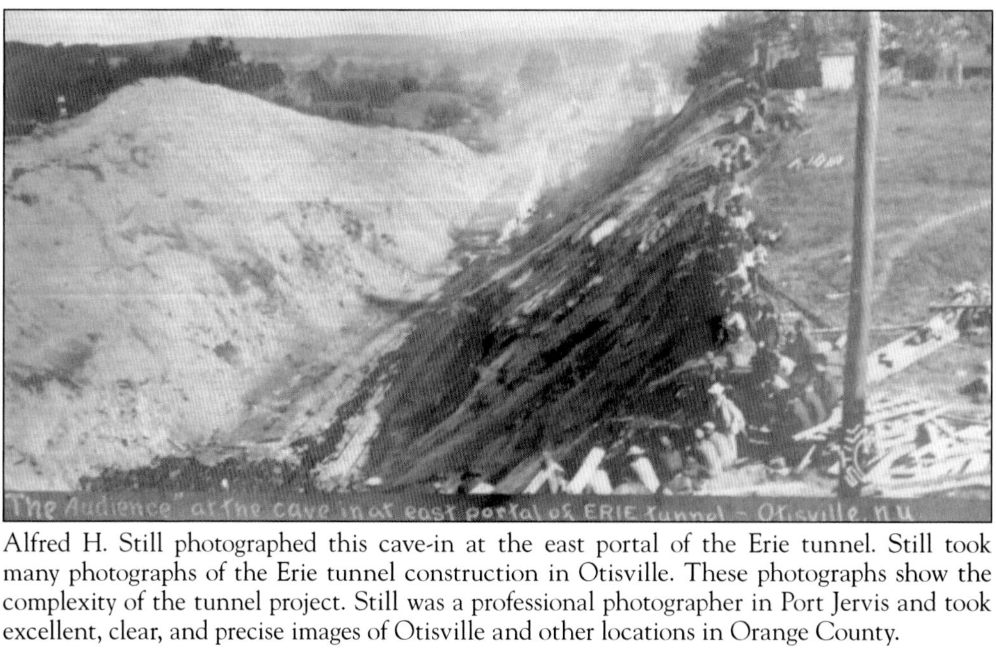

Alfred H. Still photographed this cave-in at the east portal of the Erie tunnel. Still took many photographs of the Erie tunnel construction in Otisville. These photographs show the complexity of the tunnel project. Still was a professional photographer in Port Jervis and took excellent, clear, and precise images of Otisville and other locations in Orange County.

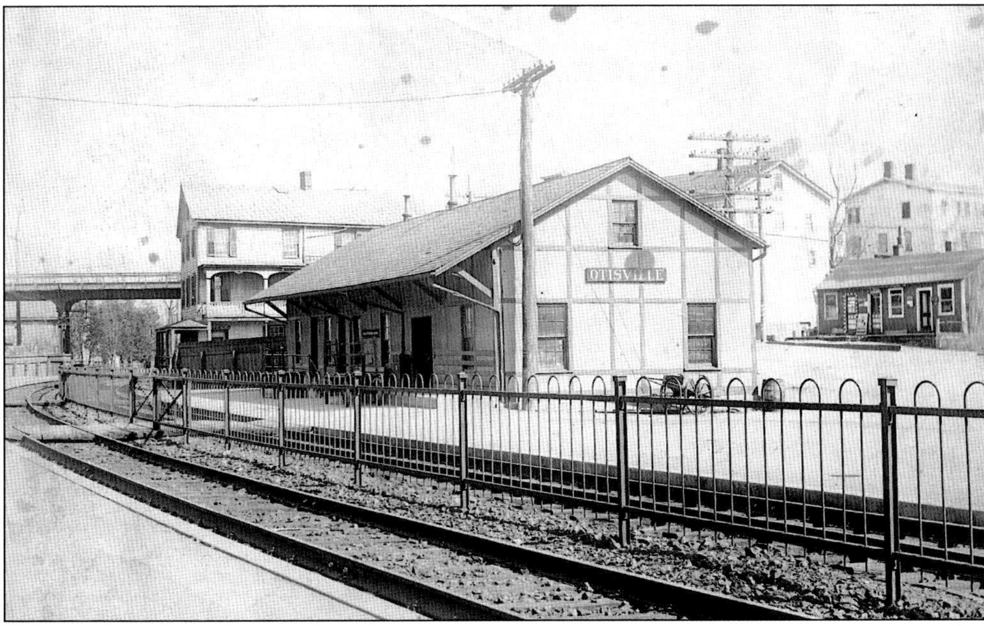

The Erie depot at Otisville has been remodeled in this later image. The clapboard siding has been removed and the depot appears to have a stucco exterior with wood trim. A wrought-iron fence separated the passenger line from the freight line in this photograph taken at the station. The fencing was installed to prevent personal injury when alighting from the train.

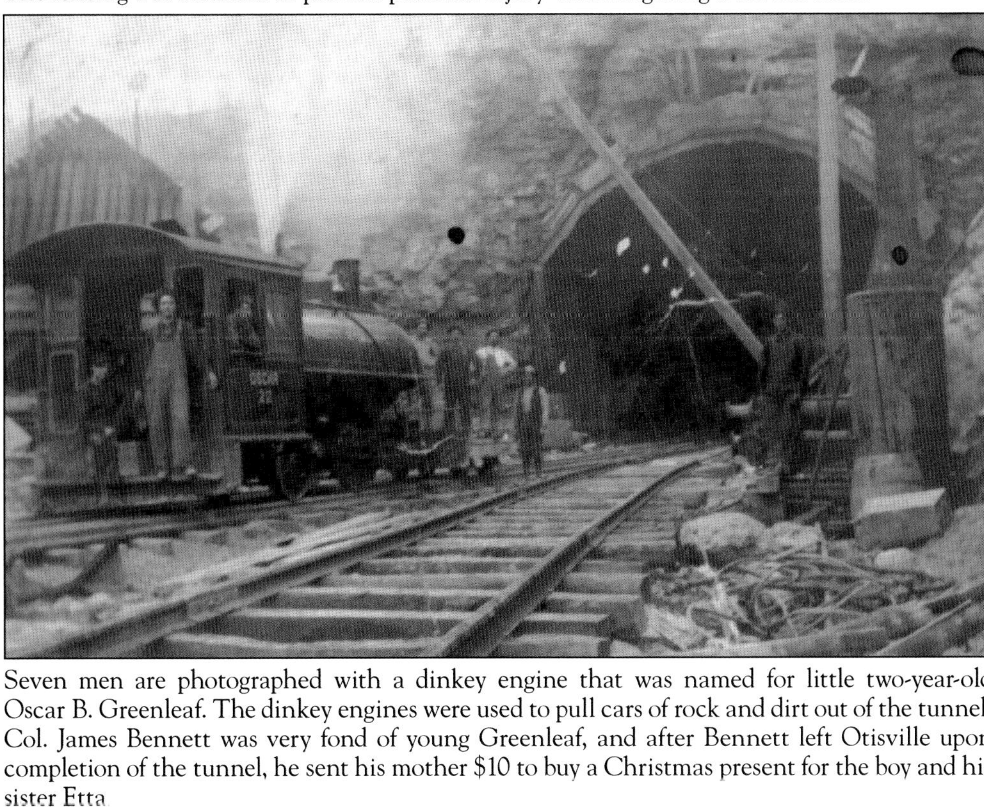

Seven men are photographed with a dinkey engine that was named for little two-year-old Oscar B. Greenleaf. The dinkey engines were used to pull cars of rock and dirt out of the tunnel. Col. James Bennett was very fond of young Greenleaf, and after Bennett left Otisville upon completion of the tunnel, he sent his mother $10 to buy a Christmas present for the boy and his sister Etta.

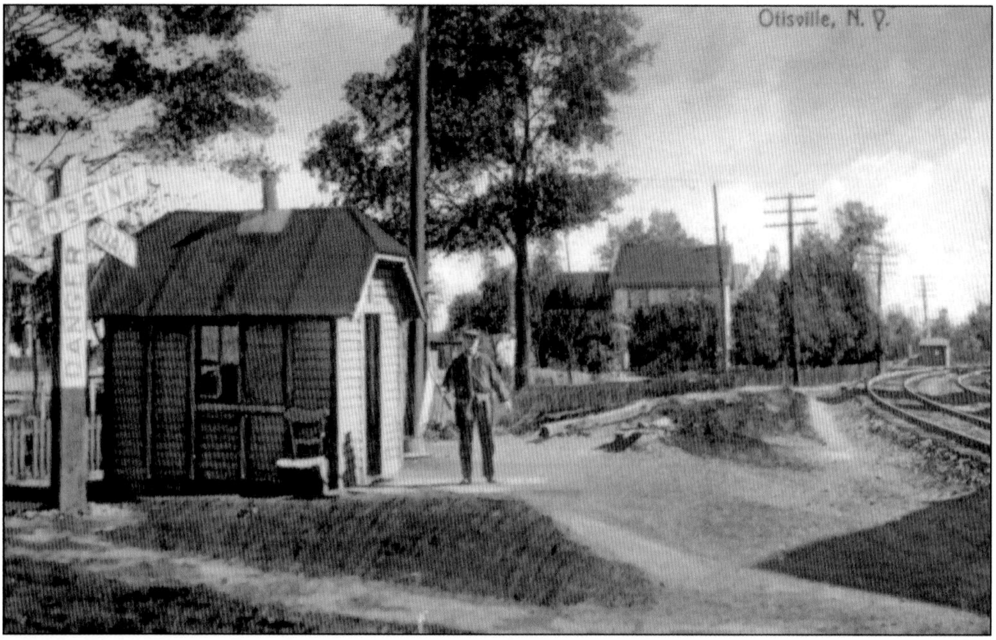

The flagman's house was located next to the Writer House hotel. The hotel was later owned by the William Loeven family. Michael Seymour lived on Hungry Hill in Otisville and was a flagman for many years. In the background of the photograph is the brick house that fronts Kelly Hill Road.

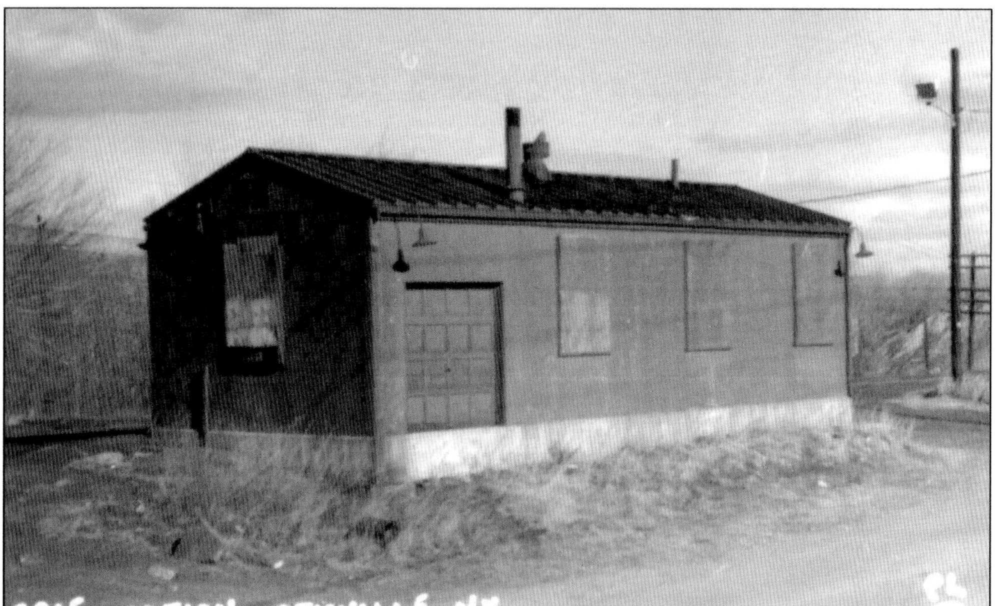

This photograph was taken of the Erie freight house in Otisville. The building was used to store freight after it was shipped by train to Otisville. The freight remained at this location until it was claimed by its owner.

Seven

OTISVILLE TUBERCULOSIS SANITORIUM, ANTITOXIN LABORATORY, AND ARMY HOSPITAL

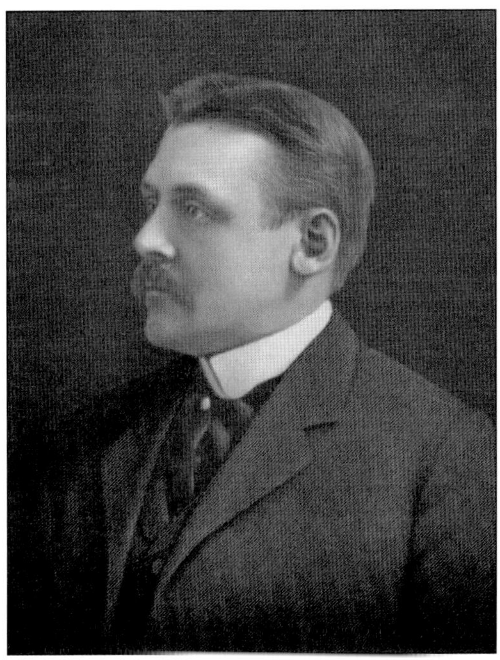

Dr. Thomas Darlington was appointed commissioner of health for New York City in 1904. In 1905, Darlington began to look for a place to build a tuberculosis sanitorium for the residents of New York City. He settled on a site two miles from Otisville, and in 1906, the first patients were admitted. Darlington believed that the fresh, cool mountain air and nutritious food would enable the patients to return to a more active life.

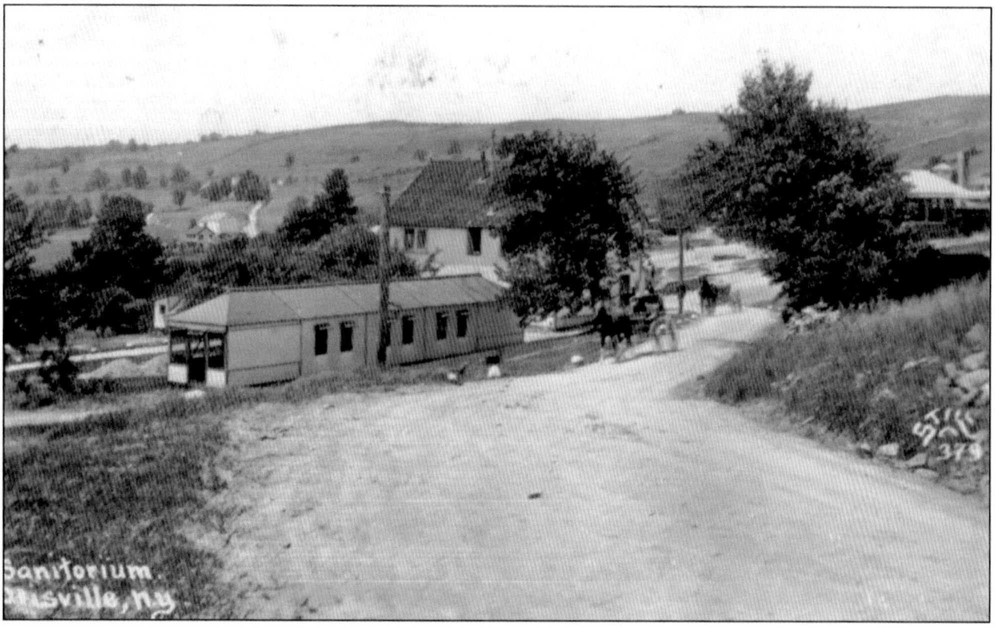

Two horses and buggies travel up the dirt road leading to the newly opened Otisville Tuberculosis Sanitorium. The sanitorium utilized several farmhouses that were located on the property. The superintendent was housed in the Tymeson house on the road that soon became known as Sanitorium Avenue. Patients arrived by train from New York City and were picked up at the Erie depot by sanitorium personnel.

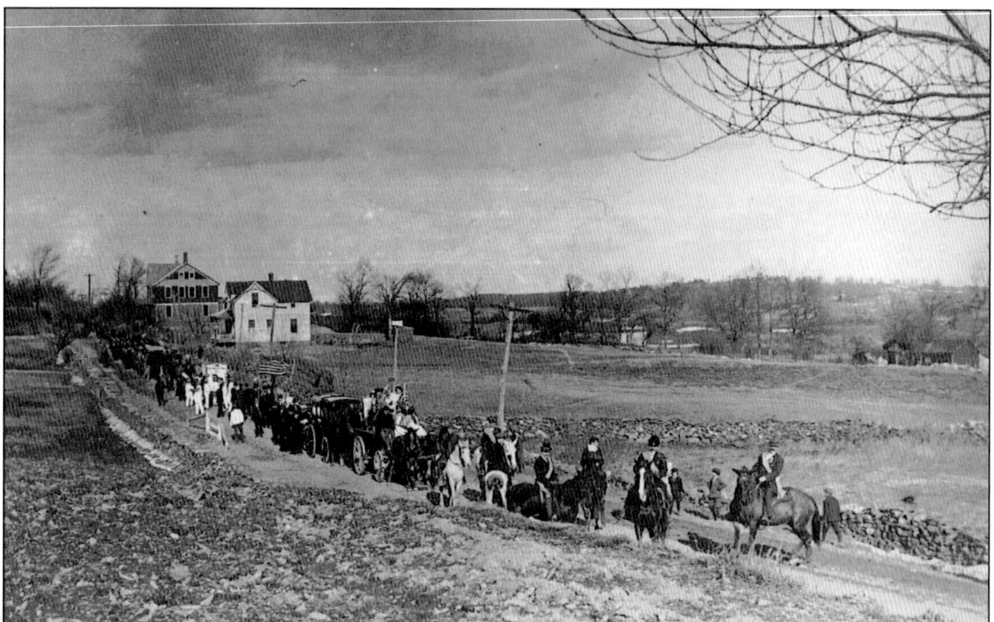

This photograph from about 1907 shows a parade of sanitorium employees and patients. Outdoor activities were encouraged by the doctors at the sanitorium. Parades were held on Memorial Day and other holidays. Horses and buggies were the chief mode of transportation in 1907.

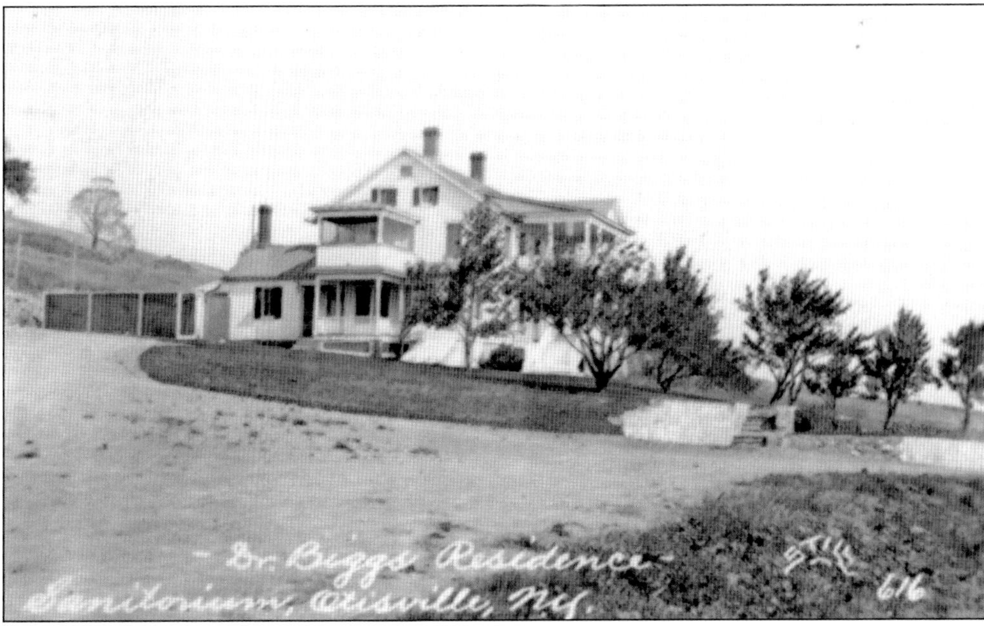

Dr. Herman Biggs resided in this spacious home on the grounds of the sanitorium when he was in residence. Biggs was chief medical officer for the City of New York and formulated a plan of care for the patients at the tuberculosis facility. His sanitary techniques were employed by other sanitoriums, and Biggs became world renown for his treatment of tubercular patients. Officials traveled from France to personally observe the techniques that were utilized at the Otisville facility.

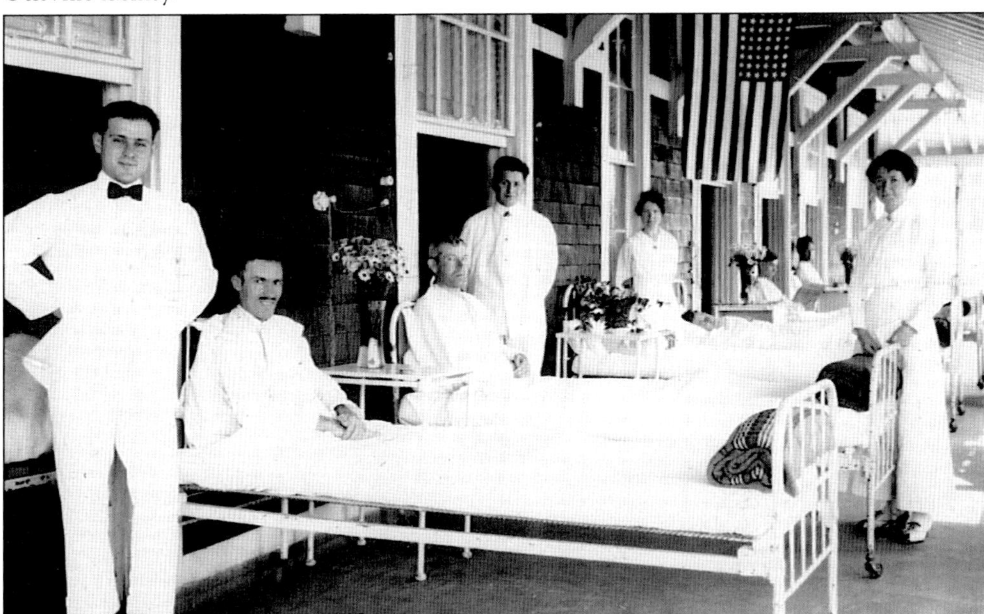

In 1917, this photograph was taken of an open-air sleeping dormitory at the Otisville sanitorium. Nurses are in attendance caring for the more delicate cases. Simple, white metal beds that could be easily cleaned were used for the tubercular patients. The nurses had a residence that was located on the sanitorium property.

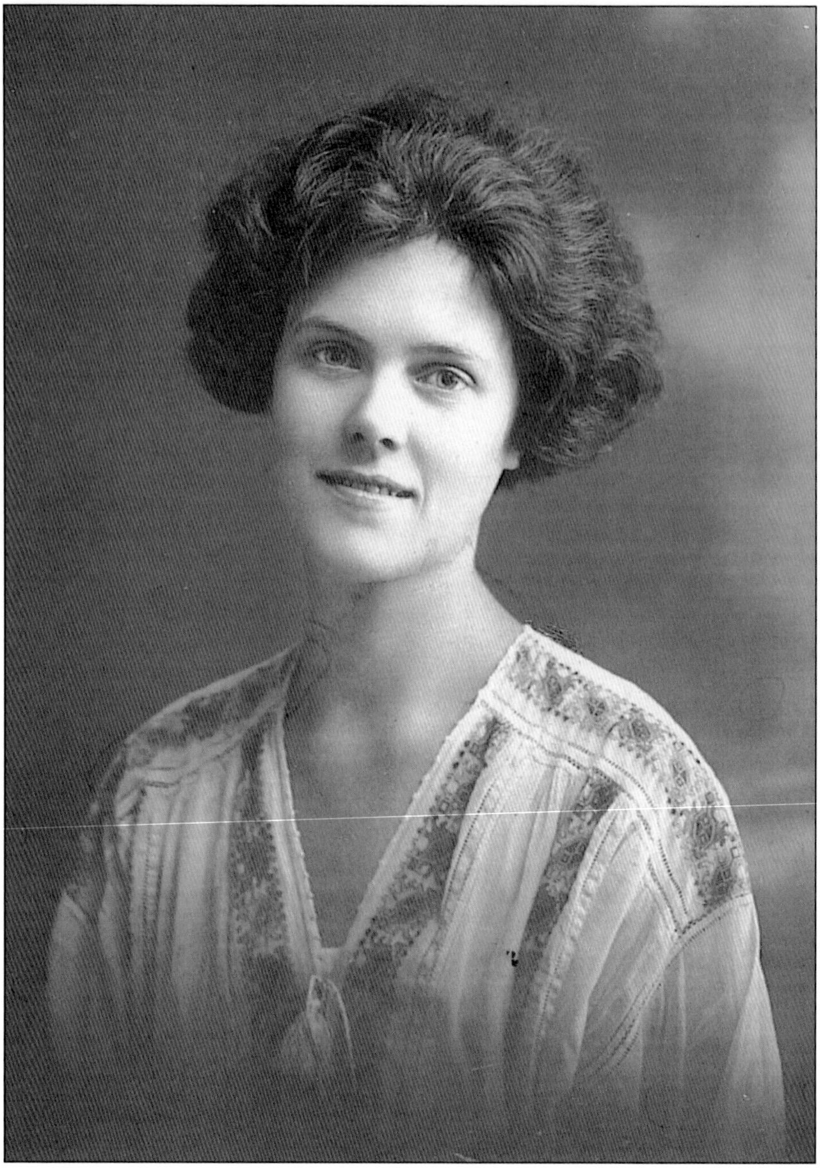

In 1917, Agnes von Kurowsky was a Red Cross nurse in Italy when a young injured ambulance driver named Ernest Hemingway was admitted to the hospital. Hemingway fell in love with Von Kurowsky during his convalescence and proposed marriage. After his recovery, Hemingway returned home but continued to pursue Von Kurowsky through his letters. She felt this was only a wartime infatuation and broke off the relationship. Hemingway was devastated. Several of his novels were based on his relationship with Von Kurowsky. In 1931, Von Kurowsky became the assistant nursing supervisor at the Otisville Tuberculosis Sanitorium. While in Otisville, she met widower William Stanfield, and they were married in 1934. William and Agnes were married for more than 50 years. After her death, photographs, letters, and a diary were donated to the John F. Kennedy Library in Boston. A movie, *In Love and War,* about the romance between Hemingway and Von Kurowsky was produced in 1996. Von Kurowsky was portrayed by Sandra Bullock and Hemingway by Chris O'Donnell. Although Hemingway once said he would cauterize the memory of Von Kurowsky from his brain, he kept all of her letters until he died.

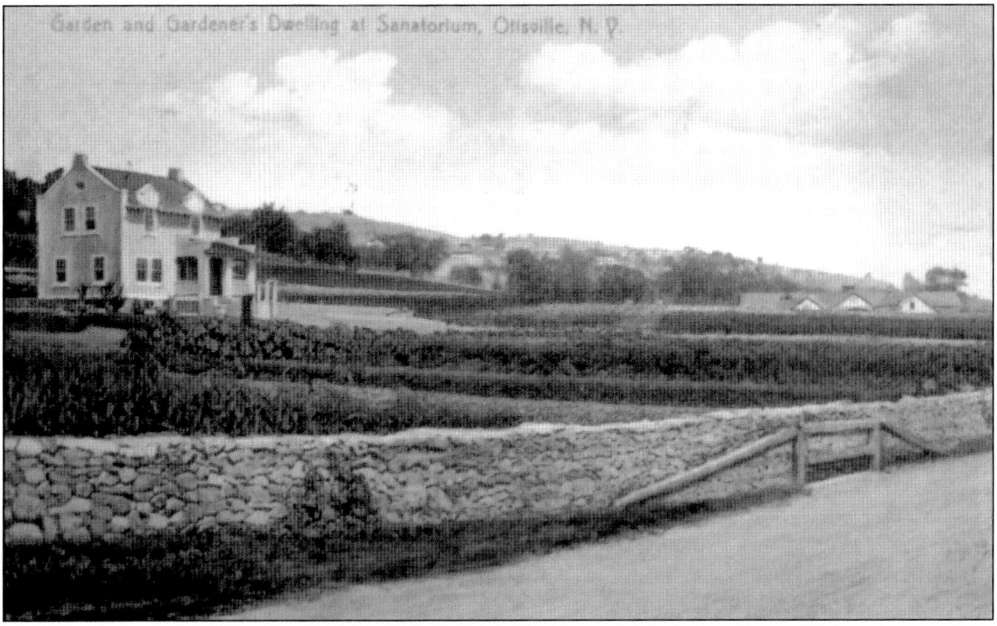

The gardener's residence was located on Sanitorium Avenue at the foot of the mountain road. The gardener and his crew, which consisted of patients from the sanitorium, grew all the vegetables that were served at the facility. Dr. Herman Biggs demanded that all the residents have fresh vegetables twice a day. The sanitorium had a chicken farm on the grounds and fresh eggs were regular items on the menu.

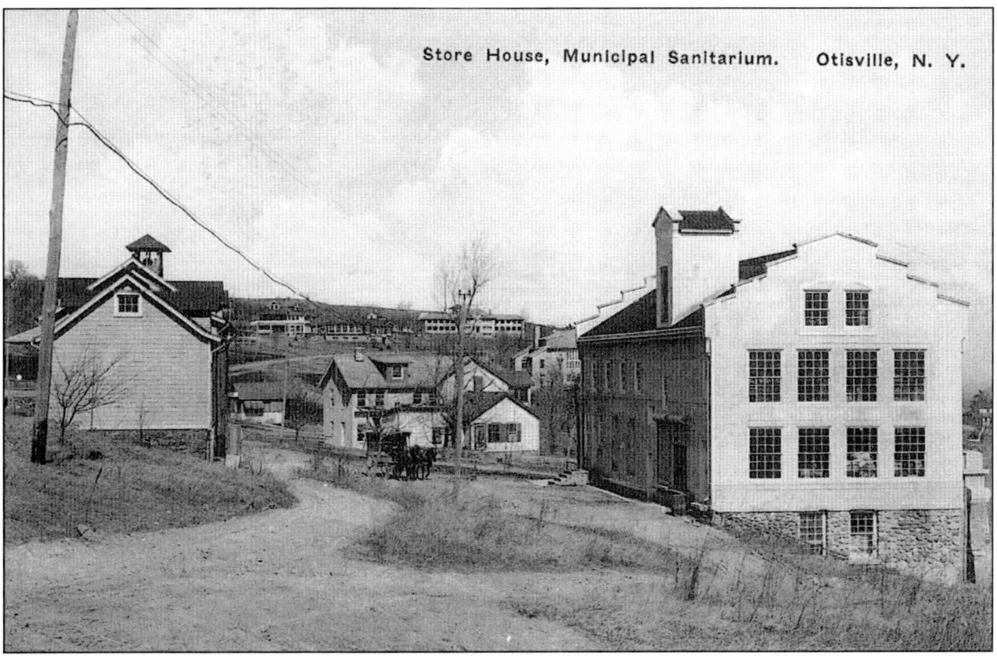

The municipal sanitorium storeroom was centrally located on the property. The storeroom placed orders and supplied sanitorium buildings with all necessary items. Each patient received a list of items to bring to the facility when admitted; however, if something was needed after admission, the facility supplied the patient with all necessities.

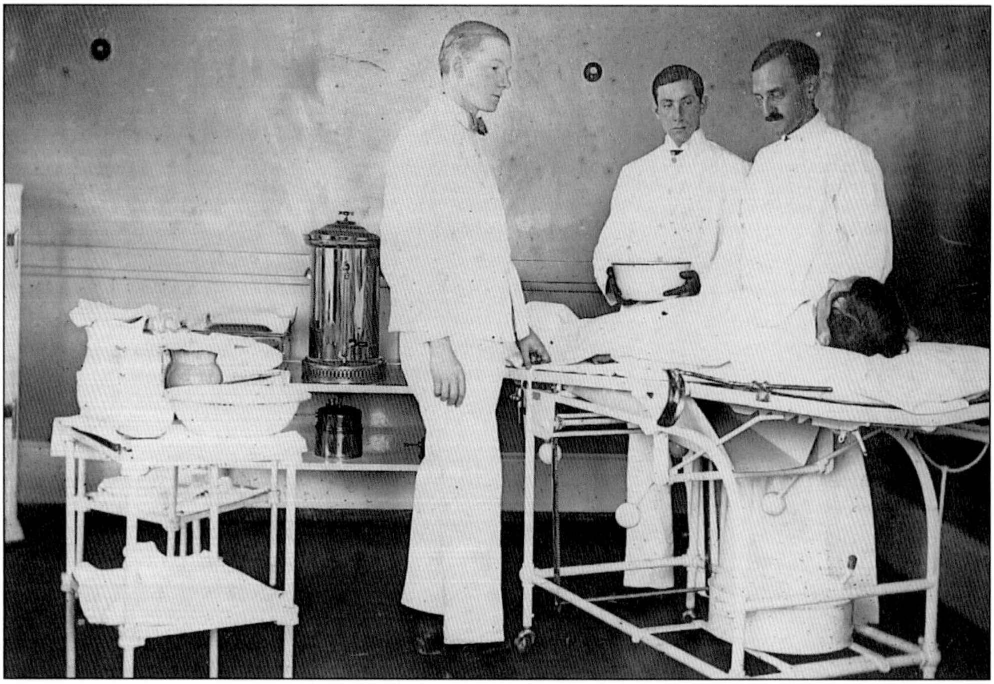

The first operation at the sanitorium is shown in this photograph. A pneumothorax was often performed on tubercular patients to put the lungs at rest. The doctors at the sanitorium had favorable results after performing this procedure, and it became accepted as a standard form of treatment at that time.

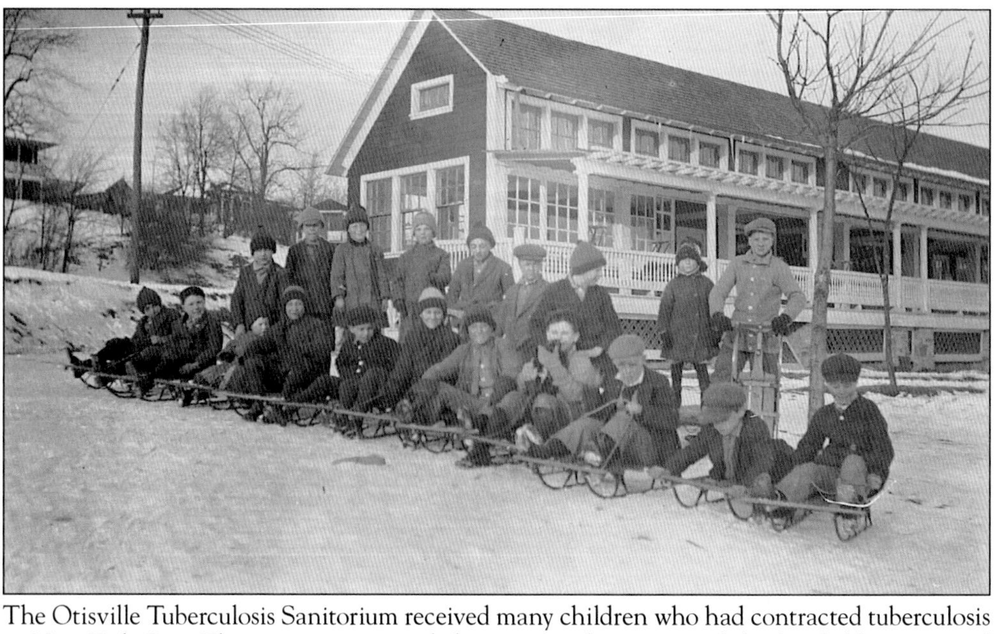

The Otisville Tuberculosis Sanitorium received many children who had contracted tuberculosis in New York City. The sanitorium provided recreational activities while the children received treatment at Otisville. In the summers, they played outdoors on the playground that was erected for their use, and in the winter, they enjoyed sleigh riding down the mountain in front of the facility.

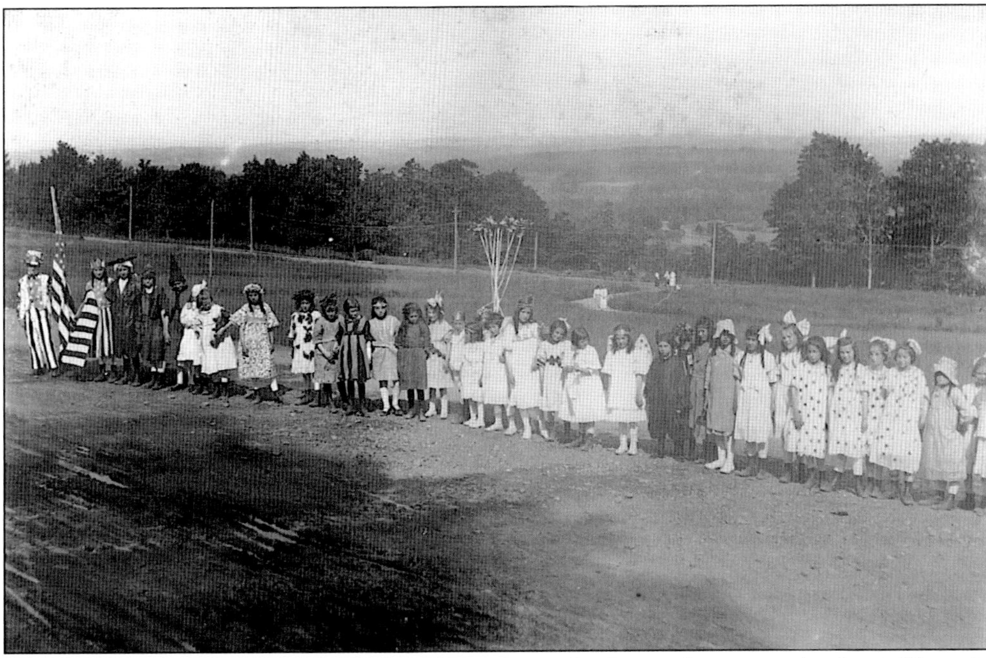

On holidays such as the Fourth of July, the sanitorium had special activities for the children. In this photograph, which was taken on Memorial Day in 1916, the children are dressed in various costumes. The boy at the front of the procession is dressed as Uncle Sam and is holding a flag, and the girl standing next to him is dressed as Lady Liberty.

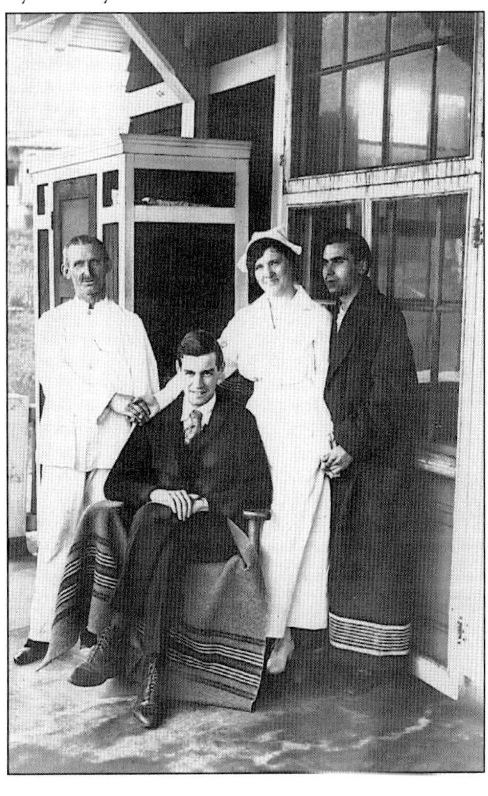

In this photograph taken around 1916, a doctor, male attendant, nurse, and patient pose in front of one of the buildings at the Otisville Tuberculosis Sanitorium. The nurse is dressed in a floor-length uniform. In earlier photographs, the nurses at the sanitorium were dressed in striped uniforms with long sleeves and white bib aprons.

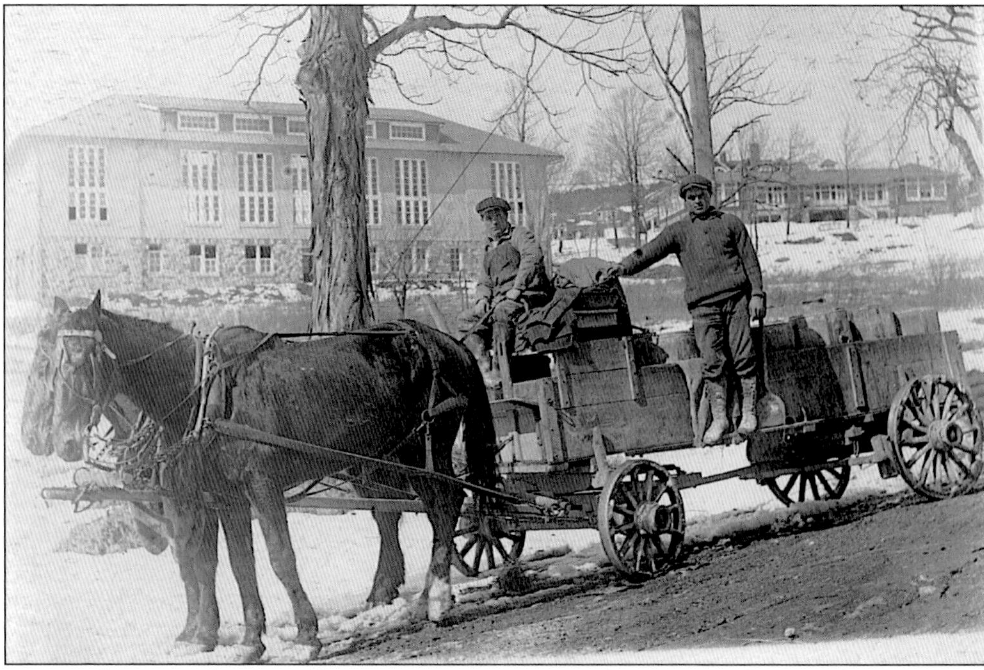

Two employees at the Otisville sanitorium are seen in this vintage photograph transporting several wooden barrels in a horse-drawn cart. Two horses are pulling the cart, which has large wooden wheels. The man standing on the cart has a small shovel in his left hand.

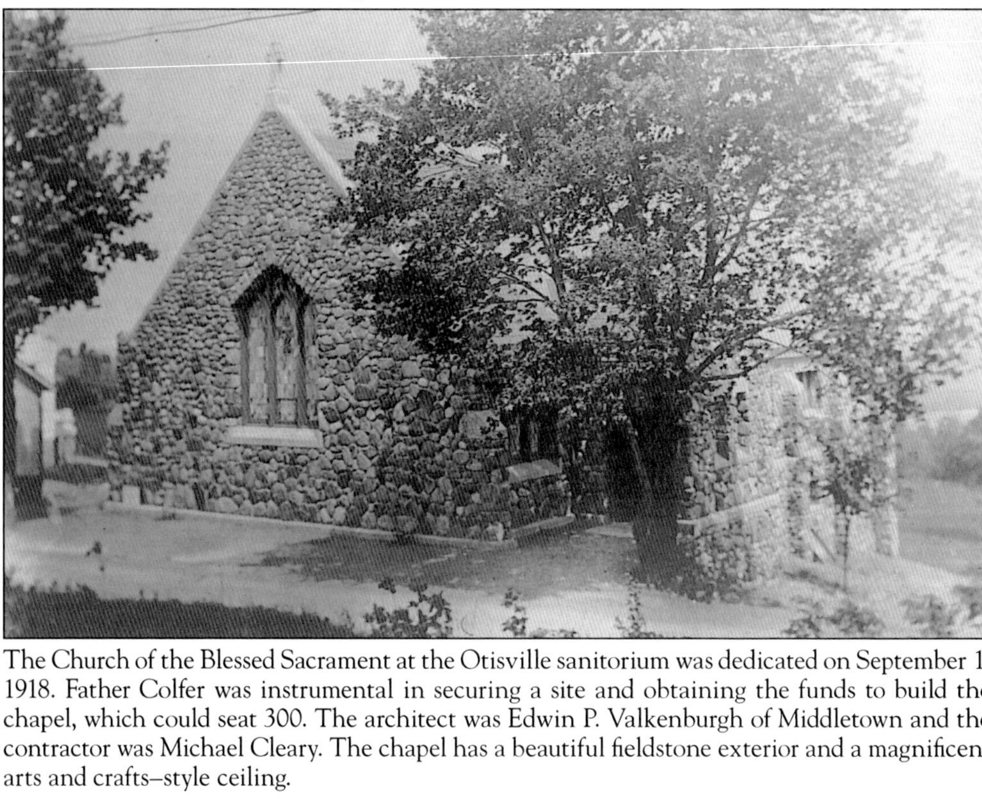

The Church of the Blessed Sacrament at the Otisville sanitorium was dedicated on September 1, 1918. Father Colfer was instrumental in securing a site and obtaining the funds to build the chapel, which could seat 300. The architect was Edwin P. Valkenburgh of Middletown and the contractor was Michael Cleary. The chapel has a beautiful fieldstone exterior and a magnificent arts and crafts–style ceiling.

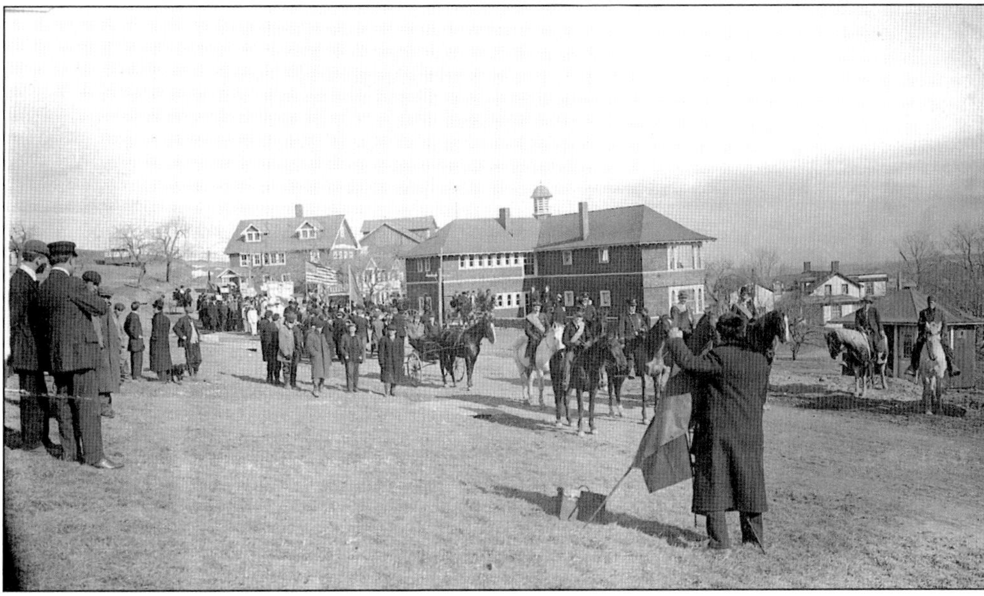

A patriotic parade is being held at the Otisville Tuberculosis Sanitorium in this early photograph. The man in the foreground of the photograph appears to be taking a picture of the procession. Many men are on horseback and one man is riding in a horse-drawn buggy. In the rear of the assemblage, a man is carrying a banner.

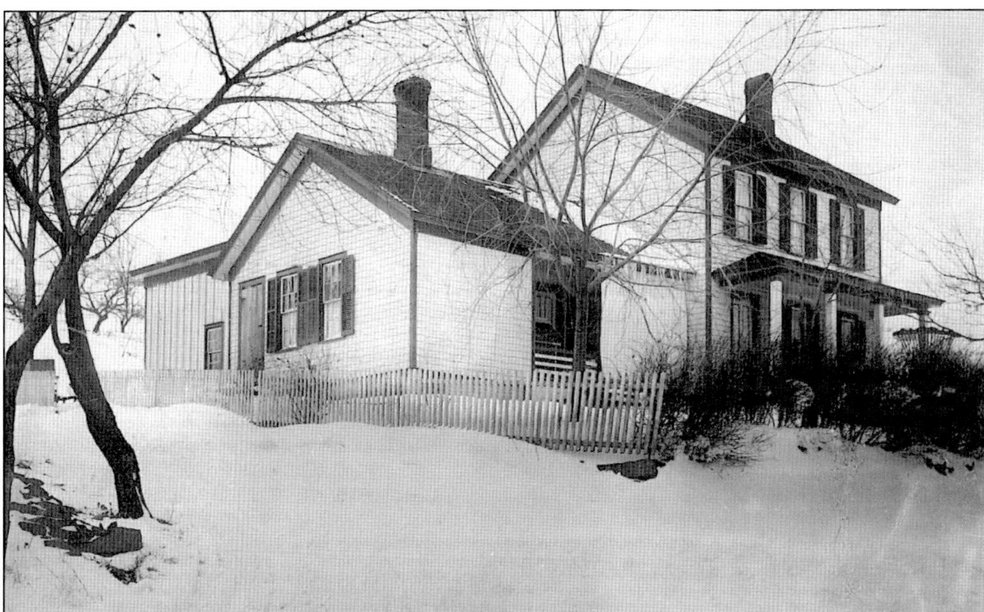

The house that originally belonged to the Glass family is featured in this early photograph. When the New York City Department of Health decided to construct their new tuberculosis sanitorium in Otisville, a large parcel of land on the mountain was required for the project. Mr. Glass sold his home, and it was incorporated into the sanitorium property. Over 1,200 acres were purchased on the Shawangunk Mountain for the tuberculosis sanitorium.

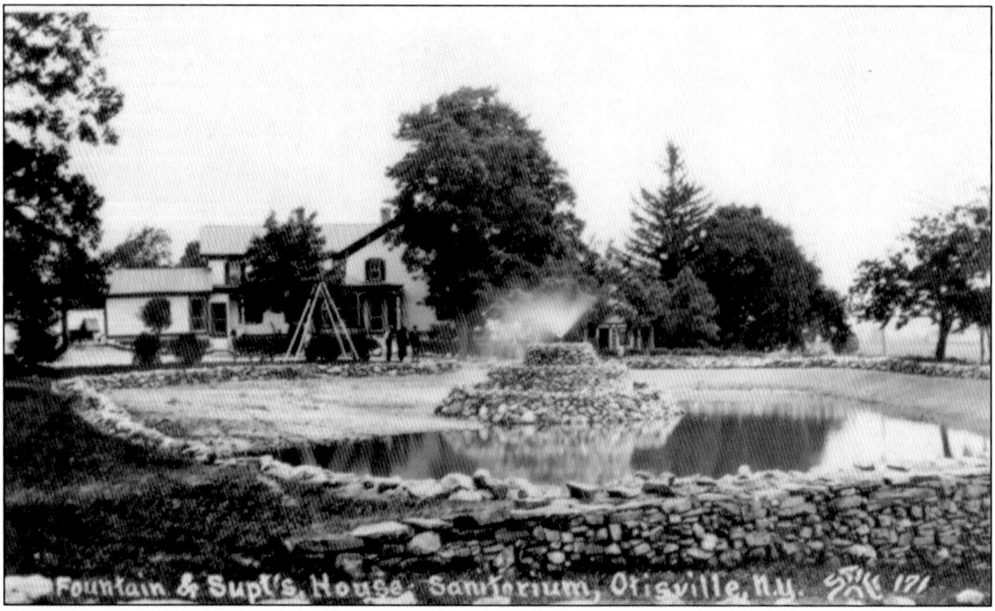

The Tymeson family once owned this charming residence on Old Mountain Road. In the summer, the Tymesons provided lodging for visitors from the metropolitan area. In 1906, it was sold and became the superintendent's house for the Otisville Tuberculosis Sanitorium. A beautiful pond with a fountain was located next to the house. A portion of the Tymeson barn was incorporated into the present horse barn next to Sanitorium Avenue.

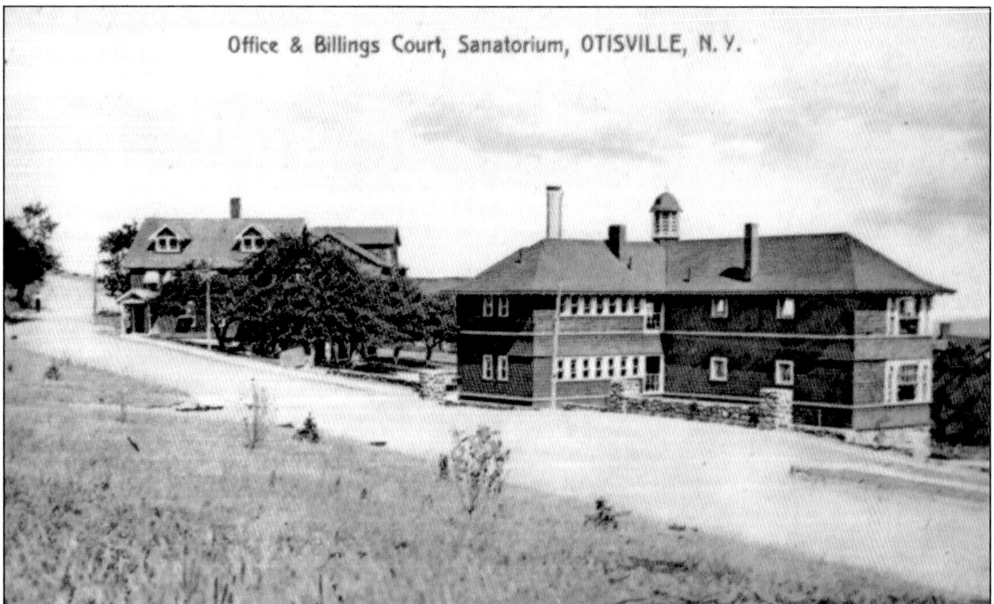

A large complex of buildings was constructed on the side of the Shawangunk Mountain in order to provide for the day-to-day operation of the Otisville Tuberculosis Sanitorium. This is a photograph of the office and billings court. The sanitorium closed in the 1950s, and the City of New York later used the property as a training school for boys.

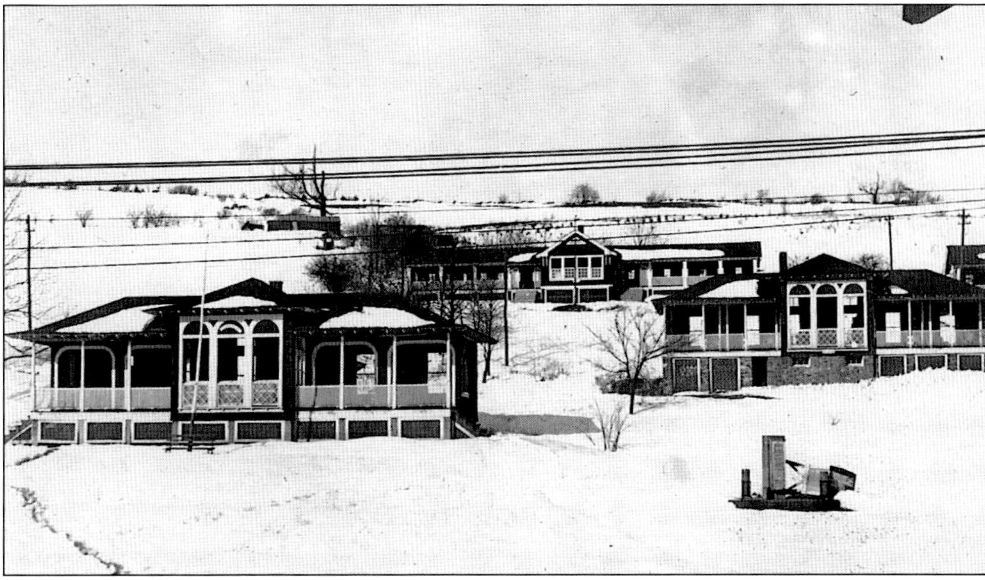

Residents of the Otisville Tuberculosis Sanitorium were photographed in front of one of the open-air cottages that were built to house residents of the facility. The patients lived and slept on porches that were open to the elements. In cold weather, they were bundled up in warm clothing. This open-air sleeping arrangement was practiced throughout the facility.

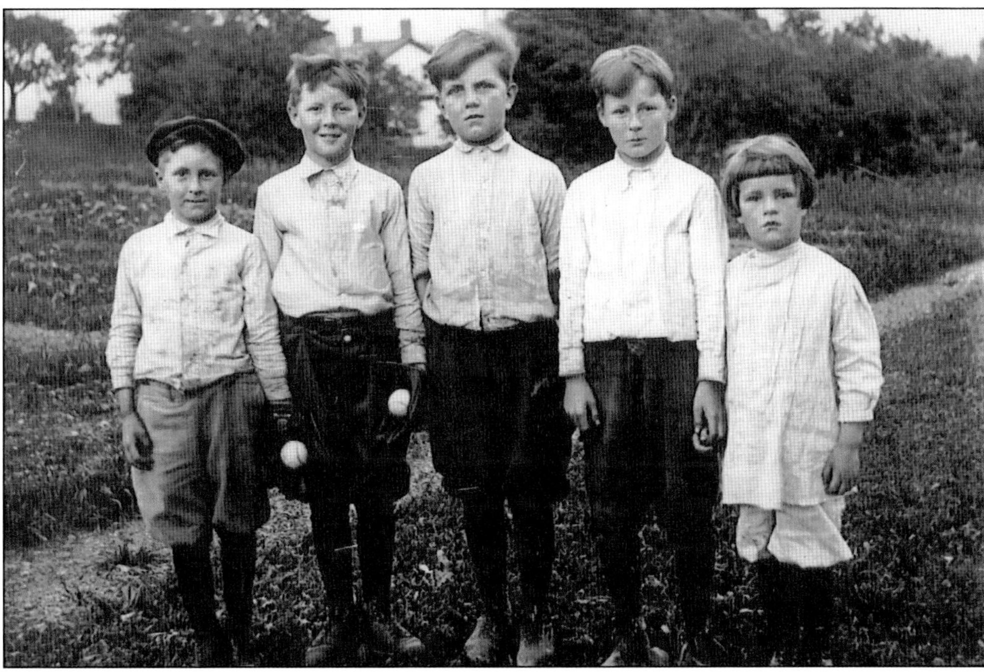

This delightful photograph was taken by Eldred Perry Carhart around 1915 at the Otisville Tuberculosis Sanitorium. These children lived on the grounds of the sanitorium with their parents who were employees. The children from left to right are Ralph Carhart, Bruce Carhart, unidentified, Eldred Carhart, and Wally Miller. Bruce and Eldred became outstanding players on the 1924 Otisville High School baseball team. In the photograph, two of the boys are holding baseballs.

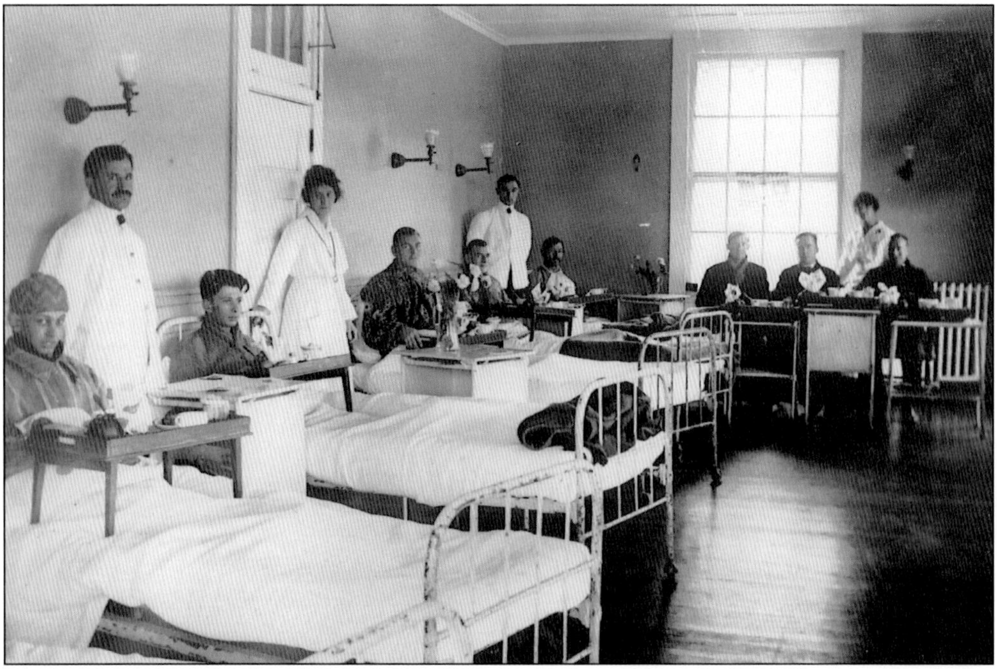

The tubercular patients in this photograph from about 1915 resided in the infirmary at the sanitorium. It was the only building where the patients slept indoors due to their medical conditions. Some patients were too fragile medically to handle the frigid living conditions on the open-air porches in the winter. In this photograph, various medical personnel are standing beside the patients' beds.

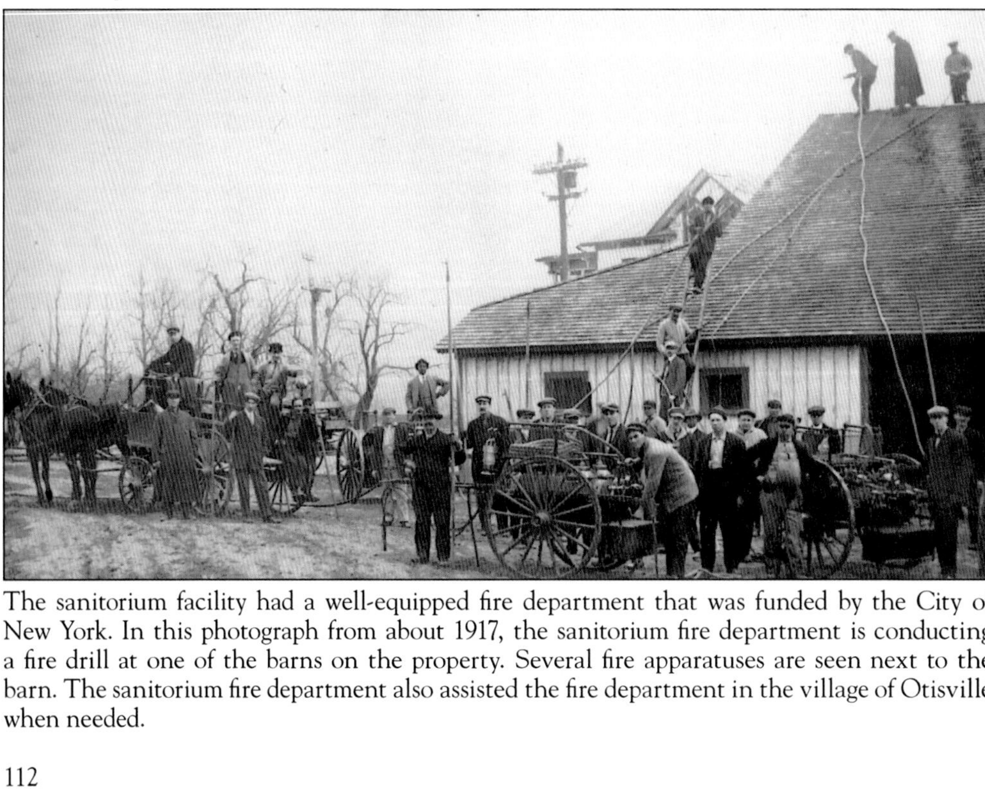

The sanitorium facility had a well-equipped fire department that was funded by the City of New York. In this photograph from about 1917, the sanitorium fire department is conducting a fire drill at one of the barns on the property. Several fire apparatuses are seen next to the barn. The sanitorium fire department also assisted the fire department in the village of Otisville when needed.

Willella and Ralph Perry Carhart were photographed around 1917 on the grounds of the Otisville Tuberculosis Sanitorium. Ralph was employed at the sanitorium and resided in a house on the property. He was an avid photographer and took many photographs of the village of Otisville and the Otisville Tuberculosis Sanitorium. After his death, his wife built a bungalow on Sanitorium Avenue where she resided.

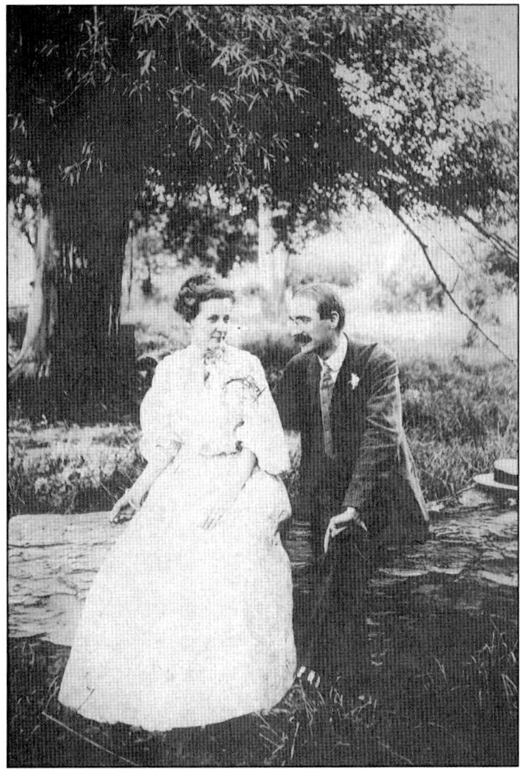

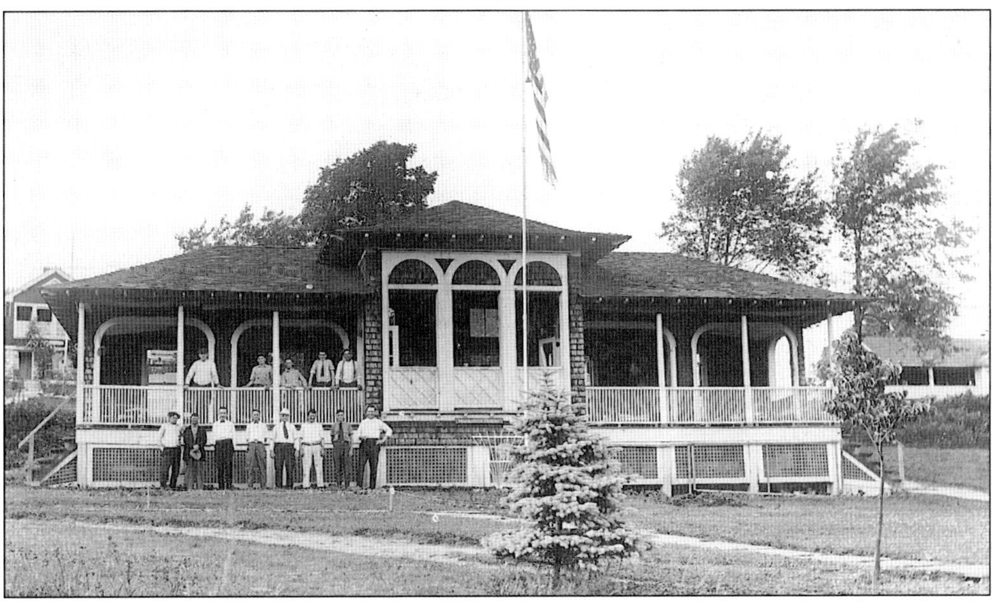

Residents of the Otisville Tuberculosis Sanitorium stood in front of an open-air bungalow for this vintage photograph. Gustave Sefranka, who was a patient and then an employee of the sanitorium, designed many of these buildings. At his funeral in 1915, Rev. Robert S. Young stated, "Morally, he rose far above the average man and professionally as an architect he was a genius." Despite his treatment at the sanitorium, he died from the ravages of tuberculosis at the age of 35.

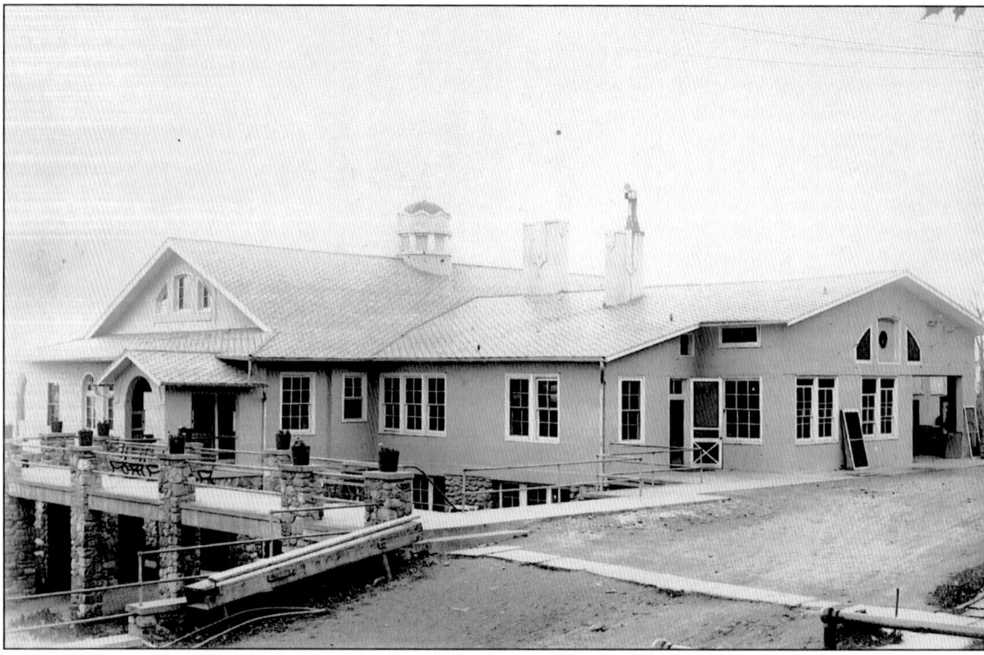

The dining hall at the Otisville Tuberculosis Sanitorium is photographed here as it appeared in the early 1900s, when it was built on the side of the mountain near Otisville. Patients were required to walk to the dining hall for their nutritious, well-balanced meals. Proper nutrition was an integral part of the cure for patients at the sanitorium.

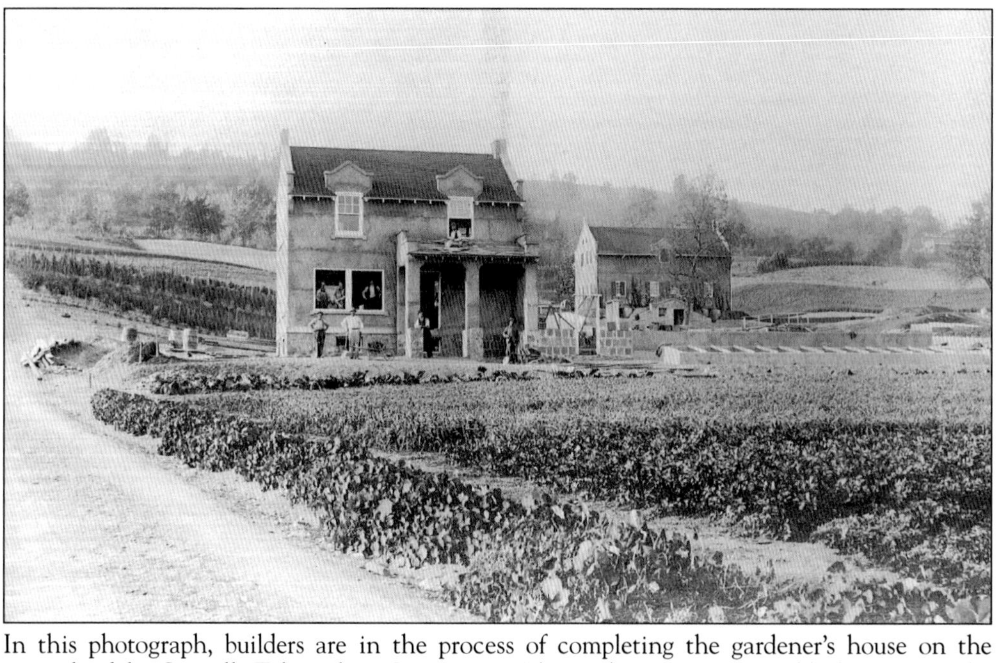

In this photograph, builders are in the process of completing the gardener's house on the grounds of the Otisville Tuberculosis Sanitorium. The gardener was responsible for growing the vegetables that were an important part of the patients' daily diet at the facility. A large barn was located behind the residence to house farm equipment. The house and barn are still located on Sanitorium Avenue.

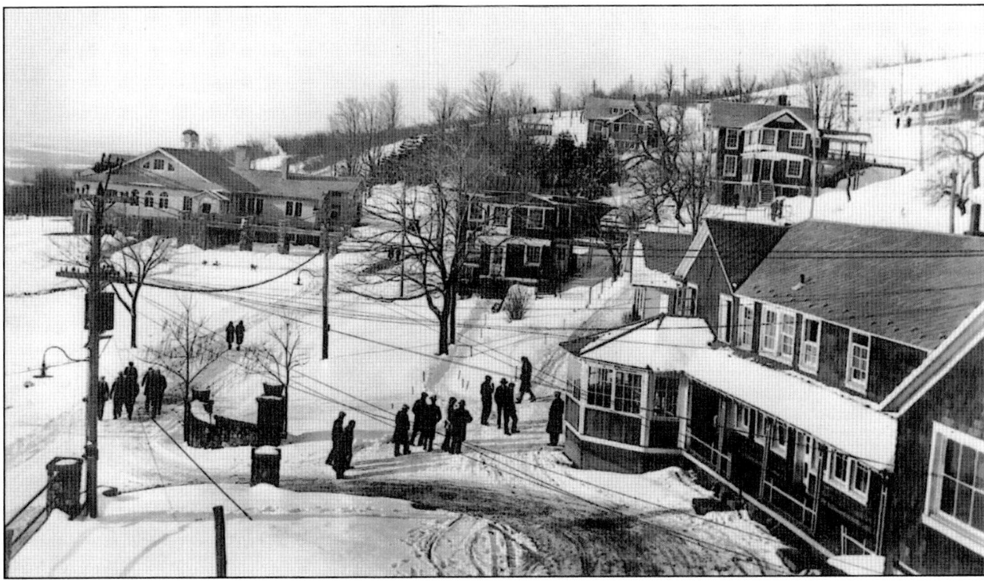

This photograph was taken from one of the roofs at the sanitorium looking out over the grounds of the facility. Residents and employees can be seen walking below on a wintry day on the mountain. Walking was encouraged by the doctors at the sanitorium and residents walked from one building to another as part of their daily exercise requirement.

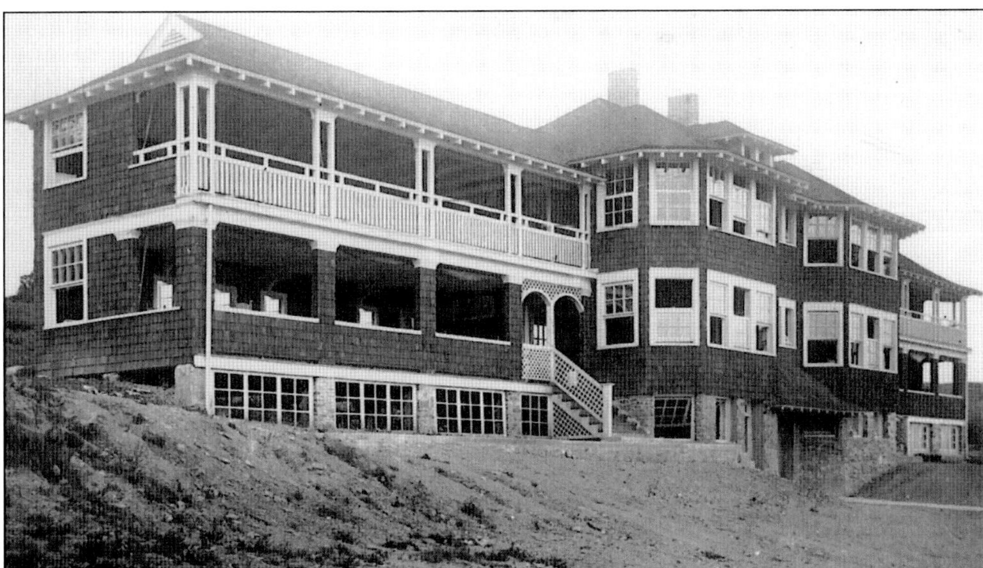

The Hudson Fulton building was an example of a large dormitory facility at the Otisville Tuberculosis Sanitorium. The building had open-air sleeping quarters in the front of the building. Patients inhaled the cool, clean mountain air and coughing episodes decreased as a result of this treatment. The exterior of the building was covered with cedar shingles.

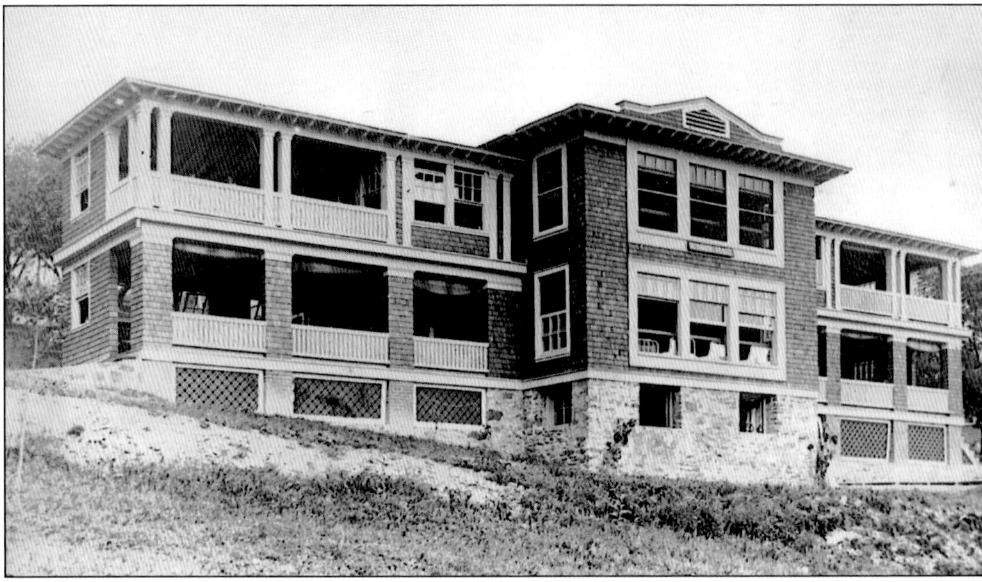

In this photograph, the Sunrise building is shown as another example of dormitory living at the Otisville Tuberculosis Sanitorium. Males and females were housed in separate dormitories. Although the open-air sleeping arrangements may seem extreme to most people today, it was found to be an effective part of the therapy that was offered at the sanitorium during the early 1900s.

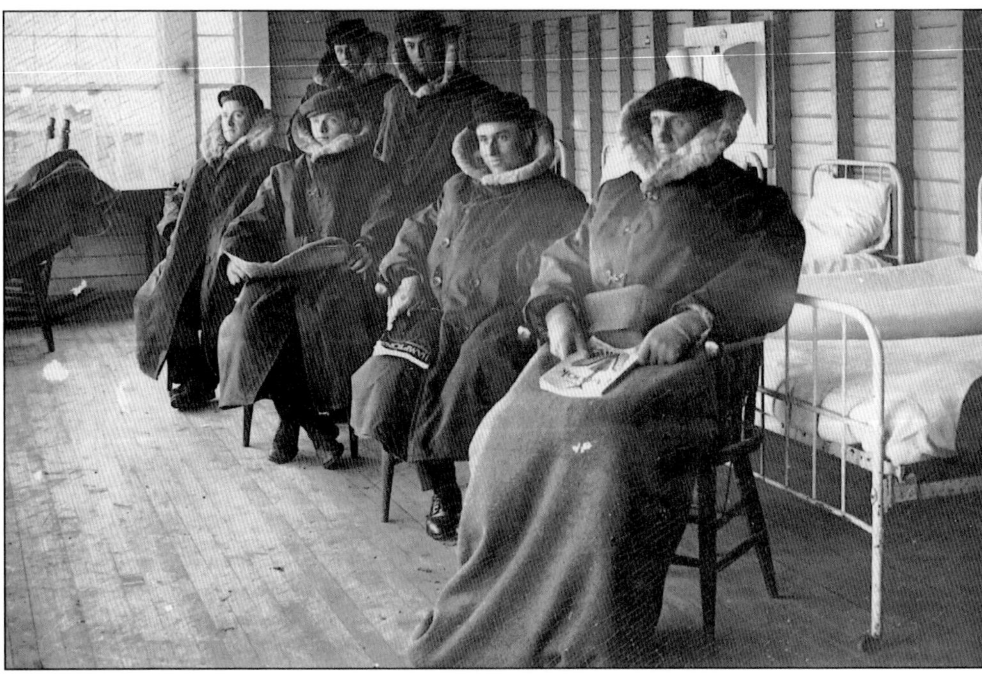

A group of patients at the Otisville Tuberculosis Sanitorium is sitting on their open-air porch where they spent a great portion of their time. They slept on the porches on cold winter nights when the temperatures dropped well below freezing. All the patients are bundled up in fur-lined coats, and one man is seen reading a magazine.

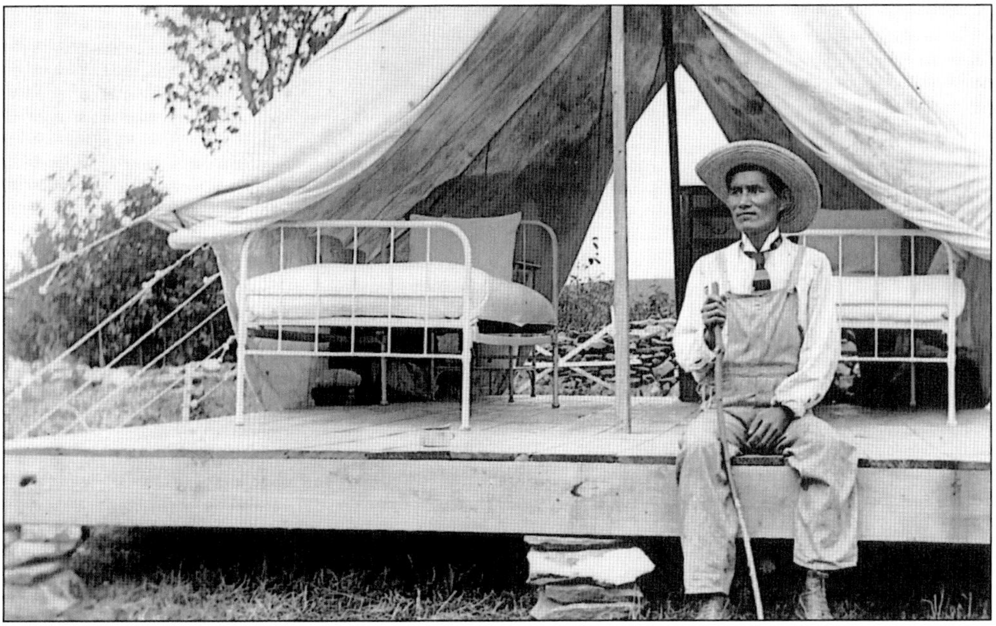

In the spring, it was pleasant to sleep in the open air. The man in this photograph is posing on the platform of his sleeping tent that he shared with another patient. There were large groups of these sleeping tents for spring, summer, and fall use in various locations on the grounds of the Otisville Tuberculosis Sanitorium. Dr. Thomas Darlington often referred to the facility as a "tuberculosis camp" when it opened in 1906.

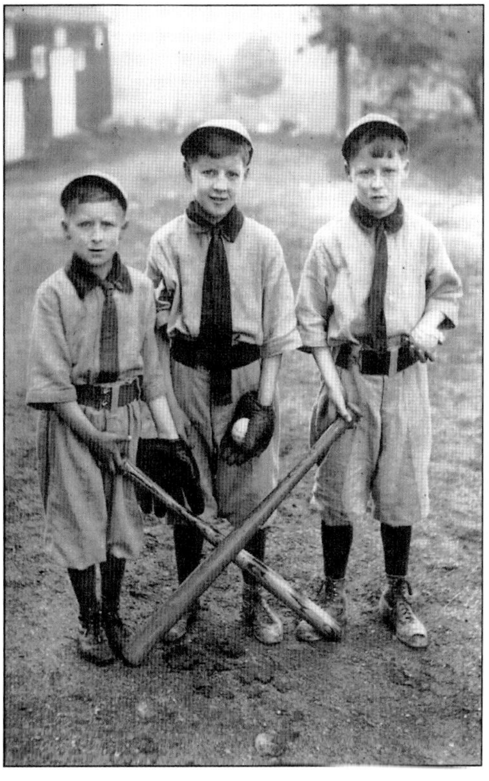

This adorable photograph of the Carhart boys in their baseball uniforms was taken in July 1911 on the grounds of the sanitorium, where they lived with their parents. From left to right, the boys are Ralph, Bruce, and Eldred Carhart. On June 13, 1925, Eldred pitched his last game for the Otisville High School baseball team, defeating Monticello High School 11-7. During his career, he pitched two no-hit games. In one game, he struck out 21 players on his way to victory for the Otisville team.

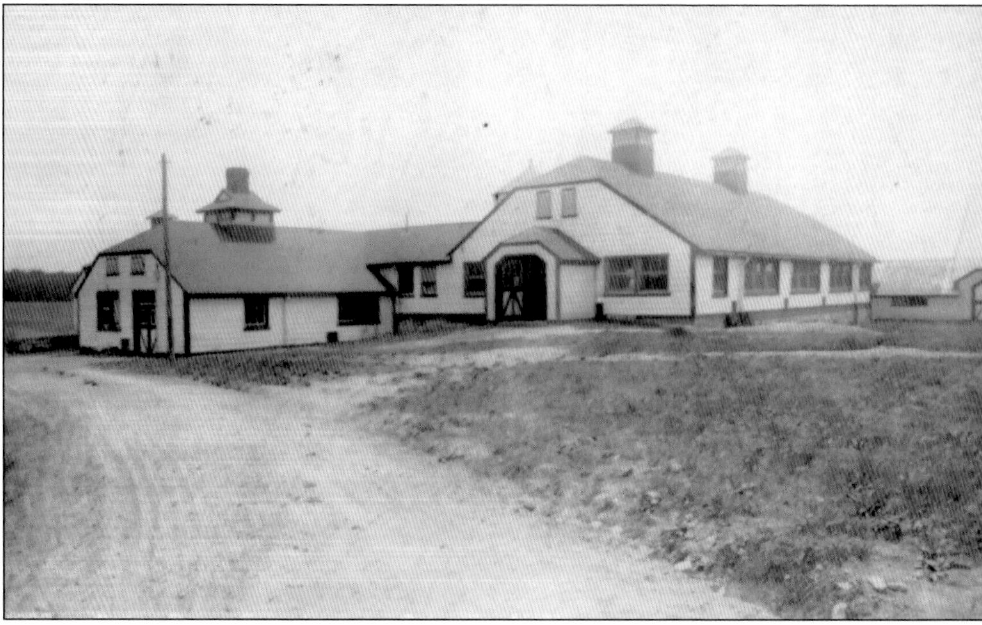

The dairy barn at the sanitorium is featured in this early photograph. The barn is still located on Old Mountain Road in Otisville. Sam Free was a dairyman who worked at the Otisville Tuberculosis Sanitorium for many years. Free was a grandson of Robert Vail, a slave in Mount Hope who belonged to the Vail family. Upon his emancipation, he took the name of Robert Free.

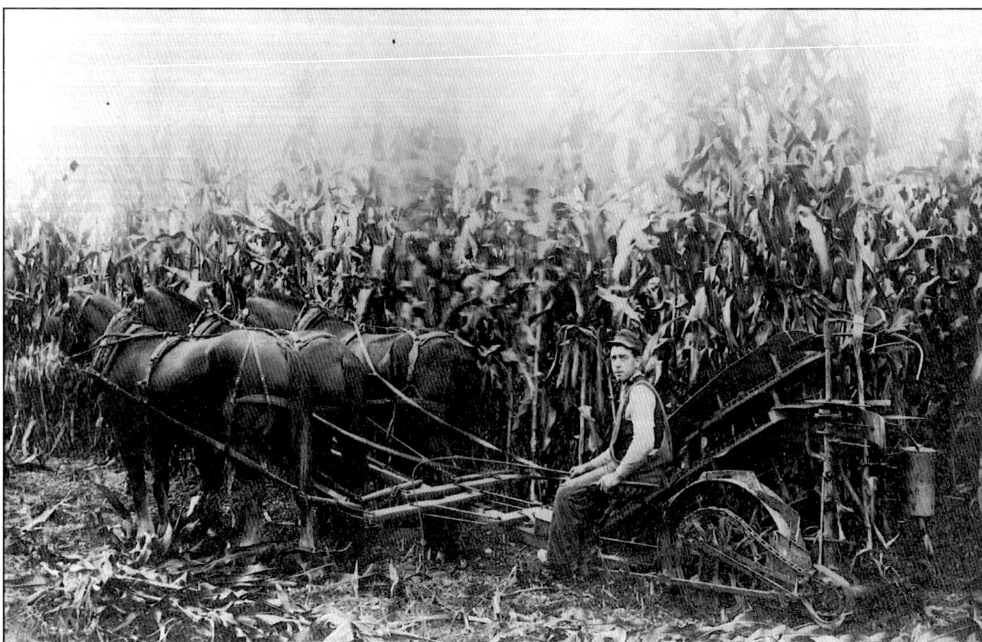

In this photograph, a man is harvesting corn using a binding machine on the grounds of the Otisville Tuberculosis Sanitorium. The machine is pulled by two workhorses. The facility was nearly self-sufficient and grew corn and other vegetables for the dietary needs of the tubercular patients who lived there.

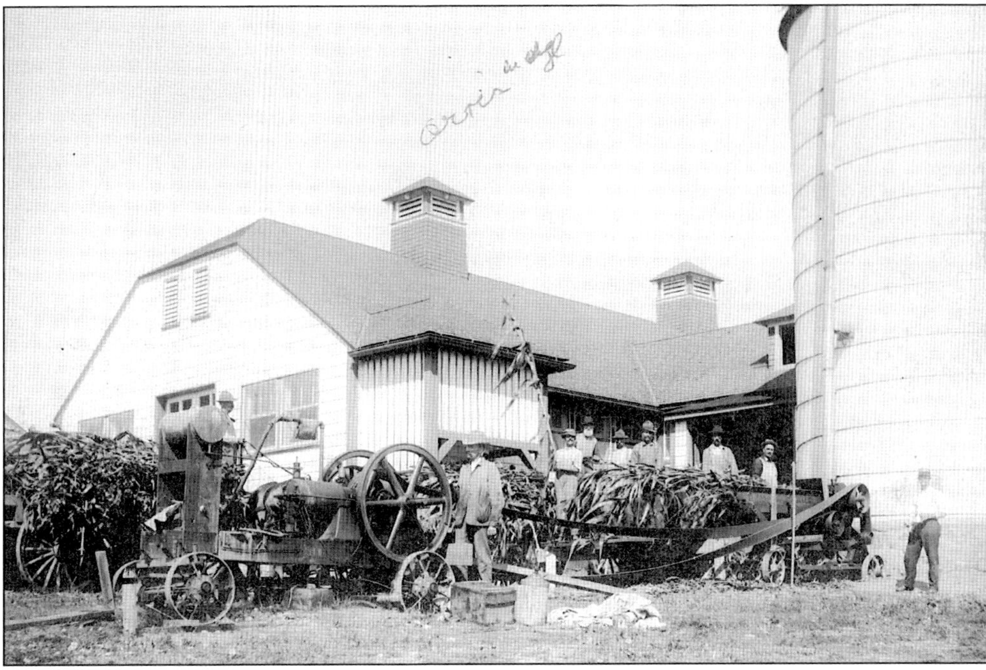

Employees of the sanitorium are chopping corn for silage in this early-1900s photograph. It was a stationary engine with a chain-driven belt that chopped the corn into silage and blew it up a pipe into the silo. The silage was fed to the cows on the farm during the winter months.

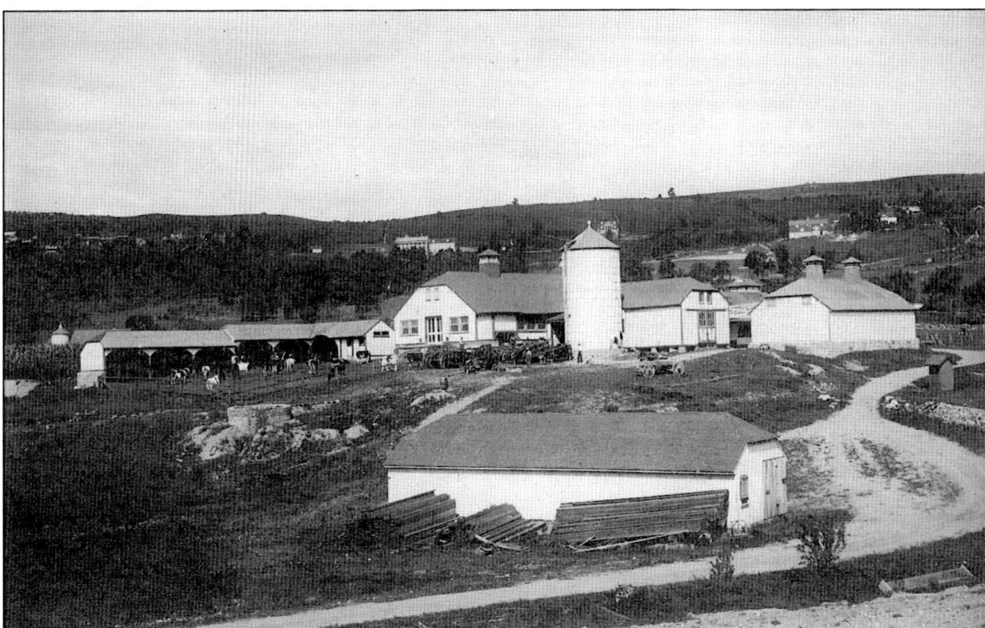

This is a view of the barns on the Otisville Tuberculosis Sanitorium and antitoxin laboratory property. The two facilities were closely related, although they were separate entities. Both operations were run by the New York City Department of Health. There was a dairy barn and horse barn at this location on Sanitorium Avenue.

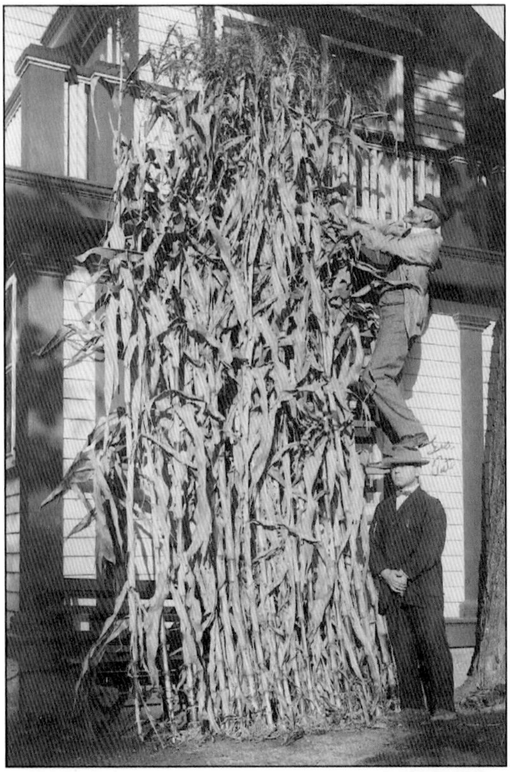

A man is standing on the head of George Tate in this photograph taken at the sanitorium in the early 1900s by Ralph Perry Carhart. The corn was very high that year, and a record of this remarkable harvest was captured in this image by Carhart, who took many photographs at the sanitorium where he was employed.

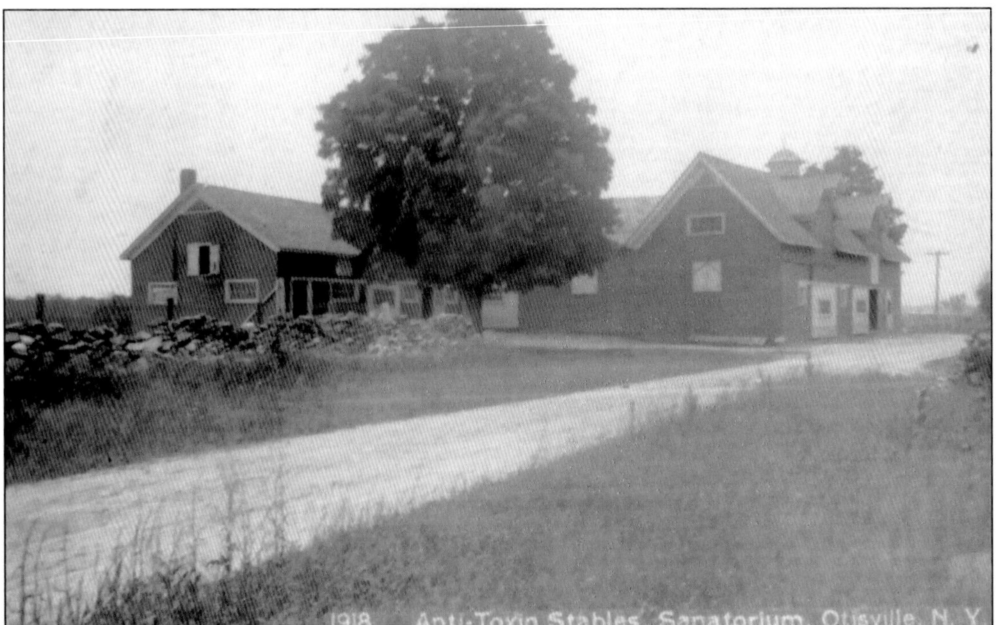

The Palmer barn was used by the Otisville Antitoxin Laboratory for various purposes. In the early years, it housed horses and farm equipment before the other barns were constructed. The barn has hand hewn beams and was part of the original Palmer farm. In later years, it was used to house small animals such as monkeys.

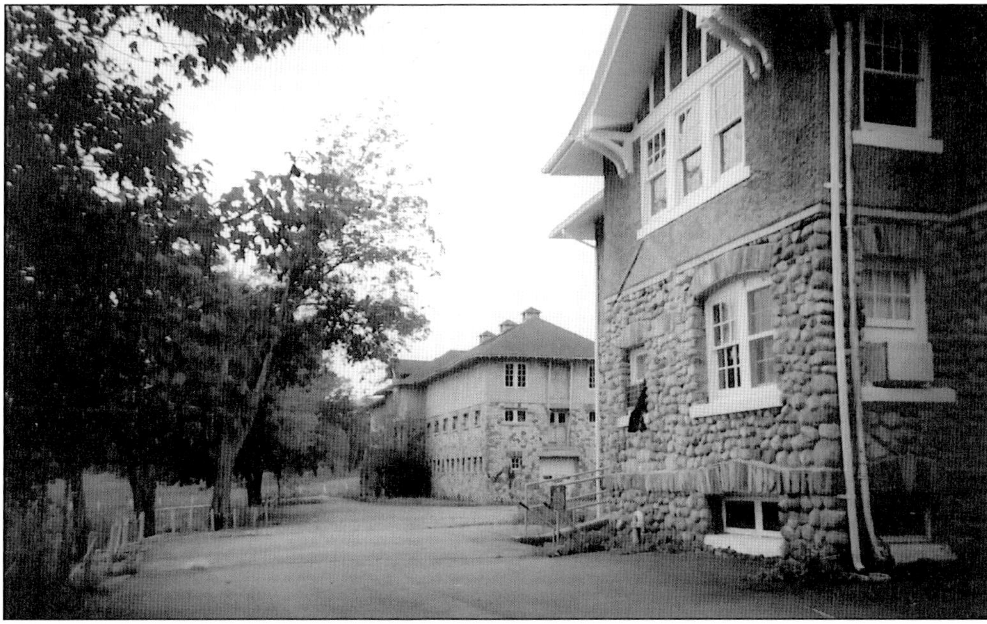

In 1906, Dr. William Hallock Park, a pioneer in the field of bacteriology and an employee of the New York City Department of Health, headed the operation known as the Otisville Antitoxin Laboratory. The facility was instrumental in producing vaccines for diphtheria and tetanus. During World War I, it provided thousands of vaccines to soldiers on the front and was responsible for saving countless lives.

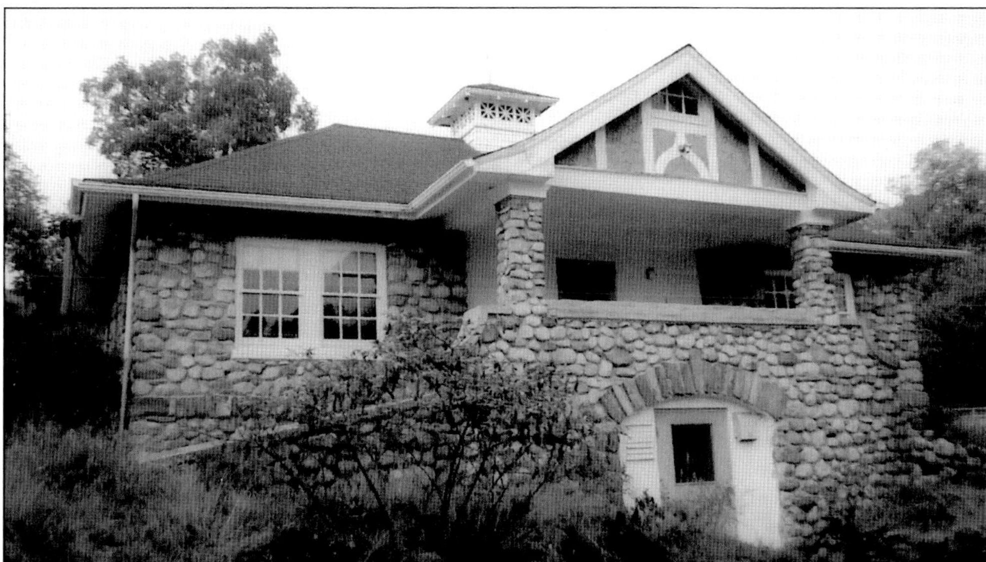

This is another example of one of the unique fieldstone buildings that made up the complex of the Otisville Antitoxin Laboratory. The horse known as number 397 was too old to clean the streets of New York City and was retired to the antitoxin farm at Otisville. By 1914, this horse, once deemed useless, had produced 282.8 million units of diphtheria vaccine worth $175,000. The laboratory in Otisville was responsible for saving thousands of lives with the diphtheria vaccine that they produced.

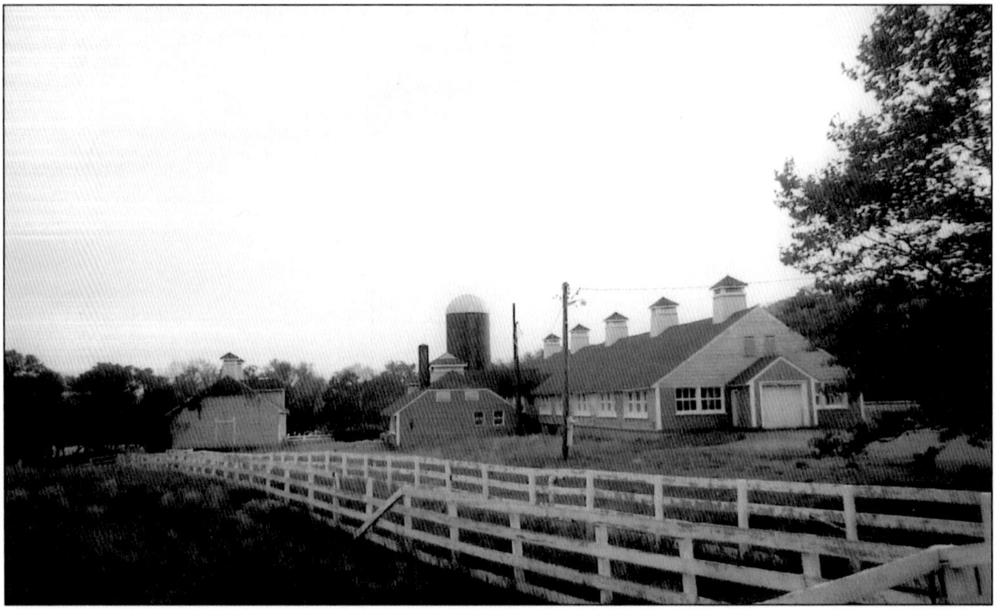

Dr. Aaron Silkman was chief veterinarian at the Otisville Tuberculosis Sanitorium and Otisville Antitoxin Laboratory. In 1914, the Otisville laboratory was the only facility in the world that produced the Flexner serum for spinal meningitis. Calves were also kept at the farm by Silkman for the production of smallpox vaccines.

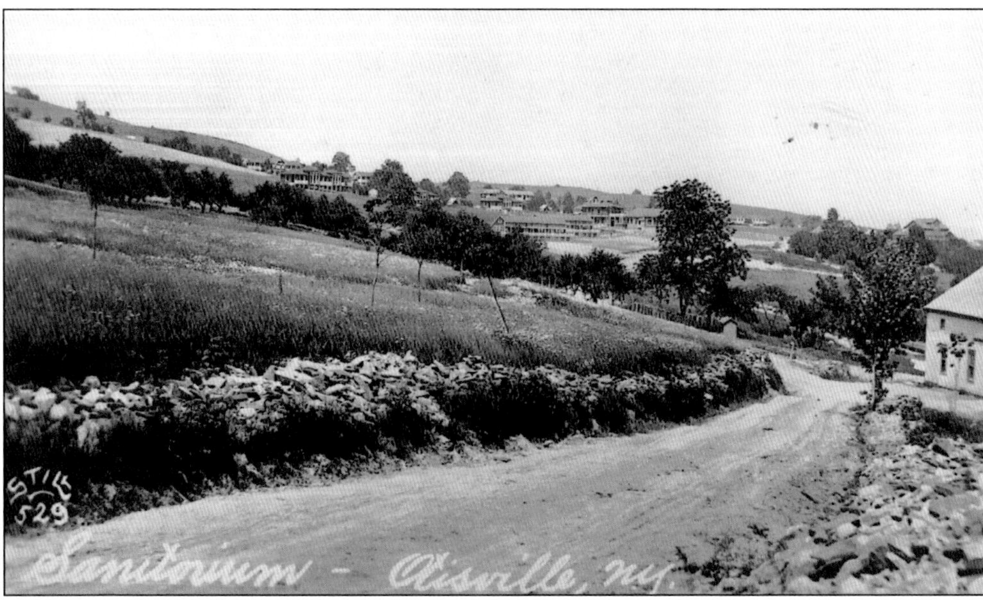

A dirt road meanders through the property of the Otisville Tuberculosis Sanitorium in this photograph. Many of the patients at the sanitorium had never lived in the country, and this was a new experience for them. Upon completion of their treatment at Otisville, several former patients decided to stay in Otisville and raise their families in this rural community.

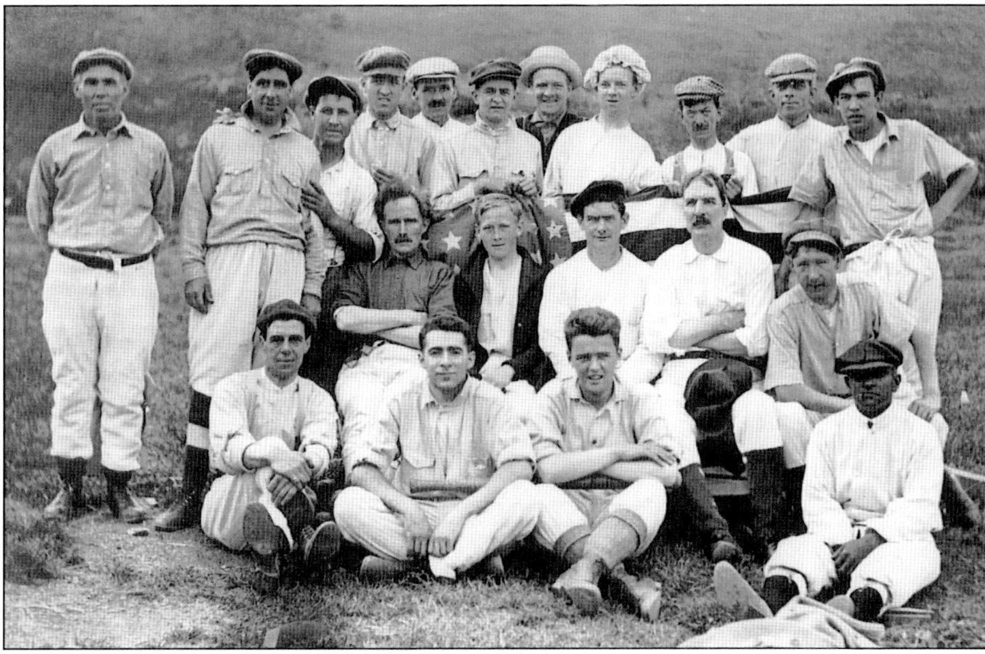

On holidays, picnics were held for the patients and employees on the parklike sanitorium grounds. This is a photograph taken around 1918 of a group of employees at the Otisville Tuberculosis Sanitorium during one of their holiday events. One of the men is holding a flag, which might indicate that it was a Fourth of July picnic.

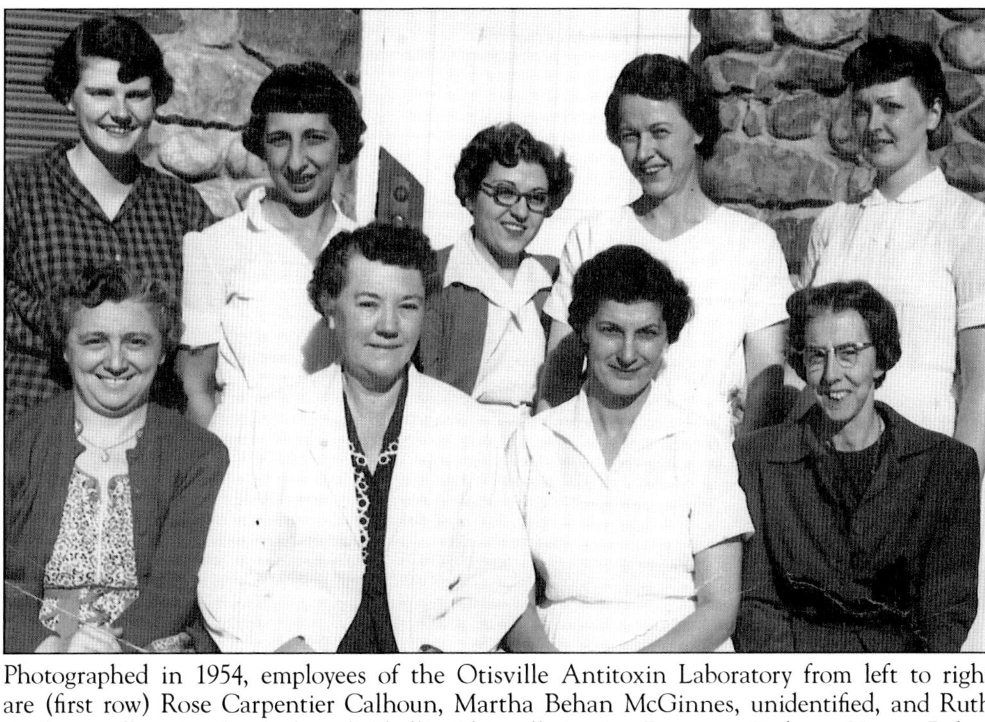

Photographed in 1954, employees of the Otisville Antitoxin Laboratory from left to right are (first row) Rose Carpentier Calhoun, Martha Behan McGinnes, unidentified, and Ruth Anderson Corwin; (second row) Phyllis Chiswell, Louise Bonanto Carhart, Honey Baker, Bernice Ketcham Wilbur, and Merici McDermott Ullrich.

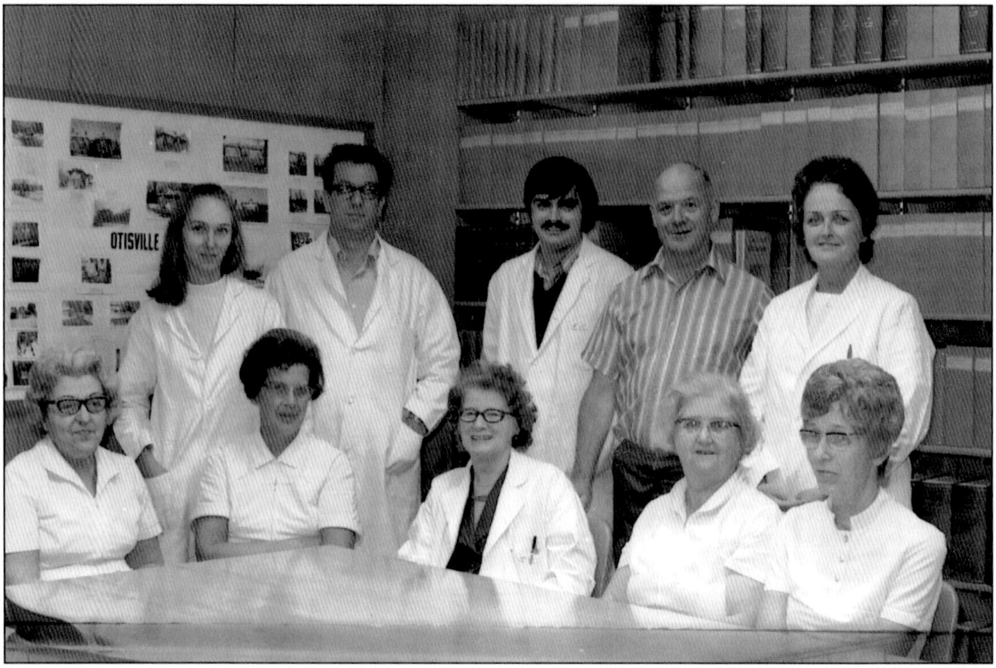

Employees of the Otisville Antitoxin Laboratory were photographed at the facility in 1978. From left to right, they are (first row) Honey Baker, Mary Lang Wilbur, Janey Stanfield, Hilda Bonagura, and Bernice Ketcham Wilbur; (second row) Paula Barber, Frank Ward, Ernie Green, Sid Green, and Merici McDermott Ullrich.

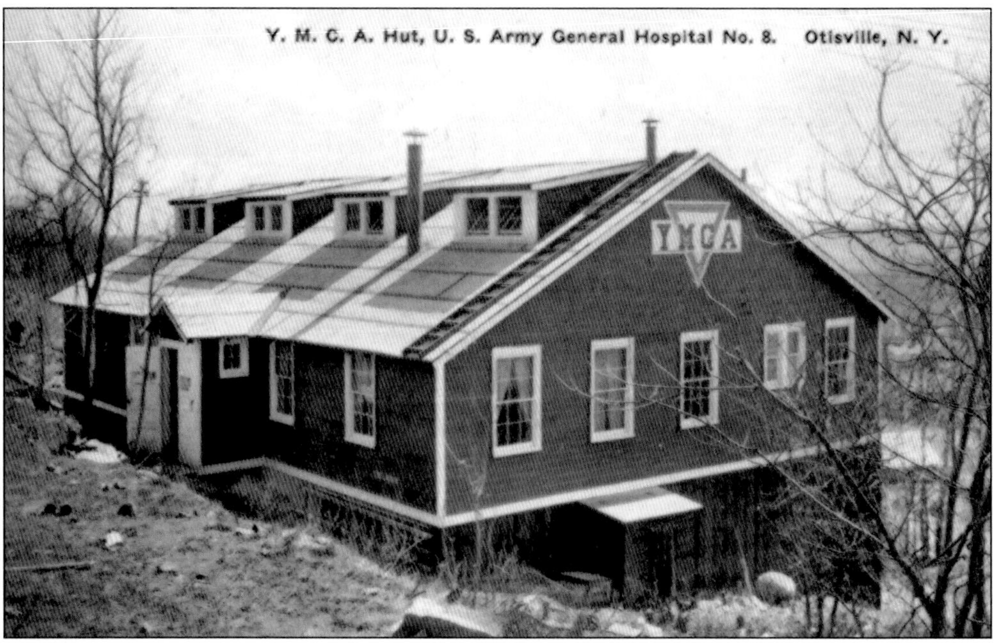

U.S. Army General Hospital No. 8 was built for World War I soldiers on the Shawangunk Mountain overlooking Otisville. This is a photograph of the YMCA hut that was part of the hospital complex. The YMCA had a reading room and theater and provided recreational activities for the soldiers who were convalescing at the hospital.

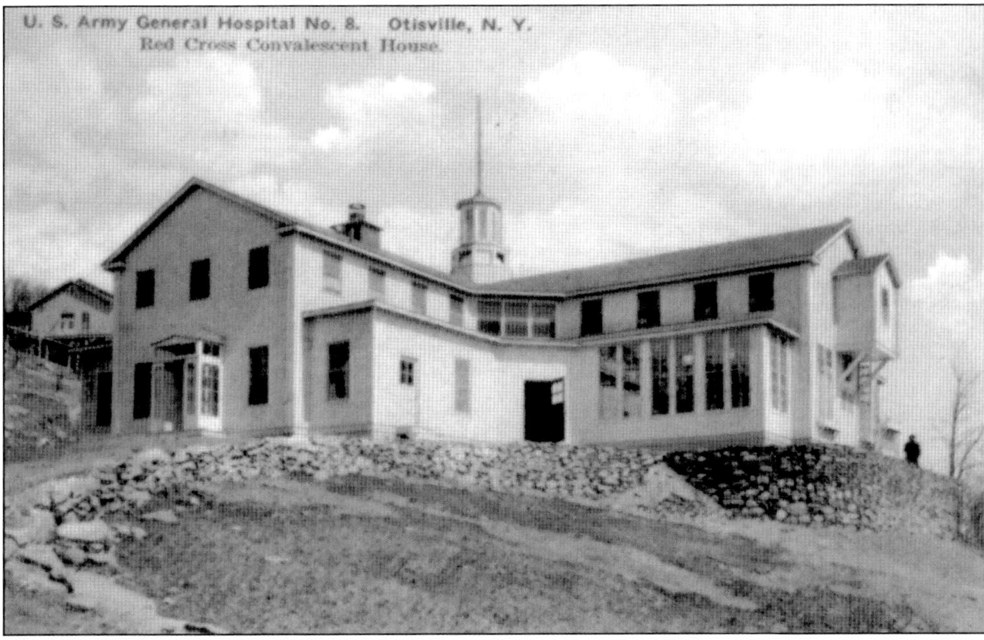

The Red Cross Convalescent House was one of the larger buildings at the hospital complex in Otisville. A canteen was located in this building for the soldiers' entertainment. The Red Cross offered many services to the soldiers at the army hospital.

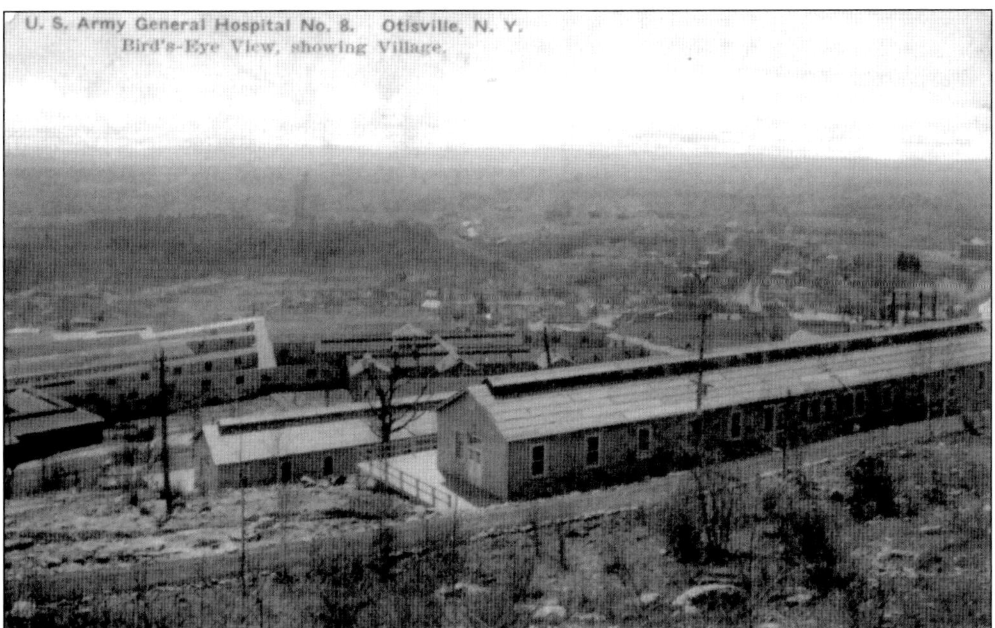

This bird's-eye view was taken from the top of the Shawangunk Mountain looking down over the U.S. Army General Hospital No. 8 and the village of Otisville. After the army hospital was dismantled, the wood was used to build many houses in the Wurtsboro area. The Pattersons used redwood from two hospital water storage containers to build an addition on their home on Orchard Street in 1922.

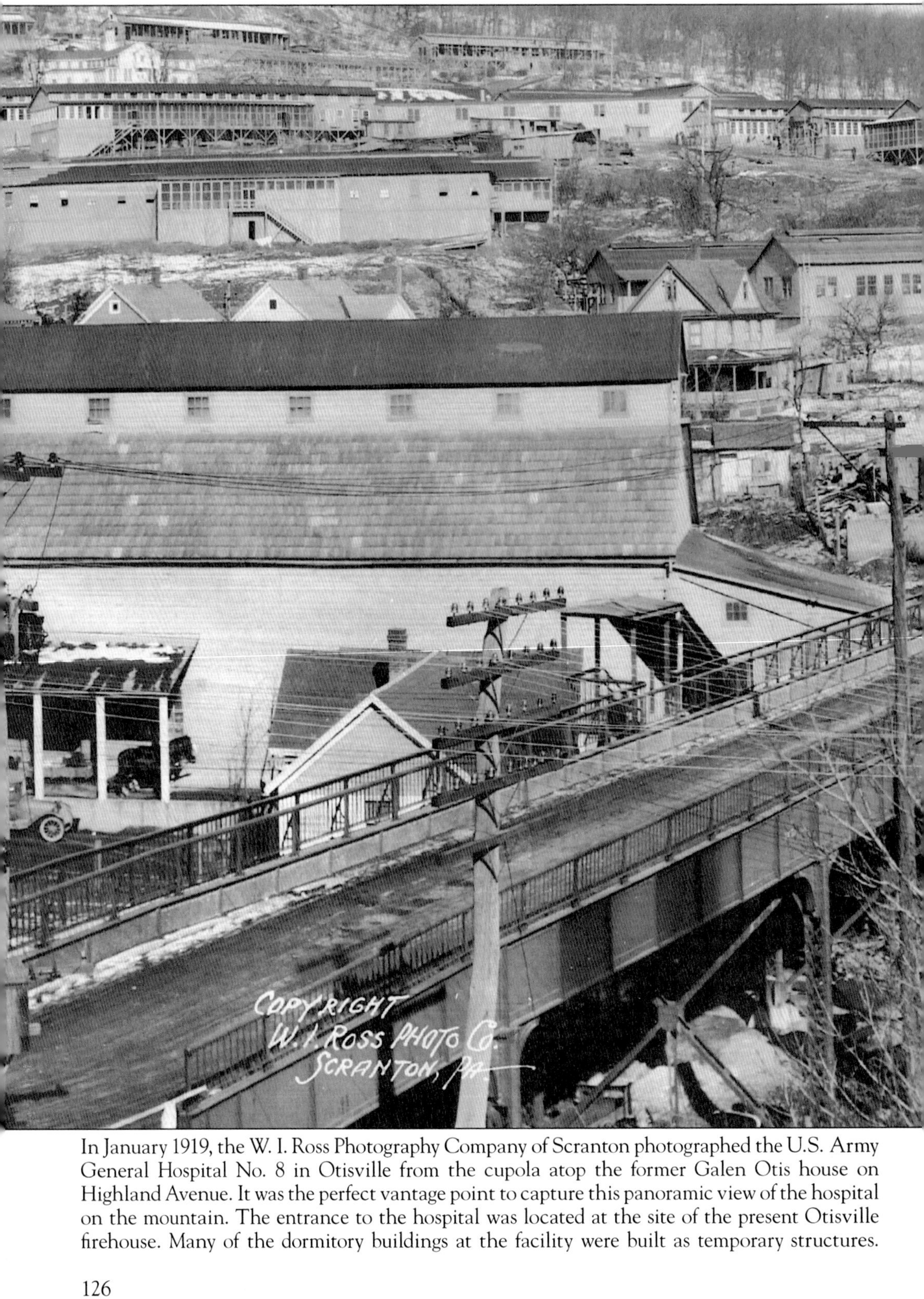

In January 1919, the W. I. Ross Photography Company of Scranton photographed the U.S. Army General Hospital No. 8 in Otisville from the cupola atop the former Galen Otis house on Highland Avenue. It was the perfect vantage point to capture this panoramic view of the hospital on the mountain. The entrance to the hospital was located at the site of the present Otisville firehouse. Many of the dormitory buildings at the facility were built as temporary structures.

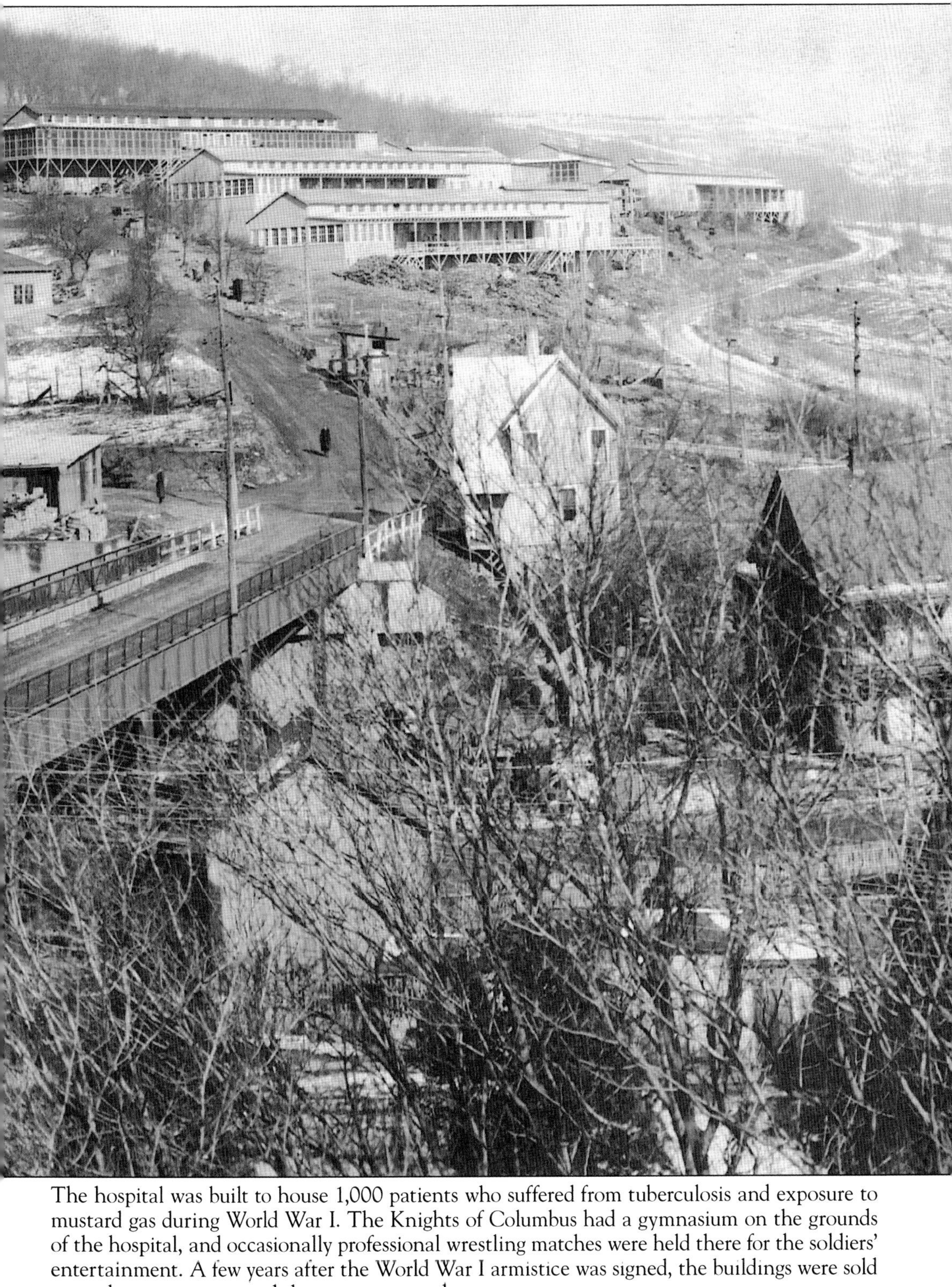

The hospital was built to house 1,000 patients who suffered from tuberculosis and exposure to mustard gas during World War I. The Knights of Columbus had a gymnasium on the grounds of the hospital, and occasionally professional wrestling matches were held there for the soldiers' entertainment. A few years after the World War I armistice was signed, the buildings were sold to a salvage company, and they were removed.

Across America, People are Discovering Something Wonderful. *Their Heritage.*

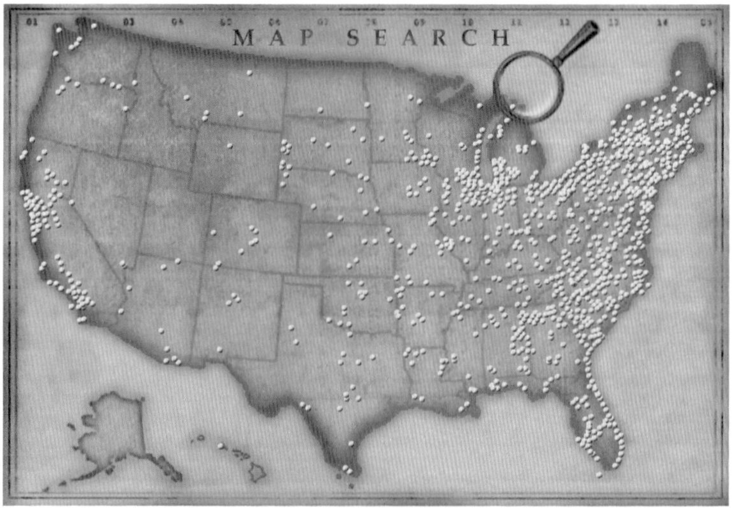